FANTASY MANAGER'S
FOOTBALL
FORM BOOK

by

Gordon Crutchley

foulsham

LONDON • NEW YORK • TORONTO • SYDNEY

foulsham

The Publishing House, Bennetts Close,
Cippenham, Berkshire SL1 5AP

ISBN 0-572-02159-3

© 1995 Gordon Crutchley

Every effort has been made to ensure that the details given in this book are accurate at the time of going to press, however the publishers cannot accept any responsiblity, and apologise, for any errors.

All photography supplied by Colorsport

Printed in England by Acorn Web Offset, Normanton, West Yorkshire

INTRODUCTION

Northern Stars Shine Brightly

At the start of the 1994/5 season the question on the lips of most football fans concerned who would win the contest for the best pair of strikers in the Premiership. Would it be one of the tried and trusted partnerships such as Cole and Beardsley, Hughes and Cantona, Wright and Smith, Hirst and Bright or Rush and Fowler? Or would one of the new pairings strike gold? Shearer and Sutton was the most fascinating one. Maybe the exciting prospect of Klinsmann and Sheringham would be more effective? Or would the potentially explosive pairing of Roy and Collymore or the new Aston Villa force of Fashanu and Saunders surprise everyone by becoming the new scoring powerhouse of the Premiership? Whichever were to prevail, there was probably a greater sense of anticipation in football in August 1994 than there had been for many a season.

Looking back, the answer is very clear, indeed it became so very early in the season. The prolific Shearer and Sutton were by far the most successful, ending the season with no less than 48 Premiership goals between them and it was largely due to this contribution that the League Championship went to Ewood Park. Apart from the goalscoring and exceptional work-rate of SAS, in the 1994/5 season , there was the very special privilege of seeing a real gentleman, as well as a master craftsman at work. Jurgen Klinsmann came with a reputation of being as good a diver as he was a striker; some would have said better! His response was to turn on his world-class skills (alongside the reliable Teddy Sheringham) to thrill and entertain everyone. Furthermore his humour and ability to win over his enemies came shining through, such as when the Spurs goalscoring celebrations took the form of ...... a dive!

Collymore, Roy, Ferdinand and of course the incredible Matt Le Tissier all contributed regular moments of goalscoring magic, but, in attack, the season belonged to Sutton and Shearer.

Another notable happening of the season was the total dominance of clubs from the North of England, and in particular from the North-West. The records will show Blackburn as Premier League Champions, Manchester United as Runners-up and Liverpool, Leeds United and Newcastle in the top six. Only Nottingham Forest, from the Midlands, spoiled a total northern dominance. Everton beat United in the FA Cup Final and Liverpool overcame the gallant Bolton Wanderers in the Coca Cola Cup Final. The automatic promotion places were won by Middlesbrough and Carlisle, from the far North, and Birmingham and Walsall from the Midlands. The best offered by the South was a battle for seventh place in the Premiership and representation in the play-offs by only Reading, Brentford and Bristol Rovers and none of them won through, even brave Reading managing to forfeit a two-goal lead and miss a penalty in order to allow Northerners Bolton Wanderers through in the play-off of the Endleigh 1st Division. The nine other clubs who contested the play-offs were all located in the geographical area between Wolverhampton, Preston and Huddersfield. Far more Southern names will be found among those clubs who were relegated. These included from the Premiership, Crystal Palace, Norwich and Ipswich and in the Endsleigh League, Swindon, Bristol City, Cambridge, Plymouth, Cardiff and Leyton Orient, with Exeter escaping the drop into the Vauxhall Conference only by a very dubious quirk in the rules of the Football League.

Unfortunately the season will probably be remembered for all the wrong reasons. This was the year of sleaze, corruption and violence not only by supporters but also by players, both on and off the field. This whole subject has been so widely covered in the media that we will avoid any further mention of it here. So far as we know, no fantasy player has deliberately given away a goal in order to forfeit his clean sheet points and there has been no report of a fantasy league manager offering bribes. Nor have there been any suggestions of violence in fantasy circles, other than morning newspapers being torn up in sheer frustration upon reading the latest fantasy scores.

Turning to the real world of fantasy football, what is there to learn from the past season? Did you win your league? If not, where did you go wrong? Whether you entered a private league or one run by a national newspaper, it would have done you no harm at all to have had the aforementioned goalscoring machine, Alan Shearer in your team. Whichever fantasy scoring system was used, he was far and away the top scorer. It is unlikely that you would have won any of the newspaper leagues without having him in your team for the majority, if not all, of the season.

Of course, neither league titles nor fantasy leagues are won by an outstanding attack alone. Whether your fantasy experience is in a private league or in one of the very public national newspaper games, you need to balance your spending correctly in order to buy the team which will combine your goalscoring attack with a mean defence and a constructive midfield which is capable of contributing a few goals. This publication is intended to provide you with all of the advice, evidence and statistics that you need in order to select your optimum team, whatever version of fantasy football you play. We hope that our contribution will assist you in having success in your selections, enabling you to enjoy a fantastic fantasy season.

HOW TO PLAY

Most people reading this book will probably already know how to play one or other version of fantasy football and therefore not a great deal of effort has been put into a detailed description of the game. What will be given in this section will be a brief outline of how the game works, and what you have to do. The main purpose of this book is to guide would-be managers in the SELECTION of their teams.

There are two main ways of playing fantasy foootball. The first is by entering a team in a league organised by one of the national (or even local) newspapers or magazines. These games which are described as "fantasy football" (or in similar terms) in newspapers do vary from one publication to another, with slightly different rules, team structures, player valuations and scoring methods. However, the general principles are very similar. Alternatively you may opt to subscribe to a specialist company who will take care of all of the organisation and administration of setting up and running your own private fantasy league for you, or even allowing you to participate in a league with other managers who could not find enough interested parties to form their own league.

In either of the two approaches, the idea of the game is that you select a fantasy league team from real players in the F.A. Carling Premiership. Each week, every player (usually only those in the Carling Premiership are eligible in fantasy leagues) will be allocated a score, based upon how they performed in their actual league match during the previous week. (Cup and other matches are not included.) This will be done throughout the season and you will be able to keep check on how your team is getting on by adding up the scores of your individual players, as printed in your newspaper, and comparing the total against others in your fantasy league.

In the case of the newspaper versions details of the top 50 to 100 fantasy teams are published including scores, team names and managers' names . There is often a valuable prize at the end of the season, but we suspect that most managers are more interested in the challenge of competing against hundreds of thousands of others and wishing to have their name published, confirming their knowledge of football, than they are in winning the prize. The odds against them doing that are really extraordinarily long.

Private League

If you decide to set up your own league by joining one of the specialist companies, you will probably have to pay approximately £30 per manager, for which you will receive guidance on how to run your league, together with reports, statistics and league tables for your league, throughout the season. It is usually recommended that a league should consist of at least 5-6 and no more than about 15 teams. Alternatively you can set up your own private league, but this will demand a great deal of effort in organisation and ongoing administration of the league. Under either set-up, the approach will be similar, although the detailed rules will probably vary.

In this version of the game, at the start of the season you will be required to attend an auction, along with the other managers. The tactics here are very different from those employed if you are entering a national newspaper league. For example only one manager will be able to play Alan Shearer in his team, the manager who puts in the highest bid. In the newspaper versions, numerous managers will select him. At the auction you will be allocated a budget (possibly £20 million), from which you must assemble a squad of players. There is often a maximum number of players, say 15, that you are allowed to have in

your squad. Care should be taken that you amass a squad from whom you are able to select a team of the structure stipulated in the rules, eg a 4-4-2 formation. Failure to do this can lead to some interesting, and maybe fatal, situations for your fantasy team.

Take the case of Mark Whittall who participated in the league arranged for charity purposes at the church attended by the author. The rules were home-made and included a clause which said that if a manager failed to buy a player for a particular position, rather than being eliminated from the league, he would be allocated the worst fantasy player that the organiser (your author) could think of. Mark managed to compose a powerful-looking squad which included a choice from Cole, Collymore and Sheringham in attack, Peacock, Lee, Magilton and Southgate in midfield and Borrows, Wilson, Vonk and Walker as defenders. Unfortunately for him, a number of managers bought two goalkeepers, so that by the time he realised what had happened, he was too late to buy one. He was allocated Craig Forrest of Ipswich! Under almost every fantasy scoring system, Craig came bottom of the list. Certainly Mark's fantasy season was in ruins and his priority for the coming season will be to ensure that he arranges to buy a complete squad. This should be your priority too at the auction.

Another tip at the auction is that you should bide

your time. Many managers will go wild at the outset, paying inflated prices for players, only to find that they cannot afford to buy the stars who appear at the end of the auction. Others who have showed more caution can often pick up bargains at the end of the evening, simply by holding on to their money until their opponents have almost run out of theirs and are therefore unable to compete with them in the bidding.

In this type of league, you are able to adjust your team, from your squad, subject to the local rules in force. Sometimes you may even be allowed to buy in unallocated players later in the season. This means that injuries or loss of form affecting players, do not ruin your season.

Newspaper Versions

Possibly the simplest way to play fantasy football is to enter one of the leagues published in newspapers. These are extremely popular, attracting hundreds of thousands of entries to each national league.

In August or early September you are required to select a team and submit your entry, either by telephone or on an entry form from the newspaper.

To enter teams in those leagues where a telephone call is required may work out rather expensive, often taking 5 - 8 minutes to enter your team, often at 39p or 49p per minute. It may well cost between £2.00 and £4.00 for each team entered. Postal entries are usually much cheaper, but here it is usually necessary to collect entry forms, which may limit the number of teams that you are able to enter. Most newspapers allow more than one entry per person, although some stipulate that entries must be in different names eg other members of the family. There is usually no limit on the number of entries per family. Later in this section are typical rules which apply in the entry of a team in a newspaper league.

Having selected your team at the start of the season, if you wish, you can simply sit back and wait for your name and that of your team to be published, although, in reality that happens to only a few managers. More likely, you will need to keep track of your score by looking each week at the results in your newspaper and watch carefully which of your players are injured, or out of form, in order to take advantage of the transfer facility which is available within most newspaper league systems.

In the following sections the main features of how to play are outlined.

Section 1.a.i)

Team Names

Usually the team name may be up to approximately 20 characters long. Care must be taken that it is not 'inappropriate' or 'offensive' or it will be removed and only the manager's name will be used.

The name is not too important and may never be seen by anyone else, but it can add a little humour and if you can offer some originality AND select a team which will get it published, then you can add to the enjoyment of the thousands who look at the published fantasy league results, as well as impress your friends and colleagues with your originality.

Section 1.a.ii)

Number of Entries

In some newspapers, only one team is allowed per person, and that must be submitted on an official form. However, there is no limit to the number of teams per household, again, provided that they each have an official, original form.

This means that, if an entrant wishes to increase his/her chances, they may submit a number of teams for all members of the family. Frequently teams are submitted in the names of infants, which will be selected and managed by dads or older brothers; this is perfectly acceptable and within the rules of most games. So, sort out your elderly aunts, grandmothers,

etc and put in a team for them. It would perhaps be advisable to get their permission and to use (c/o) your own address and telephone number, so that they do not suddenly receive letters, or even telephone calls, about their football team, which they are not expecting!

The above paragraph may sound rather sexist and that must be corrected immediately. The world of fantasy football is by no means the exclusive domain of the male sex. Many thousands of ladies enter teams and frequently put their soccer-mad husbands/brothers/fathers to shame by outscoring them.

Section 1.a.iii)

Choice of Players

There is a variety of rules regarding the selection of players depending upon the newspaper of your choice. The following are areas which are affected.

1. Team Format - You must buy eleven players; and in the format specified eg 1-4-4-2 ie 1 Goalkeeper, 4 Defenders (say 2 Full Backs, 2 Centre Backs), 4 Midfielders and 2 Strikers.

2. Restrictions Relating To Number Of Players Per Real Premiership Club – Often, it is stipulated that no more than two of the players in a team may come from the same F.A.Carling Premiership team. However, the clubs which are quoted are those for whom the player was registered at the time that the various fantasy leagues were drawn up and it is quite possible that the player may have since been transferred. In most fantasy leagues, the player concerned is considered to belong to his original

club. For example, in 1994/5 Phil Babb was described in most leagues as a Coventry player, although by the start of the season he had been transferred to Liverpool. This meant that it was valid for managers to include Babb PLUS two other Liverpool players in their team.

3. Player Values - There is normally a limit on the total value of players permitted in your team, such as £20 or £25 million. This total and the value of individual players varies considerably from one league to another. In some games there is a severe restriction on what players you can afford to include and it is necessary to go for a number of inexpensive team members, rather than the stars whom you would ideally like, if you could afford them. In other games, the total amount allocated and the price of players mean that the restrictions are far less stringent. For the purposes of this guide, we will assume that you do not have Jack Walker as your Chairman, and therefore you have to show some restraint in your spending.

The general structure of the values given to players also varies a great deal. Last season some leagues went for a wide variation, valuing players from as little as £200,000 - £300,000 up to about £7 million, whereas others valued players in a much narrower band, say approximately £1 million to £4 million. The former are probably more realistic prices considering the prices paid for Andy Cole and Chris Sutton and the likely deal involving Stan Collymore at the time of writing.

The names, identification codes (as printed) and values of the players must be either telephoned through or entered carefully onto the published entry slip and the total value for the team calculated, to check that you have not exceeded the limit. Before entering any of this information, double check that your selection does not break any of the three rules above.

When you have sent off this form you are ready to play Fantasy Football.

Section 1.a.iv)

Keeping Score

It is up to you whether or not you keep track of the points scored by your team(s). Having entered your team, you are registered on the computer and you will have your points score updated by them on a weekly basis. If your score is not printed out in the top hundred or so, in many newspaper leagues you are able to find out your points and position by telephoning a number printed in the newspaper.

However, much of the fun of being a fantasy league manager is to check out each week how your players have performed compared with those at the top of the league. To do this, you simply add the total points for all your players, as published each week, to calculate your aggregate score. You are then able to compare this to the figures published to see how near (or far) you are to (or from) the top of the table.

Matters do become a little more complicated after you have applied transfers to your team. Your score consists only of those points gained by a player when he was a member of your team, and so you need to make adjustments to the points printed in the newspaper.

Cards are provided by some newspaper leagues for you to keep your score on a week by week basis.

Section 1.a.v)

Transfers

You do not have to think about transfers at the start of the season, but they play a very important part as it progresses. Transfers are particularly useful if a player is seriously injured, or if he loses his place in the team and you consider that he is unlikely to regain it. They may also be used if a player appears to have lost his form and you think that another will make a bigger contribution to your total points score. However, as you will see in Section 1.c.v) there are dangers in doing this, so be careful.

You are usually allowed to make changes to your team, during the season, provided that you do not infringe the original selection rules, as set out in Section 1.a.iii). The strategy for transfers is set out later in Section 1.c.v). Here, we are only considering the practical steps which you need to take to effect the transfers.

You will often be supplied with official cards to enable you to do this, on which you should complete the details of the players whom you are transferring out and those of the ones whom you are transferring in. Sometimes there is the alternative of using the telephone to initiate your transfers. You MUST check that you do not infringe the selection rules, because the same rules apply as in your original selection.

Section 1.a.vi)

Documentation

Many newspaper leagues will provide you with

i) A confirmation of your team selection.

i i) A PIN (Personal Identification Number.) No. to ensure that you alone can make changes to your team.

iii) A copy of the rules.

v) Transfer cards to enable you to change your team part way through the season.

iv) Scorecards on which to keep your ongoing total.

Section 1.b

The rules

Whichever version of fantasy football you are playing, it is essential that you take a little time at the outset to read and understand the rules. Failure to do so is very likely to lead to frustration and disappointment.

A copy of the rules will always be printed in the newspaper on various occasions during August. A copy will also be sent out with your registration documents. If you are running your own private league under the guidance of a specialist company, a full set of rules will be provided. If you are running and administering your own league, it is important that rules are clearly stated and that each participating manager is fully aware of them. Failure to do this could result in much tension and argument later in the season.

For the purpose of this section of the book, we will assume that we are dealing with one of the newspaper variations, although the main principles will apply whatever version of fantasy football you are playing.

This is not meant to be a full copy of any particular set of rules, since they do vary a little and include such exciting items as the value of the stamps which you have to submit, etc. The points listed below are a summary which covers the main aspects of which you need to be aware.

1   Your team must consist of 11 players from the list published.

2   The total value must not exceed the amount stated (last season it was usually £20 or £25 million).

3   You must have no more than two players from any one F.A. Carling Premiership team.

4   Your team must consist of a set number of players of each category eg1 goalkeeper, 2 full backs, 2 centre backs, 4 midfielders and 2 strikers or 1 goalkeeper, 4 defenders, 3 midfielders and 3 strikers.

5   Transfers are permitted, only if they are actioned from the official transfer card or over the telephone, quoting your PIN (Personal Identity Number) No.

It is important for you to realise that the rules laid out above are a very brief summary of a few important points, not the official rules of any particular fantasy football game and they are far from comprehensive. You must refer to the official ones before entering your team.

Section 1.c.i)

SELECTION STRATEGY

In this section we are looking at the strategy to be adopted in the different varieties of fantasy football. However, there are a few fundamental points which apply, whatever version of the game you are playing.

Know the players

Whichever game you play, it is imperative that you do your homework and know the facts about the players in the Premiership. There is no substitute for this. For example, do you know the Manchester City midfield player who has scored 27 goals in 106 first team appearances? This book tries to help you by providing the facts and giving you some sound advice, but ultimately, you need to absorb the knowledge and make your own decision.

Watch the transfer market

During the summer period there is often hectic activity in the transfer market. We have seen it again this year. A transfer can have a dramatic effect upon the value of a player in all versions of fantasy football. It can also make an important difference to the make-up of your team. Let us take an example from last year.

In most of the newspaper games Phil Babb was described as a Coventry City defender and John Scales as a Wimbledon player, even though by the time that many of the newspaper games started, they had both been transferred to Liverpool. This had a number of effects. First of all, it meant that these two players were now considerably undervalued since they were now members of a solid defence and were therefore much more likely to produce good results and score more fantasy points. Secondly, it meant that the values of the other Liverpool defenders was also affected since they were now more likely to keep clean sheets etc. Thirdly, because they were categorised as non-Liverpool players, you could include them and two other Liverpool players, four in all in your team, and still be within the rules. Many fantasy managers noticed this and took advantage of it to gain excellent fantasy points.

Another effect that transfers may have is that a player may change from being a useful reserve into a regular first team player. Take the case of Dion Dublin last season. He moved from Manchester United to Coventry at the outset of the season and a proven goalscorer who had been languishing in a reserve team had suddenly become a potent first team Premiership striker. He was always likely to be a bargain and so it proved in many of the fantasy games.

Another example was Don Hutchison. From being a reserve midfielder at Liverpool, he became a first team member at West Ham and to add icing to the cake, he was used as a striker for some of the season (see below).

It is most important that you watch what is happening in the transfer market, particularly as the season approaches and the newspaper fantasy tables have already been published, to take advantage of transfers which have affected a player's valuation. The same point applies when you are considering introducing other players by using your transfers, later in the season.

Look out for wrongly classified players

Sometimes players are classified as defenders when

they are really midfielders. Or a player who is classified as a midfielder is really a striker or a defender. Sometimes a player changes his role. You must watch out for these to ensure that where possible you take advantage of the wrong classification, or, at least, you do not lose out by it.

The following are cases where, if the player is a suitable one, you should snap him up for your fantasy team:-

i) A midfield player (particularly one who likes to attack) is classified as a defender with a club who have a reasonably good defensive record. An example to watch out for might be Philippe Albert, who was signed as a centre back, but moved into midfield. If he is classified as a defender but plays as a midfield player, you will collect points for his considerable contribution to attack and for the defensive abilities of the improved Newcastle United back four.

ii) A striker is classified as a midfielder. The reason for signing this type of player is obvious since you are much more likely to gain points for scoring goals from a striker than you are from a midfield player. A number of players fall on the borderline. Are Matthew Le Tissier, Bryan Roy, Peter Beardsley, Ruel Fox etc midfielders or strikers? They vary from fantasy game to game, but if they are described as midfielders in your game and if you can afford them, they are the type of player to go for. These are all fairly expensive players, but there are also cheaper ones who may fall into the same type of classification query. Last year cheaper midfield players (in most of the newspaper games) who played as strikers for at least some of the season included Chris Bart Williams (Sheffield Wednesday), Dwight Yorke (Aston Villa), Don Hutchison (West Ham, originally Liverpool) and Mike Marsh (Coventry, originally West Ham). They all gave reasonable returns at cheap prices in most games. If any of them, or others who are in a similar situation, are again classified as midfielders, look at their price and make up your mind about them.

There are, however, cases where you should make sure that you avoid wrongly classified players and these are listed below:-

i) A defender who is listed as a midfielder. Here your player will get very few attacking points and he will get nothing for all of the defensive work that he does. An example of this last season was Carlton Palmer who had previously played in midfield for Sheffield Wednesday, but went to Leeds to play in the back four. He did eventually revert to midfield, but by that time the damage was done, since he picked up very few points during the first half of the season.

ii) A midfield player who is listed as a striker. Players like Rod Wallace (Leeds), Nigel Clough (Liverpool), Nick Barmby (Spurs) and even Peter Beardsley (Newcastle) are ones who may be classified as strikers or midfield players. They tend to play just behind the main striker and as such are unlikely to pick up as many points as an out-and-out striker. You should steer clear of them if they are categorised as strikers in your game.

Having considered a few points which apply to all versions of the fantasy game, let us now look at the two different approaches.

Private League

In the Private League version, whether run by a specialist organisation or organised independently by yourselves, where an auction is held, the tactics are fairly straightforward and therefore we will keep the advice on this to a minimum. You simply try to buy quality fantasy players at the best price possible. We tell you in this book who the players are who are likely to score well in fantasy football games and you choose which ones you are going to bid for. Even in this there are one or two fairly basic suggestions which you should adopt.

i) First of all, prepare yourself well for the auction. It is a good idea to prepare a list of players in whom you are interested and to know how much you think they are worth to you. Try not to go over the figure that you have set yourself when you are bidding, or you might run out of cash.

ii) Avoid going mad at the outset of the auction. There are often bargains to be picked up at the end, so do not think that you have to buy all of your team at the start of the evening.

iii) If at all possible try to get defenders who play for the clubs who are solid defensively, such as, Manchester United, Leeds United, Liverpool, Blackburn Rovers, Newcastle United or Arsenal. If you get players who play regularly for these clubs, you are unlikely to go far wrong. You may decide that there are other clubs where you are expecting good defensive performances and where you would be able to pick up defenders more cheaply eg Middlesbrough or Bolton Wanderers. That is a risk which, if it comes off, may pay rich dividends at a low price.

iv) Try to buy goalscoring midfielders. If you can get a Matt Le Tissier, Bryan Roy or Andre Kanchelskis without breaking the bank, it is almost as good as having a third striker. Alternatively, you may decide that you are going to save money here and buy only cheap midfield players so that you may spend more of your budget on two really top class strikers. The decision is yours, but plan it out beforehand.

v) Remember that you will probably get most of your points from your strikers. It is therefore sensible to be prepared to spend much of your money on those two (usually) players. If you can have Alan Shearer and Andy Cole (or one of the other top strikers) as your attacking force, it does not guarantee that you will win the league, but it certainly gives you a good start.

Newspaper versions of the fantasy game

There are two different types of game, even within this section.

As explained in "How to play", some variations give you a very large budget (say £25 million) to spend on your team and the prices of the players cover a wide range (say £200,000 to £7 million). The restrictions here are not so great. If you can find a few very cheap players, you are often able to include many of the expensive stars that you would ideally want in your team. Of course, it is still not easy and you still have to make the right choice, but at least the restrictions are not too great.

The second type of newspaper game is more restrictive. Here you have a tighter budget (say £20 million) and the range of player values is much narrower, starting say, at £1 to £1.2 million and going up to £3.5 to £4 million. These figures are not in line with current values, taking into account the reported transfers of Sutton (£5 million), Ferdinand (£6 million), Cole (£7 million) etc and there is a distinct possibility that those games will re-adjust their values to bring them more into line with current transfer fees. However the limits imposed in this type of game make it more difficult to select the team that you would ideally want and so it is upon this variation that we will concentrate in respect of strategy. If the value ranges are changed by the game organisers, it will be a fairly simple task to apply the same logic to the new values. However, there is an area of danger here which must be explored first.

Understand Player Values

One of the main confusions which leads to managers making wrong selections of players is in their valuation. The figures published in the newspapers do not necessarily bear any resemblance to the actual value of the player on the real transfer market, they are simply calculated at, by the company running the game, as their assessment of the player's "fantasy value". Let us consider how this is likely to mislead you.

The problem occurs in the game where the total budget is relatively small (say £20 million) and the range of players is narrow (say from £1 - £1.2 million to £3.5 -£4 million). It has much less effect in the other version where the budget is higher and the range of player values much wider.

The next few paragraphs include arithmetical calculations and logic which some readers may find difficult to follow. If so, simply ignore the detail and just note the conclusions.

Let us also assume that the minimum price for a player is £1.2 million and that the total budget is £20 million. If you consider buying an expensive striker who costs, say £3.6 million, and you wish to compare him with another who costs, say £2.4 million, you might expect him to gain you half as many points again. In other words, if the cheaper striker gets 80 points, you would expect the more expensive one to get 120. This is false logic which must be corrected if you are to make your decision based on fact.

Because you have to pay £1.2 million for each player, no matter how strong or weak he may be, you really should ignore that part of the price. In other words of your £20 million, the first £13.2 million (11 x £1.2 million) is already accounted for, and you only have the remaining £6.8 million to spend. Thus, the player costing you £3.6 million is taking up £2.4 of that £6.8 million whereas the player who costs £2.4 million is using up only £1.2 million of it. That means that you should expect the more expensive player to gain twice as many points as the cheaper one, not one and a half times. This argument can be continued across all values and may be worked out by calculating the "real" value of the player as follows:-

"Real" value = Published value - Minimum value

You can then know what points return you should anticipate by comparing the "Real" value of the players. A few figures are printed below based upon the criteria stated above, viz £1.2 million minimum value. These are intended to give you a guide. For other values you can do your own calculation based upon the formula above.

Cost of Player 1	Cost of Player 2	Comparison of number of points which you should expect from Player
£3.6 M	£1.6 M	6 x
£3.6 M	£1.8 M	4 x
£3.6M	£2 M	3 x
£3.6 M	£2.4 M	2 x
£3.6 M	£2.8 M	1.5 x
£3.6 M	£3.2 M	1.2 x
£3 M	£1.5 M	6 x
£3 M	£1.65 M	4 x
£3 M	£1.8 M	3 x
£3 M	£2.1 M	2 x
£3 M	£2.4 M	1.5 x
£3 M	£2.7 M	1.2 x
£2.4 M	£1.4	6 x
£2.4 M	£1.5	4 x
£2.4 M	£1.6	3 x
£2.4 M	£1.8	2 x
£2.4 M	£2	1.5 x
£2.4 M	£2.2	1.2 x

This can affect the strategy which should be adopted and will be taken further when we look at an improved strategy in Section 1 c) iii).

Standard Approach (Assuming a £20 million budget and a narrow range of player values)

In examining this, the author has researched the approach adopted by a number of managers in selecting their team and has found that surprisingly, there is an emphasis on one approach. Many managers decide that their first task will be to spend approximately £5 million on two strikers. Next they will spend somewhere in the region of £8 million on five defenders and finally approximately £7 million on four midfielders. Managers probably do not consciously put this sort of division of funds into their selection, but, they confirm that, in practice, that is what they are doing. The reason for taking this approach is logical. In most fantasy football games a manager will gain the highest returns on his/her investment from the strikers. Last season Alan Shearer scored far more points than any other player, whatever their position. Usually the next highest scorers were other strikers such as Fowler, Ferdinand or Le Tissier (the latter sometimes being described as a midfield player).

In adopting this approach, managers are making an assumption which is probably justified, but they should be aware of what they are presupposing. Their surmise is that the coming season will see another goal feast when a few top class strikers will get a rich harvest of goals. Let us look at the past three seasons.

In 1992/3 Teddy Sheringham with 22 and Les Ferdinand with 20 were the only players to score 20 or more goals. In 1993/4 no fewer than seven players exceeded 20 and Cole (34) and Shearer (31) exceeded 30. (NB These are Premier League goals only.) It was not that there were more goals scored in 1993/4, in fact, overall there were marginally less. It is just that a few forwards were scoring a larger number. In the 1994/5 season the top six scorers were Shearer (34), Fowler (25), Ferdinand (24), Collymore (22), Klinsmann (20) and Le Tissier (20).

Anyone who scores over 20 goals gives a good return, probably equivalent to the returns of a top defender or midfield player (in most leagues), over 25 will probably give you more points than a player from any other position, whilst if you find a striker who scores over 30, you have struck gold. Apart from buying other strikers who have done similarly, you could not have bettered your points tally. (In saying all of this we are over-simplifying, as we need to do for the sake of simplicity. Obviously there is the question of assists, which also have to be taken into account. A player like Le Tissier, who takes corners, free kicks, etc is likely to score many more points from assists than a Collymore or a Fowler and therefore may well score more fantasy points overall.)

The lesson that you should learn is that you need to assess, at the start of the season whether you think that there will be another glut of goals in the coming season. If you believe that there will be strikers who score 30+ goals then the above approach is a valid one to adopt. If, however, the top scorers are only going to find the net on about 20 occasions (as in 1992/3), then their points tally is only likely to be the equivalent of the top defenders or midfielders and this approach should be modified.

The evidence of the past two seasons is that with the new breed of strikers (Shearer, Fowler, Cole, Collymore, Sutton etc) there are many who have the potential to score 30 or more goals in a season. For this reason, we will pursue the logic of the "standard approach", but we will also look at other possibilities.

Selecting Strikers

In selecting their strikers, managers will usually choose one expensive, top class striker such as Shearer, with another, who is much cheaper. The vast majority of the managers spoken to said that they would choose Shearer "at all costs". In the games where the top price (and Shearer will certainly be that!) is £3.5 to £4 million, that leaves only £1 to £1.5 million for the second.

Expensive Strikers

Is it right to think of Shearer as the only possibility as the expensive striker? Certainly no-one could argue against selecting him, but in 1993/4, although he scored 31 goals, Cole outscored him. We will therefore examine other contenders who may compete with Shearer for the honour of being leading goal scorer.

We will look at Andy Cole, Tony Yeboah, Les Ferdinand, Robbie Fowler and Stan Collymore.

Cole has done it before and therefore must come into the reckoning. He has now settled in at Manchester United and is likely to have the prompting of Cantona to give him a service similar to that which he enjoyed at St James' Park from Peter Beardsley. With the help of the classy and hard-working midfield, plus feeding from the scraps from Denis Irwin's free kicks and even latching onto the first time clearances from goalkeeper Peter Schmeichel, it is not unreasonable to expect Cole to return to his prolific goalscoring ways of 1993/4. The one question which remains is with regard to his injuries. Has he fully recovered from the shin splint problem? This has recurred at the tail end of the 1994/5 season and must cast a doubt over his future. Even if he is able to play, will he recover the sharpness which made him such a goalscoring force? Make up your own mind.

The impact that Tony Yeboah made at Elland Road when he began playing for them in February was quite dramatic. From 16 starts he scored 13 goals and he looked the complete striker. Of course, for those who knew his track record this did not come as a surprise as he had scored 61 goals in 109 games for Eintracht Frankfurt in Bundesliga matches. He took no time at all to adjust to the English style of play and one wonders just how many goals he might score next season. There was a suggestion that he would not re-sign for Leeds, but any problems were successfully overcome and he is now looking forward to the possibilities for 1995/6. So are the Elland Road fans. It is our opinion that you must find room somewhere for Tony in your fantasy team, and he may well be not quite as expensive as Shearer.

Les Ferdinand has averaged 20 league goals per season over the past three seasons and had his best year so far last season. The supply line at Loftus Road has not always been at the highest level and he has done exceptionally well to achieve this level of consistency. Now that he has moved to Newcastle, with the support of Beardsley, Sellars, Fox, Lee, Gillespie and others, the sky really is the limit. Expect Les to break his personal best for goals scored in a season. Perhaps the key to just how many times he will score lies in how he combines with Paul Kitson. You must give due consideration to Ferdinand when you choose your team.

Robbie Fowler seems to have been around for years, but he is still only 20. After being dogged by injury the previous season, he was an ever-present member of the first team in 1994/5 and responded by scoring 25 goals. He has the benefit of playing alongside the veteran Ian Rush and this will undoubtedly stand him in good stead for the future. With the burgeoning talent of the young Liverpool midfield, it seems that his goalscoring feats can only get even better. He is a likely 30+ striker for next season and you have to consider him.

Finally, in this group, we have "Stan the Man". At the time of writing, it is not known where he will be playing next season. It now seems inevitable that he will leave the City Ground, but his destination is uncertain. His talents cannot be doubted. Collymore scores goals that probably no-one else in the Premiership could convert. His speed off the mark and his eye for goal are phenomenal. Yet there must be a doubt regarding his personality. There has been a long-running saga between Stan and Frank Clark, and his team mates stopped celebrating with him when he scored. This must cast a shadow over his footballing feats. Nevertheless, he scored 22 goals and if he joins a club where the service is right for his type of game, he could improve on that. After all, he is only 24.

Behind this group come a batch of others including Beardsley, Bright, Cantona, Holdsworth, Rush, Sheringham, Stein, Sutton and Wright, all of whom are reliable strikers, but arguably not quite on the same level as the group mentioned above when it comes to scoring goals. They are all likely to be fairly expensive,

Inexpensive Strikers

If our budget for strikers is £5 million and we have spent £3.5 to £4 million on one of the above, we have to find a much cheaper one to make up our partnership.

One way of doing this is to look for a proven goalscorer who is languishing in the reserves at one of the top clubs, who may either force his way into the first team or alternatively may be transferred to another Premiership clubs. Last season Dion Dublin was just such a case. He had always been a prolific goalscorer and at Cambridge had hit the target on 69 occasions in 162 starts. As we recommended last year, he was one to look out for. At the time of writing that, we did not know that he would be transferred to Coventry City and become a bargain buy in virtually all of the fantasy leagues. Certainly the author included him in his fantasy teams, and if you did too, you would have been rewarded with an excellent goals per £ ratio.

Another approach is to look for young strikers with high potential who are likely to break into the big time from early on in the season. There are three outstanding candidates who fall into this category; the talent among young Premiership strikers at present is amazing.

Probably one of the reasons why Ray Wilkins was prepared to allow Les Ferdinand to go to Newcastle was the tremendous ability shown by young Kevin Gallen. He scored 10 league goals from 36 starts, which may not be as impressive as some of the other strikers mentioned, but he has been a prolific scorer in youth and reserve teams and it is highly likely that that rate will improve. Furthermore he has contributed with numerous assists for Les Ferdinand. There is talk that Roberto Baggio may come to Loftus Road. Maybe their fans are playing their own game of fantasy football! Whether their dreams are fulfilled or not, Kevin Gallen has a tremendous future and he could score lots of goals in 1995/6.

At Elland Road, Noel Whelan is only 20 and has scored 7 goals from only 19 starts. He is a lanky youth with great skill who has a tremendous future in the game. He is unfortunate to be competing with Yeboah, Deane and Massinga for a place in the starting line-up and bearing in mind Howard Wilkinson's apparent aversion to giving youth a chance (with the notable exception of Gary Kelly), he may not get too many chances. If he does get in, playing alongside Yeboah would give his career the lift-off that it needs and he could well make a real breakthrough. Alternatively, he may be the "Dublin" of 1995/6, transferring to a club where he will be given his chance to make his mark. Check what happens as the season is about to start.

The third of the young hopefuls is the hugely talented Paul Scholes. He has appeared mainly as a substitute (11 times), having started in only 6 games, but he has scored five goals. He also scored twice on his debut in the Coca Cola Cup against Port Vale in October. Last year our comments about him were "You read it here first! This young man will be a star! United's Young Player of the Year 1993/4, he is a good dribbler, fights for the ball and scored 25 times in 25 appearances for the 'A' team. Watch this space." He has started on his first team career and with what success! However, with Cole, Cantona and Hughes around, what chance does he have, other than the occasional game as substitute? Another situation to watch carefully. One thing is for sure, if he gets the games, he will get the goals.

Selecting Defenders

The selection of defenders is much more dependent upon the team for whom they play than is the selection of midfield players and strikers. The attacking flair of defenders, which brings extra points, should only be thought of as a bonus on top of the main means of acquiring points for defence, which is by keeping clean sheets. Under no circumstances should a defender be selected purely on the basis of his attacking capabilities. An example should demonstrate this. Mark Bowen is an excellent attacking defender, but despite his abilities in attack, the leaky Norwich defence meant that in most of the newspaper games, he finished with a very poor points score at the end of the season.

Table 1, in Section 1.c.ii) shows clubs in order of the number of goals conceded throughout the season. It also gives the number of clean sheets. Table 2 shows the same information, but for only the last ten games of the season. Also shown are the equivalent figures for 1993/4.

In the "Standard Approach" you have approximately £8 million to spend on your five defenders, that is an average of £1.6 million per player. Where should you look for them?

It would be nice if you could simply select the most powerful defensive teams and then select all of your defenders from there. Unfortunately, life is not that simple. You will be unable to fill your defence with players from these highly-organised defences and you may have to select just one, or at the very most two, from these highly-priced defenders if you are to remain within your budget. We will therefore look at which of these should be our prime target, and whether there are others who are good defensive prospects, but at a much cheaper price.

Expensive Defenders

The first place that you should look for the one or two top class defenders that you will be able to include, is in the teams which have a consistently good defensive record. These include Manchester United (who were outstanding in this respect in 1994/5), Liverpool, Leeds United, Blackburn Rovers and Newcastle United. To this list might be added Arsenal, who were outstanding during the previous season, but who had a poorer record last year. Everton and Sheffield Wednesday also did well defensively and may move into the top category; you must decide.

Last year in the various newspaper games, the most highly-priced defenders usually came from Arsenal, Blackburn Rovers and Manchester United. Those from the last two named will undoubtedly be expensive again. It is just possible, though rather unlikely, that one or two fantasy games might reduce the price of the Arsenal defenders, in view of their relatively poor 1994/5 season. If so, you may find a bargain, since it is most unlikely that they will do as poorly again.

In selecting an expensive defender you should first consider the club for whom they play, and whether you feel that they will keep a good number of clean sheets in the coming season. Clean sheets score good fantasy points in most games and it is important to gain these if you possibly can. However, assuming that you are choosing from the teams mentioned above, you need have few doubts about their defensive abilities. There is another area to be

considered. To take maximum returns from your investment, you should seek a player who will also score points for either scoring goals or for assisting by "making" a goal. Thus, wherever possible, you should avoid a totally defensive player.

Defenders from the top defensive teams who get forward and occasionally score include Adams, Le Saux, Wetherall, Scales, Ruddock, Bruce, Pallister, Irwin, Albert, Elliott, Howey, and Nolan. You should also add the name of Stuart Pearce of Nottingham Forest, who were just out of the top batch of clubs, but Pearce's goalscoring record is second to none among defensive players.

As was mentioned at the start of this section, particular attention should be paid to Philippe Albert, who will probably be classified as a defender, but will play in midfield. If that is the case, he is a must for selection. Others who would be towards the top of the list of star defenders would be Graeme Le Saux, who sometimes plays on the left hand side of midfield and also takes shots at goal from free kicks. The incredible goalscoring record of Stuart Pearce must also be considered seriously, and if you think that Nottingham Forest will improve just a little on their impressive first season back in the Premiership, then he could be an important member of your team.

Others who had a very impressive season last year were Andy Hinchcliffe and Peter Atherton. They will undoubtedly be more expensive in 1995/6, and may be less cost-effective.

Without knowing the cost of each individual player for 1994/5 it is impossible to make a final selection, but, looking at a mixture of expensive and good mid range priced defenders, we would probably be choosing from the following:-

Tony Adams	Denis Irwin
Philippe Albert	Graeme Le Saux
Peter Atherton	Ian Nolan
Warren Barton	Gary Pallister
Steve Bruce	Darren Peacock
Robbie Elliott,	Neil Ruddock
Andy Hinchcliffe	John Scales
Steve Howey	David Wetherall

We said earlier that you would be able to afford, at the most, two of those expensive defenders, so let us examine cheaper options.

Inexpensive Defenders

Often the best bargains may be obtained by finding players who are not sure of their place at the start of the season. Last year Stig Bjornebye found himself as a regular member of the Liverpool defence, when at the start of the season that would have seemed unlikely. He gained good points and in most fantasy leagues, he was very reasonably priced. Who will be the equivalent in 1995/6?

There is just a possibility that one of the list given above may fall into this category. Robbie Elliott of Newcastle made only 10 appearances in the season, partly due to injury, but also because he has not yet regained his place at left back from John Beresford. Fans at St James' Park rate him very highly and this could be the year when he breaks through and wins a regular place. He may be a little cheaper than the other Newcastle defenders and as such, be an excellent buy.

One of the best sources of cheap defenders is from promoted clubs. Last year both Nottingham Forest and Crystal Palace (even though they were relegated) did reasonably well defensively. Furthermore, they were inexpensive. The evidence from the Endsleigh League Division 1 results is that the teams being promoted this year are of a better quality defensively. As you will see from their write-ups, the comparison of their defensive performances, as compared with those of other clubs promoted in recent years, are as follows:-

1994/5	Played	Goals Conceded	Clean Sheets
Middlesborough	46	40	18
Bolton Wanderers	46	45	19

The defensive records compare favourably with those of the clubs promoted the previous season, which were as follows:-

1993/4	Played	Goals Conceded	Clean Sheets
Crystal Palace	46	46	14
Nottingham Forest	46	49	15
Leicester City	46	59	12

Crystal Palace and Nottingham Forest acquitted themselves very well defensively in the Premiership, Palace were relegated because their goalscoring dried up rather than because of defensive inadequacies. From the above records, it would appear that Middlesborough and Bolton Wanderers are likely places to find inexpensive, effective defenders.

The players who may also contribute fantasy points for attacking involvement include Stubbs (if he remains at Bolton), Green, Pearson, Vickers and Cox. Goalkeepers Miller and Branagan should also be included.

Selecting Midfielders

Under the "Standard Approach", we are looking for four midfielders totalling about £7 million, ie an average of £1.75 million. In effect, this means that if a top class goalscoring midfield player such as Matt Le Tissier or Bryan Roy is selected, the other three midfielders will have to be inexpensive ones. Alternatively, you may be able to afford two medium priced ones, say approximately £2 million each and two cheaper ones. Therefore we need to look at this category of player in three price ranges.

When selecting midfield players, the club for whom they play is largely irrelevant, although where a player is in a team where a large number of goals are scored, that can mean that he has a greater opportunity to be involved in assists. However, it is interesting that many of the midfield players who scored high points in fantasy leagues are from clubs in mid-table, or even near the bottom.

The selection of midfield players is often where a fantasy league is won and lost. Often an "unknown" player will emerge to score well and make all the difference to your score. Likewise, a star midfielder would have a bad season and mean that you have wasted a great deal of money. Who, for example, would have said at the start of last season that Steve Stone of Nottingham Forest would score five goals and get plenty of assists (helping Roy and Collymore) and would easily outscore the much more expensive Ryan Giggs, who managed only one league goal?

Expensive Midfielders

By this we mean midfielders who cost more than, say £2.25 million, although this figure will vary from game to game.

The top player in this group is undoubtedly Matt Le Tissier. There are many who will be prepared to pay the extra for him because his goalscoring record, plus his contribution with assists, means that you virtually have another striker in your team. We cannot argue with that, except that you must expect to pay a high price for the privilege of having him.

With him in the expensive group are likely to be Ryan Giggs, Bryan Roy, Ruel Fox, Gary Speed, Steve McManaman, Darren Anderton and Andre Kanchelskis. All of these have their backers and you simply have to make your choice and find the money.

Medium Priced Midfielders

Here we are thinking of players whose value is approximately £1.75 to £2.25 million. This will probably include a number of well-known midfielders such as Barnes, Bart-Williams, Batty, Bohinen, Dozzell, Earle, Gillespie, Hutchison, Keane, Kennedy, Lee, McAllister, Magilton, Merson, Moncur, Gavin Peacock, Ripley, Sellars, Sharpe, Sherwood, Sinclair, Sinton, Stone, Waddle, Wilcox, Wise, Woan and Yorke.

Of these, one or two deserve special mention. Hutchison and Yorke have each played a number of games as striker and have done so quite successfully. Check whether they are still classified as midfielders and if so, see whether they start the season in attack. Even if they do not, in view of the fact that the experiment last season was successful, they may well play there again in the future. In any case ,they are both goalscoring midfielders and so you are unlikely to lose out by selecting them.

Wilcox is a genuine left winger who is a good crosser of the ball (and with Shearer and Sutton waiting for it in the middle, that can lead to plenty of points) who also has an eye for goal. He was unlucky with injury last year, otherwise his goal tally, and more especially his fantasy points tally, would have been much more impressive. Expect much more from him this year.

Peacock of Chelsea and Earle of Wimbledon are both goalscoring midfield players who had a poor season, and as a result may be much cheaper for 1995/6. They may well be reduced in price and available as a bargain. Their Premiership goalscoring records are as follows:-

	1992/3	1993/4	1994/5
Peacock	12	8	4
Earle	7	9	0

Earle was out for much of the season through injury, playing in only nine league games. Peacock has been less influential this season and must surely do better in 1995/6.

Lee began last season in great form, scoring 11 goals in his first 11 games (both league and cup). His run then dried up and he scored only twice more during the whole of the season. Strange form indeed; fans believe that his season fell apart after he was injured while playing for England. Do you have the confidence to buy him, assuming that he will show his early season form again in the coming season?

Gillespie is another Newcastle midfielder who has lots of talent. Early indications are that he will not score enough goals to justify his selection in your team, although he contributes well with assists.

Finally in this section, there is Paul Merson. Hopefully his drugs and other problems are behind him and he can concentrate on his football. He scored 4 goals in the 14n games after his rehabilitation and really looked the part again. His is an undoubted talent which may develop even further this year under a new strict management.

Inexpensive Midfielders

These are the players who cost less than £1.75 million, or thereabouts. So where do we look for our cheap midfielders?

Players who have already made an impact in the Premiership but have fallen away into some obscurity in the reserves include Darren Caskey (Spurs), Clark (Newcastle), Gemmill (Nottingham Forest), Meaker (QPR), Ryan Jones (Sheffield Wednesday) and Jason Dozzell (Spurs). All of these have considerable talent and know where the goal is. The question is whether they will be able to win back their place in the team. If they do, they are likely to be inexpensive and worth snapping up.

There are also a few midfield goalscorers at Manchester City. Paul Lake has an outstanding strike record, but has been plagued by injury for about four years. It really is make or break time for him as the rumours suggest that he is ready to return. If he does, will his knee stand up to the rigours of top class soccer? If so, you could get a real bargain for a known goalscorer who will be dirt cheap. Then there is Steve Lomas, sadly missed when he was injured at the start

of 1995. He should return to be, with Flitcroft, the dynamo of the City midfield, and to score the occasional goal. Garry Flitcroft is probably the most likely member of your team; he still managed five goals, even though the team struggled. Furthermore, he should not be too expensive.

So where do we look for up-and-coming talent this year? The promoted teams each have effective midfield players who can score. Check up on Richard Sneekes and Alan Thompson of Bolton, and Alan Moore, Jamie Pollock and Craig Hignett of Middlesbrough. All can score goals, particularly Craig Hignett, although he has the problem of not being able to hold a regular place in the first team. If he manages to do so, he is the ideal fantasy player.

Finally, there is a bright young midfield star at Everton named Tony Grant. He was drafted into the England U-21 squad for the game against Latvia in April and has played a few games (mainly coming on as a substitute) in the Premiership. Here is one for the future, and just maybe for this coming season.

Step by Step Guidelines

If you decide that the "Standard Approach" outlined in this section is the one that you would wish to adopt, you will find brief guidelines to give you an "assist" in Section 1d). Alternatively, you may wish to consider an "Improved Strategy" which is outlined in Section 1 c) iii).

Figures in respect of Middlesbrough and Bolton Wanderers in the Endsleigh League 1st Division are as follows:-

1994/5	Played	Goals Conceded	Clean Sheets	Goals Scored	Points
Middlesbrough	46	40	18	67	82
Bolton Wanderers	46	45	19	67	77

The defensive records compare favourably with those of the clubs promoted the previous season which were as follows:-

1994/5	Played	Goals Conceded	Clean Sheets	Goals Scored	Points
Crystal Palace	46	46	14	73	90
Nottingham Forest	46	49	15	74	83
Leicester City	46	59	12	72	73

Both Crystal Palace and Nottingham Forest acquitted themselves very well defensively in the Premiership, Palace were relegated because their goalscoring dried up because of rather than any defensive inadequacies. From the above records, it would appear that any potential problems which lie in store for Middlesbrough and Bolton Wanderers are likely to lie in their goalscoring abilities rather than in their defence. However, Middlesborough have attempted to overcome this with the signing of Jan Fjortoft and the promise of more signings to come.

1994/5 DEFENCE STATISTICS

(1993/4 figures in brackets)

Table 1 (42 games)	Goals conceded	Clean sheets
Manchester United	28 (38)	24 (17)
Liverpool	37 (55)	17 (9)
Leeds United	38 (39)	17 (18)
Blackburn	39 (36)	16 (18)
Newcastle United	47 (41)	15 (15)
Crystal Palace	49 (N/A)	15 (N/A)
Everton	51 (63)	14 (11)
Sheffield Wednesday	57 (54)	14 (10)
Coventry City	62 (45)	14 (13)
Nottingham Forest	43 (N/A)	13 (N/A)
West Ham United	48 (58)	13 (14)
Arsenal	49 (28)	13 (21)
Chelsea	55 (53)	13 (11)
Wimbledon	65 (53)	12 (12)
Aston Villa	56 (50)	11 (13)
Tottenham Hotspur	58 (59)	11 (7)
Norwich	54 (61)	10 (10)
Queen's Park Rangers	59 (61)	10 (10)
Manchester City	64 (49)	10 (12)
Southampton	63 (66)	9 (6)
Leicester City	80 (N/A)	4 (N/A)
Ipswich Town	93 (58)	3 (14)

1994/5 DEFENCE STATISTICS

(1993/4 figures in brackets)

Table 2 (Last 10 games)	Goals conceded	Clean sheets
Manchester United	6(8)	6(5)
Everton	8(19)	6(3)
West Ham United	5(14)	5(2)
Nottingham Forest	7(N/A)	5(N/A)
Wimbledon	11(10)	5(3)
Leeds United	8(7)	4(5)
Aston Villa	10(19)	4(2)
Southampton	12(20)	4(1)
Queen's Park Rangers	9(19)	3(1)
Liverpool	11(12)	3(1)
Newcastle United	12(8)	3(5)
Chelsea	13(12)	3(3)
Crystal Palace	15(N/A)	3(N/A)
Sheffield Wednesday	17(9)	3(4)
Blackburn	12(12)	2(4)
Arsenal	13(11)	2(2)
Coventry City	15(7)	2(4)
Leicester City	15(N/A)	2(N/A)
Tottenham Hotspur	16(13)	2(3)
Manchester City	16(9)	1(4)
Norwich	18(15)	1(3)
Ipswich	21(20)	1(1)

1994/5 ATTACK STATISTICS

(1993/4 figures in brackets)

Table 3 (42 games)	Goals scored	Points gained	League position
Blackburn	80 (63)	89 (84)	1 (2)
Manchester United	77 (80)	88 (92)	2 (1)
Nottingham Forest	72 (N/A)	77 (N/A)	3 (N/A)
Newcastle United	67 (82)	72 (77)	6 (3)
Tottenham Hotspur	66 (54)	62 (45)	7 (15)
Liverpool	65 (59)	74 (60)	4 (8)
Queen's Park Rangers	61 (62)	60 (60)	8 (9)
Southampton	61 (49)	54 (43)	12 (18)
Leeds United	59 (65)	73 (70)	5 (5)
Manchester City	53 (38)	49 (45)	17 (16)
Arsenal	52 (53)	51 (71)	12 (4)
Aston Villa	51 (46)	48 (57)	18 (10)
Chelsea	50 (49)	54 (51)	11 (14)
Sheffield Wednesday	49 (76)	51 (64)	13 (7)
Wimbledon	48 (56)	56 (65)	9 (6)
Leicester City	45 (N/A)	29 (N/A)	21 (N/A)
West Ham United	44 (47)	50 (52)	14 (13)
Everton	44 (42)	50 (44)	15 (17)
Coventry City	44 (43)	50 (56)	16 (11)
Norwich	37 (65)	43 (53)	20 (12)
Ipswich Town	36 (35)	27 (43)	22 (19)
Crystal Palace	34 (N/A)	45 (N/A)	19 (N/A)

1994/5 ATTACK STATISTICS

(1993/4 figures in brackets)

Table 4 (Last 10 games)	Goals scored	Points gained
Nottingham Forest	26	26
Southampton	17	18
Arsenal	16	11
Leeds United	15	21
Manchester United	14	19
West Ham United	14	17
Tottenham Hotspur	14	11
Blackburn	13	17
Newcastle United	13	12
Manchester City	13	11
Liverpool	11	16
Queen's Park Rangers	11	16
Everton	11	15
Wimbledon	11	14
Coventry City	11	11
Crystal Palace	11	11
Chelsea	10	14
Leicester City	10	8
Sheffield Wednesday	9	8
Norwich	7	4
Aston Villa	5	10
Ipswich Town	5	4

Section 1.c.iii)

IMPROVED STRATEGY

The scoring systems of most of the newspaper fantasy football games and our 'Standard Approach' seem to make a few assumptions which we should examine. The scoring systems seem to have been set in order to allow the best strikers and defenders to gain approximately the same number of points if the top scorers in the league get 20 to 25 goals.

In 1992/3 Teddy Sheringham with 22 and Les Ferdinand with 20 were the only players to reach that range. In 1993/4, no fewer than seven players exceeded 20, and Cole (34) and Shearer (31) exceeded 30. In 1994/5 Shearer scored 34 goals again, whilst five others exceeded 20.

What will happen in the coming season? Will the defences have rumbled Shearer and know how to handle him? Or will he and maybe others break the 30 goals per season barrier again? The answer to these questions should determine the strategy which we decide to adopt. If we are to see leading strikers again scoring 25 to 35 goals, then, on the basis that the most fantasy points are scored by strikers in that scenario, the correct tactics must be to spend sufficient money to buy two major goalscorers, whatever the price, and fill up the team with lower value players in defence and/or midfield. If so, we must review our approach.

However, it may be that one of the lower priced strikers breaks into the big time, and so we are able to get top points at a lower cost.

We must also take into account the segment "Understand Player Values" in Section 1 c) i), which demonstrates that it is better value for money to buy a striker for £2.4 million who will score say 80 - 90 points than one at £3.6 million who gets 150.

It is our opinion that there are a number of strikers who have the potential to score over 30 goals. Our suggested list would include Shearer (inevitably), Cole, Ferdinand, Yeboah, Fowler and Collymore (depending upon which club he joins). An outside possibility to add to this list might be Wright, if Bruce Rioch raids the transfer market for someone to give him the service which he needs. All of these are likely to be expensive in most newspaper variations for the coming season.

There is the chance that a cheaper striker might develop rapidly and if you could find one, then you would really have struck gold. If all of the conditions for this were right, the ones most likely to do this are Scholes, Gallen or Whelan although, as we have pointed out elsewhere, they are not guaranteed their first team place and something dramatic would have to happen if they are to achieve the breakthrough that we are talking about.

The other possibility is the importing of a top class striker from abroad. A world-class figure like Jurgen Klinsmann was expensive when he was put in the fantasy lists, but a lesser known one, Yeboah, was less expensive when he was introduced into some of the games, even though his goalscoring potential was probably higher than that of the German. Watch out for other foreign strikers joining the Premiership, and do your homework to assess whether they are likely to give good returns.

We are going to consider three variations on the Standard Approach, each of which might pay very good dividends. Remember that the Standard Approach was based upon an expensive striker (£3.5 - £4 million), who was expected to score 30+ goals and a cheap striker (£1 - £1.5 million) who might score 10 - 15 goals. The three variations are as follows:-

	Approximate values of strikers	Anticipated no number of goals	Amount for Midfield	Amount for Defence
1	£3.5 million	30+		
	£3.5 million	30+		
Total £7 million			£6 million	£7 million
2	£3.5 million	30+		
	£2.5 million	20+		
Total £6 million			£7 million	£7 million
3	£2.5 million	20+		
	£2.5 million	20+		
Total £5 million			£7 million	£8 million

Variation 1

If you are able to find two strikers who will break the 30+ barrier, then you are on the way to a very high points total under any fantasy football game. However, if they are experienced top-class strikers, as is likely, they will be expensive. Assuming that you have to pay a total of say, £7 million for them, your budget for defenders and midfielders will be reduced to £6 million and £7 million respectively. This means that you have an average of only £1.5 million per midfielder and £1.4 million per defender. You will be forced to find nine inexpensive players for the privilege of fielding two star attackers. Nevertheless, it has been proved in the past that it is possible to come up with cheap defenders and midfielders who will give an excellent return on a very low investment.

The method for this variation is simple. Take a lot of time to get your strikers right! This is the most crucial aspect. Then examine our comments carefully, check on the past records of the cheaper players whom you fancy, and try to balance your budget. Some compromise will almost certainly have to be made. Managers usually find that they end up a few hundred thousand short of what they need to buy the team that they would ideally like.

Do not forget to watch out for the wrongly-classified players and those recently transferred, as explained in Section 1 c) i).

Variation 2

Here you opt for an expensive top-class striker who will score more than 30 goals, with a medium-priced one who will get over 20. Remember the lesson learned in the segment "Understand Player Values". A top striker costing £3.6 million needs to score twice as many goals as one costing £2.4 million, in order to justify his price tag.

Thus, if you expect your top striker (costing, say £3.6 million) to score, say 120 points, in your fantasy game, then any points in excess of 60 scored by a striker costing only £2.4 million, is a bonus. If you adopt this variation, you will have another £1 million to spend on your midfielders which, if invested wisely, may bring better returns that spending it on your second striker.

Variation 3

This could be the optimum solution. Do you have the courage to ignore the Alan Shearers of this world and the other very highly-priced ones? If you can find two strikers costing a total of around £5 million, each of whom could score three-quarters of the points scored by the top-price stars, you have really found a winner. This will leave you enough to include one or more players of the quality of a Le Tissier or a Roy to give your score a big boost from midfield. This could be the winning formula.

The only way of improving on this is to find a genuine goalscorer among the very cheap strikers (such as Dublin in 1994/5) to combine with either a star striker or a medium-priced one. This way your returns may be even higher.

The secret of getting the best value for money is to check the "Real" value of your players against the points that you expect them to gain, and then to calculate whether you are getting a good return on your investment.

Evaluating your Potential Returns

This segment takes the logic of "Understand Player Values" one stage further. Once again, it involves some mathematical ability which might be a problem to some readers. If so, ignore the section and base your selections on the outline given above.

We have already seen how to calculate the "Real" value of a player, that is, the amount by which the player's price exceeds the minimum price of a player in your newspaper game. Thus if the minimum price of a player is £1 million and your player costs £4 million, the "Real" price (by our definition) is £3 million. It is possible to calculate a rate of return for a player by taking the number of points scored by him and dividing that by the "Real" value.

$$\text{Rate of return} = \frac{\text{Points scored}}{\text{"Real" value (in £100,000s)}}$$

For example if, in a league where the minimum value per player is £1.2 million, a player costing £3.6 million scores 120 points, the calculation would be as follows:-

"Real" value = £3.6 - £1.2 million = £2.4 million

$$\text{Rate of Return} = \frac{120}{24} = 5 \text{ points per £100,000 spent.}$$

In fact you could use this type of calculation to indicate what return was gained by a player last season and use it in working out your hoped for return in the coming one. For example, you could use the above calculation as a base to indicate what points you should expect for various values.

At the above rate you would expect the following return:-

Price of Player	"Real" value	Expected no. of points return (at 5 points per £100,000)
£1.5 M	£.3 M	15
£1.8 M	£.6 M	30
£2 M	£.8 M	40
£2.4 M	£1.2 M	60
£2.7 M	£1.5 M	75
£3 M	£1.8 M	90
£3.3 M	£2.1 M	105
£3.6 M	£2.4 M	120

If 120 is the return that you would expect from a top striker costing £3.6 million, then any points score which is higher than the one listed for a particular value is, in fact, a better pro rata return. Thus medium-priced strikers (approximately £2.5 million) scoring 70 to 80 points are a better investment than your top striker. However, this is only the case if the money that you save can be spent on another investment who also has a better return than your top striker.

Perhaps the highest return will be from a striker costing only, say, £1.5 million, and scoring 30 to 40 points. Here again the advantages have to be weighed against whether you are able to use the money saved to buy other players who will also give you a rate of return better than the one which you have set as your requirement.

Therefore the advice is, set a rate of return (say 5 points per £100,000 as above) at which you are aiming and select players who you think will exceed that rate. This may lead you to a better total score than simply paying for top strikers.

Warning:- It should be noted that as the players' values get very close to the minimum (here £1.2 million), the calculations can become rather misleading.

Step by Step Guidelines

You will find help in Section 1 d) to lead you through the stages of selecting your team under the variation which you adopt.

Timing of Entry

The strategy here is simple and not at all sophisticated. Nevertheless, it can make a dramatic difference to the success of your fantasy football team.

The recommendation is that you leave it AS LATE AS YOU POSSIBLY CAN, within the rules, before submitting your selected team. This will not make you (or me!) popular with the various fantasy organisations, but it must be obvious that it is to your advantage to have every bit of available information that you can, before making your final selection.

Players may get an injury, or late signings may be made, or all sorts of other eventualities may occur which will harm your selection, unless you leave it as late as possible.

If you are able to delay your submission into the start of the season, you will be able to see which players have gained an early place in Premiership teams, and you may even gain some idea of which individual players have made an early impact on the fantasy scene.

The only problem that this may cause is if you make a mistake in your selection, say by exceeding the total value allowed, or accidentally selecting more than two players from the same club for your team. If the newspaper fantasy game organiser tightens up on their rules you may find that you do not have time to resubmit your team, resulting in it being eliminated. On the other hand, it may result in you having even more time.

Sect 1.c.v)

Transfers

Some fantasy games allow the transfer of players, others do not. Where transfers are allowed, they are often on the basis of 2 - 4 players up to three times per season.

The use of transfers can be very important, particularly if one of your players is injured or loses his place in the Carling Premiership team. However, managers should avoid the temptation to use up their transfers too soon. Even if a player is injured, it may well pay to wait for a short time before transferring him out, particularly if he is the only player in your team who is injured or who has lost his place (maybe through a loss of form). The use of transfers towards the end of the season can give a manager a very big advantage.

A further important consideration is whether the transferring out of players who are not gaining points is the right approach. It is often players who have picked up a LARGE NUMBER of points who should be considered for transfer out. An example from the past season might explain the principle.

If you had been very brave (or foolhardy) and decided at the beginning of March to transfer out Alan Shearer and transfer in Andy Cole, you would in fact have improved your goalscoring, and probably your points total at the end of the season. From 1st March to the end of the season, Cole scored 10 goals whereas Shearer scored only eight. Now that may not have seemed to be a sensible thing to do and there was probably no good reason for doing so, but the fact remains that you would have gained points.

The principle of this applies more to other situations. The point of all this is that it is not a good idea to chase after points which have already been scored. You are looking for points in the future, not in the past. Of course, it may be that one player who has scored well in the past will do even better in the future, but it is also possible that the very team members whom you would consider to be your most reliable point scorers, suddenly dry up.

Transfers should be used carefully and thoughtfully.

Sect 1.d.i)

Step by Step Guidelines

The following is a guide to the stages through which you should go in order to carry out your selection in a thorough and organised way. You should use the chart over the page to get more detail in how to carry out these steps.

It should be noted that these guidelines assume that the prices of players and total amount allowed will be as explained in the sections relating to strategy, viz Total Budget = £20 million and Range of Values for Players = approx £1million to £4 milllion. If this is not the case, it will be necessary to adjust the figures quoted accordingly.

Stage 1

Determine your strategy:-

i) If you think that you will be able to find an inexpensive striker who will be able to score 10 to 15 goals and a top class striker who will approach 35 goals, adopt the "Standard Approach".

ii) If you think that once again there will be a number of very high-scoring forwards (25 to 35 goals in the season), go for two forwards, preferably one of them from the medium-price range (approximately £2.5 million), if such a bargain is available. This will be Variation 1 or 2 of the "Improved Strategy".

iii)If you can find two medium-priced strikers (approximately £2.5 million) who will score 25+ goals, this could be your best solution. This is Variation 3 of the Improved Strategy.

Stage 2

Select your short-lists:-

There will be a number of lists for the different positions. You will probably need to compile lists for "Star", "Medium Price" and "Budget" players for each position. These can be thought of as shortlists of players from whom you will make your final selection. Forms to assist you are included at the end of the book.

i) Follow the order shown in the chart to select shortlists of strikers from which you will make your final selections. If you are entering more than one team, it is useful to have all of the possibilities to enable you to have a variety of choices.

ii) Follow the instructions on the chart for defenders who will be on your short list.

iii) Do the same for midfield players.

iv) Write your selections onto the appropriate shortlist sheets in the appendix in Section 5. You have forms for each of the categories Goalkeeper, Full back, Centre back, Midfield and Striker. Write on the name of the player, his club, price and the code given in the newspaper.

Stage 3
Make your Prime Selections:

i) Under either strategy there will be 'Prime Selections', which you will need to make, which are the fundamental 'Banker' players in your team. Once again, the detail of this is shown in the chart. This will certainly include your strikers, plus any other defenders or midfield players who are fundamental to your team. This is where you will spend most of your money and great care must be taken.

ii) Enter these selections onto your 'Proposed team' sheet in pencil. They should not be changed, since they are the players who are fundamental to your team. However, every manager changes his/her mind or tactics sometimes, and so it is best to keep your options open by using pencil.

iii) It is essential at this and at all subsequent stages that you ensure that you do not select more than two players from any one Premiership club.

Stage 4
Check your finances:-

i) Having completed Stage 3, you will now need to keep one eye continually on your expenditure. Work out how much you have spent on your 'Prime Selections' and how much of your £20M remains.

Stage 5
Select your remaining players:-

The chances are that by now you are having to watch your spending carefully. It is likely that most of your selections here will be cheaper defenders and midfielders. You have already produced your shortlists, so now you examine those to make your final selections.

There will be need for compromise here. You certainly will not be able to afford all of the players whom you would like to have. Therefore you will probably have to select untried youngsters or unproven players moving up from a lower Division. Do not be put off by this. Every other manager will have the same problem. It is likely that this is the selection which will decide the eventual winner. Many will get the right strategy and the correct 'Star' players, but expertise and a certain amount of good luck will be needed to choose relatively unknown players who are about to make the grade. We hope that this book will help you.

Finally, enter these selections onto your 'Proposed team' sheet and check that you have not exceeded the £20M limit.

Stage 6
Double check

i) Cross check the value of each player selected to make sure that you have not written down a wrong value.

ii) Check the total to ensure that you have added it correctly.

iii) Check that you have not included more than two players from any one club.

iv) Check that you have the correct make-up of the team eg:

     1 Goalkeeper

     2 Full backs

     2 Centre backs

     4 Midfield players

     2 Strikers

v) Submit your entry and settle down to wait for your name and that of your team to be printed in your newspaper.

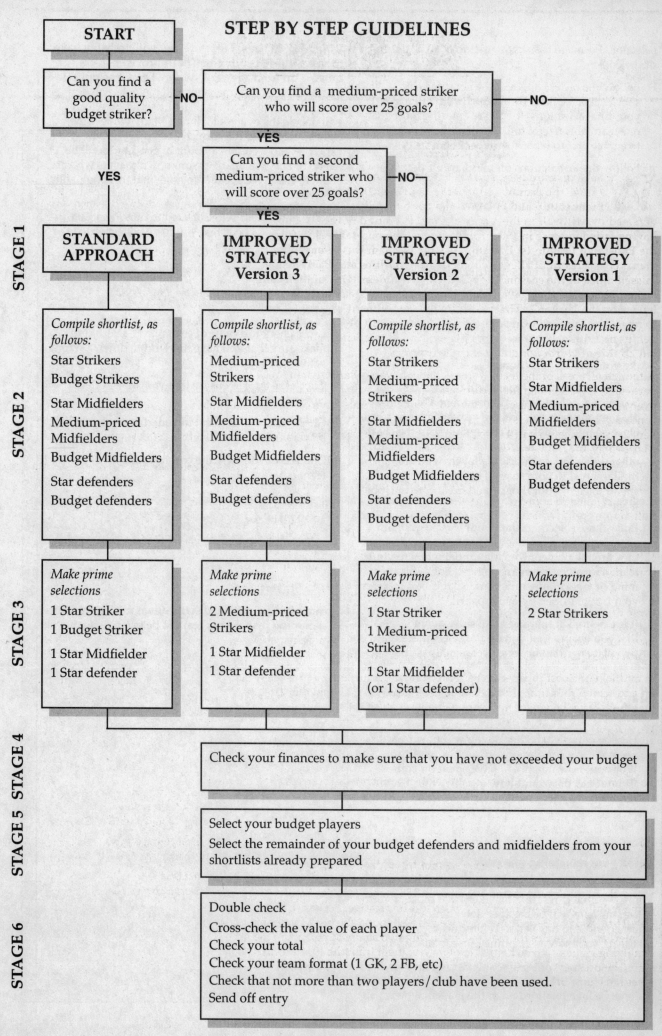

STEP BY STEP GUIDELINES

START

STAGE 1

Can you find a good quality budget striker? —NO→ Can you find a medium-priced striker who will score over 25 goals? —NO→

YES (Can you find a second medium-priced striker who will score over 25 goals?) —NO→

YES

STANDARD APPROACH

IMPROVED STRATEGY Version 3

IMPROVED STRATEGY Version 2

IMPROVED STRATEGY Version 1

STAGE 2

STANDARD APPROACH	IMPROVED STRATEGY Version 3	IMPROVED STRATEGY Version 2	IMPROVED STRATEGY Version 1
Compile shortlist, as follows: Star Strikers Budget Strikers Star Midfielders Medium-priced Midfielders Budget Midfielders Star defenders Budget defenders	*Compile shortlist, as follows:* Medium-priced Strikers Star Midfielders Medium-priced Midfielders Budget Midfielders Star defenders Budget defenders	*Compile shortlist, as follows:* Star Strikers Medium-priced Strikers Star Midfielders Medium-priced Midfielders Budget Midfielders Star defenders Budget defenders	*Compile shortlist, as follows:* Star Strikers Star Midfielders Medium-priced Midfielders Budget Midfielders Star defenders Budget defenders

STAGE 3

STANDARD APPROACH	IMPROVED STRATEGY Version 3	IMPROVED STRATEGY Version 2	IMPROVED STRATEGY Version 1
Make prime selections 1 Star Striker 1 Budget Striker 1 Star Midfielder 1 Star defender	*Make prime selections* 2 Medium-priced Strikers 1 Star Midfielder 1 Star defender	*Make prime selections* 1 Star Striker 1 Medium-priced Striker 1 Star Midfielder (or 1 Star defender)	*Make prime selections* 2 Star Strikers

STAGE 4

Check your finances to make sure that you have not exceeded your budget

STAGE 5

Select your budget players

Select the remainder of your budget defenders and midfielders from your shortlists already prepared

STAGE 6

Double check
Cross-check the value of each player
Check your total
Check your team format (1 GK, 2 FB, etc)
Check that not more than two players/club have been used.
Send off entry

ARSENAL

COMMENTS

What a disastrous season for the Arsenal! After fourth place in 1993/4, they could do no better than twelfth in the Premiership and fourth of the London clubs! They were defeated by Millwall in the replay of the third round of the FA Cup, having failed to score in 180 minutes against the mid-table club from the Endsleigh League 1st Division. George Graham was removed as manager as a result of alleged financial irregularities and Paul Merson missed much of the season through a drugs problem . One of their fans writes, "Maybe if they gave points for scandals and sleaze, we would have won the League!". Their ultimate disappointment was the failure to retain the European Cup Winners Cup, as a result of a moment of genius or a fluke, (from ex-Spurs player, Nayim,) depending upon which side of North London you come from.

Although all areas of the team were probably adversely affected, in particular, the decline in the performance of the defence in particular over the whole of the seaso, was quite dramatic, and must give cause for concern. The same players, who in 1993/4 conceded only 28 goals and kept 21 clean sheets, let in 49 goals and kept the score sheet blank on only 13 occasions the following season . In the previous season they had appeared impregnable, now they were only average.

For next season Bruce Rioch has been brought in (as second choice when the Board failed to land Bobby Robson) after his sterling work in leading Bolton from being an average 2nd Division side to Premiership status in under 3 years.

Where does one look for fantasy points? The obvious place to start is in defence. Look out for the prices of Arsenal's back five this season. In virtually every version of fantasy football last season, they were the top-priced defenders in the whole of the Premiership (possibly along with those from Manchester United). There is just a chance that their values may fall slightly as a result of their mediocre results in 1994/5. Surely they cannot do as badly again? Tony Adams or Lee Dixon at a price which is less than the maximum fantasy price has to be a good deal.

In midfield, the best prospect is Paul Merson who returned after his lay-off and scored four times in fifteen games. If he could maintain that rate for a full season he would be a very valuable acquisition for your team.

Ian Wright scored 18 league goals (plus a massive 12 in cup competitions) from only 30 appearances. Assuming that he avoids injuries and cuts down on suspensions, he can improve significantly on that.

To summarise, Arsenal can reasonably expect a much more successful season than last year. (Some would say that it could hardly be worse!)

P.S.

As we go to press, the exciting news comes through of the signing of Dennis Bergkamp by Arsenal, from Inter Milan for £7 million. Dennis is a world class striker who scored 103 goals in 185 games for Ajax before going to Italy, where his record has been less impressive. He has scored only 11 times in 52 Serie A matches. He has also found the net 23 times in 39 international games for Holland, including two against England, in the qualifying games, which helped to eliminate them from the 1994 World Cup. The prospect of Wright and Bergkamp together for a full season gives fans hope of better things to come.

FACTS

Key players
Tony Adams, Steve Bould, Lee Dixon, David Seaman, Nigel Winterburn, Paul Merson, Ian Wright, John Hartson, Dennis Bergkamp

Premier League record

	Points gained	Goals scored	Goals conceded	Clean sheets
1994/45	51	52	49	13
1993/4	71	53	28	21

Club strengths
Usually reliable defence
Very well organised
Solid midfield
Good youth policy

Club weaknesses
Need for creativity in midfield
Need for settling-in period for new management
Defence vulnerable to lobs from 50 yards

New Players
Dennis Bergkamp

Top goal scorers

1994/45		1993/4	
18(12)	Wright	23(12)	Wright
7(1)	Hartson	14(5)	Campbell
		7(5)	Merson

Who takes

	Penalties?	Corners?	Attacking free kicks?
1)	Wright	Merson	Schwarz
2)	Dixon	Schwarz	Merson
3)		Helder	Winterburn

Attacking midfielders	Attacking defenders
1) Merson	Dixon
2) Schwarz	Winterburn
3) Helder	
3) Parlour	

Defenders who join the attack for corners
Adams, Bould, Linighan, Keown

Promising young players
Marshall, Read, Shaw, Dickov

Goal makers
Merson, Schwarz, Helder

ASTON VILLA

Key players

Dwight Yorke, Steve Staunton, Ian Taylor, Ugo Ehiogu, Savo Milosovic

Premier League record

	Points gained	Goals scored	Goals conceded	Clean sheets
1994/45	48	51	56	11
1993/4	57	46	50	13

Club strengths

Younger players introduced
New attacking force likely
Likelihood of goals from midfield

Club weaknesses

Deterioration in defence
More cover needed for ageing players

New Players

Gareth Southgate from Crystal Palace for £2.5m
Savo Milosovic from Partisan Belgrade for £3m

Top goal scorers

1994/45		1993/4
15(2)	Saunders	10(6)
Saunders		
6(1)	Yorke	8(7)
Atkinson		
5	Staunton	5(2)
Richardson		

Who takes

Attacking Penalties? Corners?
kicks? free

1) Saunders	Staunton	Staunton
2) Staunton		Saunders

Attacking midfielders	**Attacking defenders**
1) Taylor	Charles
2) Yorke	Ehiogu
3) Staunton	Wright
4) Townsend	

Defenders who join the attack for corners

Ehiogu, McGrath, Teale

Promising young players

Fenton, Farrell

Goal makers

Taylor, Yorke, Staunton

There can be no argument with the general view which comes from fans at Villa Park, that the 1994/5 season was a very disappointing one. Villa failed to prosper in their second successive year in Europe, being eliminated from the UEFA Cup by unfashionable Trabzonspor (on away goals) in the second round, having eliminated the mighty Internazionale in the first, on penalties. Ron Atkinson had to pay the price for failure and he was sacked in November, only seven months after winning the Coca Cola Cup, being replaced by Brian Little. If Ellis was seeking to get a firmer defence, his new manager's record at Leicester was hardly a great commendation. Nor was the "direct route" style which had been adopted there, likely to improve the attendances, if introduced at the Villa.

The reaction of fans to the sacking of Big Ron was mixed. He was hero-worshipped by many, yet most of the fans had become very uneasy through his reluctance to give the younger element a chance. Nevertheless, it is hard to argue with his record. He had brought European football to Villa Park for two years and won a piece of silverware.

Brian Little's achievements since arriving could hardly be described as outstanding. However, he did preserve the Premiership standing by lifting the club the one place necessary from 19th, when he took over, to 18th, which meant safety. Out have gone the thirty-something brigade of Houghton, Richardson and Whittingham (and Parker, who will be 30 in September) and a younger squad have been signed including Wright (age 23), Johnson (24), Charles (25), Taylor (27) and Carr (28).

There has been much talk of the impending arrival of a new striker to partner Dean Saunders. This has now been resolved with the signing of Savo Milosovic from Partisan Belgrade for £3m. He has an amazing strike record, having scored 174 goals in 213 games since he was fifteen. He has scored 79 first team goals in three seasons, including 30 last season. In his five internationals, he has scored three times. Although his transfer has come too late to include a pen-picture, you have to consider him very seriously.

So where can we pick up fantasy points? If Steve Staunton is classified as a full back, he is a must for your team. Following the introduction of Alan Wright, the whole defence may improve next year. Staunton scored five goals in the season, most of which from full back, and if he plays in midfield he will undoubtedly get more.

Dwight Yorke made an impressive switch from midfield to play as a striker in the final few matches. Some fans feel that this is the exciting young player's best position. He may not play up front regularly, but after such a successful experiment, he is almost certain to be used in that position if either striker is injured.

The other possible fantasy star to consider is Ian Taylor who has always scored goals in his career, but managed only one for Villa and one for Sheffield Wednesday, last season. He will certainly score more now that he has settled in and has won a regular place in the Premiership side.

P.S.

Gareth Southgate, who played a very solid role in the midfield/defence for Crystal Palace has been signed. He will do something similar for Villa, releasing Yorke and Taylor to play more of an attacking role.

BLACKBURN ROVERS

COMMENTS

Blackburn Rovers achieved the ultimate when they took the FA Carling Premiership Championship, beating Manchester United in the run-in to end up victors by just one point, despite having the jitters in the last few games, and having taken only 10 points from their last seven games in April and May. Fortunately for them, Manchester United failed to take advantage of the opportunity presented to them and so Kenny Dalglish became only the third manager to win the English Championship with two different clubs. He also picked up the Manager of the Year Award.

Everyone will associate their success with Sutton and Shearer (SAS), although it depended upon much more than just the strike force. Nevertheless, the problem posed by the attack was rarely solved by opposition defences; Rovers failed to score in only 5 league matches.

Shearer scored 34 league and 3 cup goals and is now the number one striker in Britain. Many claim that he is the best in Europe, although that is still to be proved in international and European tournaments. He will have a few opportunities to press this claim in the season ahead. Sutton made a huge contribution in feeding Shearer, although he will probably be disappointed with his league goal tally of 15.

The club had little success in cup competitions, including the humiliating defeat at the hands of Trelleborgs in the UEFA Cup. However it could be said that the early exit from the knock out competitions probably helped the team to concentrate on the Premiership.

The 1994/5 season was not without its injury problems. Most unfortunate was undoubtedly Kevin Gallacher who, after a broken leg, was out until April and then played just 65 minutes before suffering a similar injury. Other unlucky ones included Jason Wilcox, David Batty, Stuart Ripley and Nicky Marker. The loss of Batty and Wilcox was of particular importance and Rover's results were certainly affected.

What does the future hold? It is important that Kenny does not fall into the trap that some feel was encountered by Alex Ferguson. At Old Trafford a squad has been assembled with a large contingent of foreign (non English) players. It appears that Dalglish has carefully considered this as he has brought his squad together.

So among this galaxy of talent, where do we look for our fantasy players? The attack is obviously the place to start. Shearer will be in most people's team, and who could argue with that? However, it may be that Sutton will be a better bargain in 1995/6. His price may well drop, and surely he will score more than 15 goals next year. Check him out.

All of the defenders will gain good points, but will anyone be good value for money? The player to look out for is Graeme Le Saux. He has set his sights on goal from a few dead ball situations and more fantasy points will come from there. If he does find his way to play in midfield and is classified as a defender, you must purchase him at all costs. Also, he has started to score more goals as a result of having been moved into midfield for some games. Flowers and Hendry should also be considered.

In midfield watch out for Jason Wilcox. He is a fine crosser of the ball and with SAS in the middle waiting for the inviting centres, that will produce points. Furthermore, he knows the way to goal, his five league goals coming from only 27 matches.

FACTS

Key players
Graeme Le Saux, Jason Wilcox, Alan Shearer, Tim Flowers, Colin Hendry, Chris Sutton

Premier League record

	Points gained	Goals scored	Goals conceded	Clean sheets
1994/45	89	80	39	16
1993/4	84	63	36	18

Club strengths
Dependable defence
Well-balanced midfield
Exceptional attacking attack
Plenty of money
Wise management

Club weaknesses
Lack of opportunity for younger players

New Players
None at time of going to print

Top goal scorers

1994/5		1993/4	
34(3)	Shearer	31(3)	Shearer
15(6)	Sutton	7(1)	Wilcox
6	Atkins	6(1)	Wilcox
6	Sherwood	6(2)	Newell
6	Wilcox		

Who takes

Penalties?	Corners?	Attacking free kicks?
1) Shearer	Wilcox	Shearer
2)	Ripley	Le Saux
3)	Slater	

Attacking midfielders	Attacking defenders
1) Wilcox	Le Saux
2) Ripley	Berg
3) Sherwood	Kenna

Defenders who join the attack for corners
Hendry, Pearce

Promising young players
Pearce

Goal makers
Wilcox, Ripley, Sutton

BOLTON WANDERERS

FACTS

Key players

Alan Stubbs, Simon Coleman, Scott Green, Keith Branagan, Richard Sneekes, John McGinlay, Alan Thompson

Endsleigh League
Division One record (46 matches)

	Points gained	Goals scored	Goals conceded	Clean sheets
1994/45	77	67	45	19
1993/4	59	63	64	10

Club strengths

Sound defence

Promising young players

Club weaknesses

Lack of experience

Uncertainty regarding the new manager

Danger of losing key players

New Players

None at time of going to print

Top goal scorers

19944/5		1993/4	
16(6)	McGinlay	25(8)	McGinlay
13(3)	Paatelainen	7(10)	Coyle
7(2)	Thompson	6(2)	Thompson
6(2)	Sneekes		
5(3)	McAteer		
5(1)	Coyle		

Who takes

Attacking Penalties?	Corners?	free kicks?
1) McGinlay	Thompson	Sneekes
2) Sneekes	Patterson	Stubbs
3) Thompson		

Attacking midfielders	Attacking defenders
1) McAteer	Stubbs
2) Sneekes	Green
3) Thompson	Coleman

Defenders who join the attack for corners

Coleman, Stubbs, Green

Promising young players

De Freitas, Whittaker

Goal makers

McAteer, Paatelainen, Thompson

COMMENTS

1995/6 is the season when a very famous footballing name returns to the stage where it rightly belongs. The name is Bolton Wanderers and the stage is the top tier of football in England. Up until 1964 Bolton Wanderers' name was almost permanently in the 1st Division of the Football League. Since then they have returned to the top flight only once, in 1978, and stayed there for just two seasons.

Their illustrious history seems to be inextricably linked to some of the most memorable moments in English cup football and includes four FA Cup triumphs. Their first victory was also the first final to be held at Wembley Stadium in 1923 when the crowd overflowed onto the pitch and a few mounted policemen, one on the famous white horse, maintained some sort of control. They were there again for the "Stanley Matthews" final in 1953 and their last victory there was in the 1958 final, playing against the Manchester United side which had been devastated three months earlier by the Munich air crash. Certainly the history of the F A Cup and the name of Bolton Wanderers will never be separated.

Many famous names have turned out in their white shirts, including David Jack, sold to Arsenal in 1928 for the then record fee of £10,890, Eddie Hopkinson (a record 519 appearances) and of course, the present President of the club, the great Nat Lofthouse.

What is the future for Bolton in the Premier League, and where should we look for fantasy points? Will Bolton do a Swindon, Crystal Palace and a Leicester and return immediately to the 1st Division, or will they follow the achievements of Newcastle United and Nottingham Forest to become a force to be reckoned with in the Premiership?

The signs are that their defence will probably hold firm against most Premiership attacks. They conceded 45 goals last season in the Endsleigh League Division 1 (only 13 in 23 home games), compared with the 46, 49 and 59 conceded the previous season by Crystal Palace, Nottingham Forest and Leicester City respectively when they won promotion.

With Bruce Rioch gone, Colin Todd's problem may well be in attack where they scored only 67 goals in 46 games in the 1st Division. John McGinlay was top scorer with 16 league goals, followed by Paatelainen with 13. Fabian De Freitas, signed from Holland, is young, fast and very popular with the fans. He has good potential, and he scored two goals in his seven first team starts. He may well oust Paatelainen in the coming season and may prove to be the answer to the scoring needs.

In midfield the strength and durability of Jason McAteer is well known. Perhaps less well publicised is the outstanding ability of Richard Sneekes (pronounced Sneakers), from Fortuna Sittard in Holland, coached by Johann Cruyff. He is a great passer of the ball, with an outstanding shot and has been described enthusiastically by Bolton fans as the "Glenn Hoddle" of Bolton, and as a "revelation". With 6 league goals from 37 starts, plus two in cup matches, he is one to watch. Another goalscoring midfielder is Alan Thompson, who is a young left winger who loves to take on his defender and who possesses a great shot.

Bolton probably do not have the financial backing to build a team which can challenge for the Premiership Championship, but they have a solid-looking team which might reasonably expect to finish in mid-table. They also have good strength in depth, their reserves having won the Pontins League for the first time in 40 years.

CHELSEA

COMMENTS

If you have been a Chelsea fan for any period of time, you will know all about false dawns. Just because you start the season well does not mean that everything will continue to prosper!

Having reached the FA Cup Final the previous season and qualified for the Cup Winners' Cup by courtesy of Manchester United having won the double in 1993/4, Chelsea had high hopes. They seemed to be justified as they shot up the table to occupy fifth place at the end of September. The slide down the table then began, and although they never really looked like being relegated, towards the end of the season there were one or two anxious moments. They eventually finished in eleventh place. The fans claim that a massive injury list was the main reason for the decline in their fortunes. For the match against West Ham on 2nd October, they had no less than 13 of the first team squad injured. It was at this point that their form began to suffer.

The highlight of their season was certainly their performance in the European Cup Winners' Cup. They made their way through to the semi-final losing out to the eventual winners Real Zaragoza by an aggregate 4-3 scoreline. A disastrous 3-0 away defeat proved too much to make up at home, although a 3-1 victory was a valiant attempt.

At least the fans enjoyed the more cultured approach to football which Glenn Hoddle has introduced, although with the introduction of Furlong into the attack, there is now the option to hit the long first-time ball into the danger area. One negative which this has created has been the effect which this has had on the runs through the middle of Gavin Peacock. Whereas in 1992/3 he scored 12 goals for Newcastle and in 1993/4, 8 for Chelsea, last season he played a more subdued role and contributed only 4 strikes.

A major problem at Stamford Bridge is the dependency of the Blues on one man, Dennis Wise. When he is out, not only is the midfield supply line cut, but without his motivation the whole team looks fragile, falling to pieces when things go wrong.

Maybe this will change in 1995/6. There is a 32-year-young newcomer called Ruud Gullit who has been showing a great deal of promise and looks as though he could have a future in the game. The talk is that he will start out in a mainly defensive role, either just in front of or just behind the central defenders. Will it be a Beckenbauer-type of role, or more of a Hoddle variation? Whatever the approach, I cannot imagine that when Chelsea desperately need a goal in the last ten minutes of a game, Ruud will be able to resist the temptation to go forward; nor would Hoddle want him to. This could mean that if, as a result of him joining Chelsea, their defensive record improves and he scores even a small proportion of his potential strikes, he may score a mass of points in fantasy games.

In terms of where to look for talent for the fantasy game, Stamford Bridge is fairly restricted. Unless you are totally convinced about the "Gullit factor" you have to steer clear of their fragile defence. Their goalscoring strikers, are reliable rather than prolific and so it seems that we have to look in midfield. Presumably Gavin Peacock's price will be reduced and it could be that Gullit's defensive role will release him to make more of those penetrating runs which have brought him so many goals in his career. Of course there is Wise, who can be relied upon to gain a reasonable number of points for you, but he will be fairly expensive.

FACTS

Key players
Gavin Peacock, Ruud Gullit, Dennis Wise

Premier League record

	Points gained	Goals scored	Goals conceded	Clean sheets
1994/45	54	50	55	13
1993/4	51	49	53	11

Club strengths
Creative attacking midfield

Club weaknesses
Inconsistent defence
1994/5 produced numerous injuries which highlighted a lack of cover

New Players
Ruud Gullit

Top goal scorers

1994/5		1993/4	
11(3	Furlong	13(1)	Stein
11(2)	Spencer	8(6)	Peacock
8(2)	Stein	4(0)	Cascarino
6(1)	Wise	4(2)	Wise
4(2)	Peacock		

Who takes

	Penalties?	Corners?	Attacking free kicks?
1)	Wise	Wise	Wise
2)	Spencer	Rocastle	Burley
3)	Stein	Minto	Lee
4)			Furlong

Attacking midfielders	Attacking defenders
1) Wise	Clarke
2) Newton	Minto
3) Burley	

Defenders who join the attack for corners
Johnsen, Kjeldberg, Sinclair

Promising young players
Duberry, Myers

Goal makers
Wise, Spencer, Rocastle, Peacock

COVENTRY CITY

FACTS

Key players
None

Premier League record

	Points gained	Goals scored	Goals conceded	Clean sheets
1994/45	50	44	62	14
1993/4	56	43	45	13

Club strengths
Potentially lethal strike force
'Big Ron' factor

Club weaknesses
A leaky defence
A hard working but not terribly
creative midfield
A lack of goals
An excess of mediocre players

New Players
None at time of going to print

Top goal scorers

1994/5		1993/4	
13(3)	Dublin	11(0)	Ndlovu
11(2)	Ndlovu	8(1)	Quinn
		6(0)	Wegerle
		5(0)	Darby

Who takes

Penalties?	Corners?	Attacking free kicks?
1) Ndlovu	Cook	Cook
2)	Wegerle	

Attacking midfielders	Attacking defenders
1) Marsh	Borrows
2) Flynn	

**Defenders who join
the attack for corners**
Rennie, Pressley

Promising young players
Christie, Hall

Goal makers
Ndlovu, Dublin

COMMENTS

Coventry escaped relegation by the skin of their teeth and fans are divided as to where the blame lies for the problems they have had to endure. Some blame Phil Neale for the defensive approach which he adopted and believe that, with "Big Ron" at the helm, the future looks much brighter. Others point out that in the 1994/5 season Neale improved the defensive record dramatically from the previous year and it was only because he had to sell Phil Babb (to Liverpool) and Peter Atherton (to Sheffield Wednesday) in order to raise funds, that his record in that area deteriorated. They also cite the purchase of Dion Dublin, top scorer with 13 league goals, as an inspired purchase which helped them to stay up.

What does the future hold with Atkinson in charge? Certainly there is much optimism, indeed there is evidence of considerable "Ron mania". There is talk among fans of a place in Europe and possibly winning a cup. Is this a realistic possibility?

One thing is for sure, there will inevitably be a big clear-out of players from Highfield Road. Far too large a squad has been assembled under Phil Neale and now Ron Atkinson, and there must be a number who will be made available for transfer in a summer clear-out.

Putting aside the bias of the Coventry faithful for a few moments, let us look at the probability of success without partiality. There can be no argument that "Big Ron" has achieved much with former clubs and that at Aston Villa he took them into Europe for two successive years. There is also plenty of evidence that he is a great motivator for one-off matches and that he is a wonderful front-man. But the Premiership clubs where he has had success have been much more secure financially than Coventry. Some of the Villa fans have highlighted what they feel is one of his major failings, viz that he sticks with older, well-established players for too long. At Villa Park, and that the elderly midfield including Houghton, Townsend and Richardson got in the way of development of bright youngsters like Yorke and Fenton and led to the transfer of other good potential such as Cox (to Middlesbrough) and Froggatt (to Wolves).

Already he has brought in Richardson Shilton and Strachan, the latter primarily as coach, but still playing a few games (extremely well) at the end of the season. There are rumours that he is trying to persuade Sir Stanley Matthews to come out of retirement. It would be a pity if the promising younger element was held back from developing.

It would seem that there are very few, if any, fantasy stars at Highfield Road. Other than Dublin (13) and Ndlovu (11), no-one scored more than four goals and are therefore not worth inclusion as either strikers or midfielders. With the defence so uncertain, we could not recommend anyone from there either.

Unfortunately our lack of optimism with regard to choosing Coventry players for fantasy teams is matched by our feelings about the Premiership season ahead. Last year we rightly predicted, before the season began, that Leicester and Ipswich were doomed to be relegated. Whilst we are not quite so definite in our predictions about Coventry, we certainly do not have the confidence that some of the fans have. Of one thing we are confident, "Ron mania" will not prevent Coventry City from having another very unsettled season ahead. We feel that the best that they will achieve is another last match escape from the big drop for Big Ron.

EVERTON

COMMENTS

What a season! By the end of October Everton were bottom of the Premiership, yes, even below Leicester and Ipswich, having scored only 9 goals in 14 games, and Mike Walker was about to lose his job as manager after only 10 months in charge. Joe Royle took over on 10th November and the change was dramatic. A run (actually started under Mike Walker) of seven matches without conceding a goal, took them to Christmas in a much better state of mind and six points clear of the bottom two. The league season still proved to be a struggle and safety was finally assured only in the last match against Coventry.

However in every other aspect, the season flourished, particularly with an outstanding cup run which saw them eliminate Newcastle United and Spurs, among others, before the final conquest of Manchester United at Wembley. So a season which promised disaster ended in dramatic triumph, with the FA Cup in the Trophy Room and a place in Europe.

In addition, confidence returned to the players and there were notable improvements in form and enhancement of reputations. Duncan Ferguson was signed from Rangers and has made such an impact that he is being compared with Dixie Dean and Bob Latchford; praise indeed. Fans are expecting 25+ goals from him next season.

There is talk among fans that Everton might save a few million by bringing in two bright young stars from the reserves. Watch out for an impressive young midfield playmaker named Tony Grant, who was called up for the England Under-21 squad at the end of April, after just over four hours first team football. He also knows the way to goal, having scored 5 goals from 21 starts in the reserves. Neil Moore is a young defender who will also make a few appearances in the first team in the coming season.

The likely midfield will be Limpar and Hinchcliffe wide and Horne and Parkinson in the centre. All of these had a good season in 94/5, although Anders Limpar was the most inconsistent.

In attack there are mixed views on Paul Rideout. Both Daniel Amokachi and Stuart Barlow have their backers, particularly "Amo", who has great skill, but is said not to be a favourite of Joe Royle. The question is "Who will partner Ferguson in attack?".

In defence, Southall has one more year left on his contract and on the evidence of last season is hardly likely to be challenged. The general view is that Matthew Jackson is the best right back who has been unfortunate to have been left out since Earle Barrett arrived. At left back, Gary Ablett has continued to be a valuable servant to the club. With Hinchcliffe having moved into midfield, he has made this position his own, although it may be that this is one area where Royle will spend. Watson and Unsworth look certain to be the centre back pairing. Ablett is able to deputise there if required.

In terms of fantasy football, there are few opportunities to collect a great amount of points cheaply. Hinchcliffe was a bargain in many versions last season, but do not expect the same again in 1995/6. Ferguson is the obvious target man, not only for Everton, but also for fantasy managers, but do not expect him to be cheap. Your best bargains may well come from fringe players, particularly midfielder Tony Grant who may well push his claim for a first team place from the start of the new season. Watch out for him!! The other possibility is that Matthew Jackson might win back the right back place, and at a reasonable price to you.

FACTS

Key players
Tony Grant, Matthew Jackson, Andy Hinchcliffe, Duncan Ferguson, Dave Watson, Gary Ablett

Premier League record

	Points gained	Goals scored	Goals conceded	Clean sheets
1994/45	50	44	51	14
1993/4	44	42	63	11

Club strengths
Confidence level high
Effective management
Improved defence
Excellent support

Club weaknesses
Very poor goalscoring record
Lack of midfield creativity

New Players
None at time of going to print

Top goal scorers

1994/5		1993/4	
14(3)	Rideout	16(3)	Cottee
7(1)	Ferguson	6(5)	Rideout
4(2)	Amokachi	4(1)	Beagrie
		4	Ebbrell

Who takes

	Penalties?	Corners?	Attacking free kicks?
1)	Unsworth	Hinchcliffe	Hinchcliffe
2)	Watson		Limpar
3)	Hinchcliffe		

Attacking midfielders	Attacking defenders
1) Limpar	Watson
2) Stuart	Ablett
3) Hinchcliffe	

Defenders who join the attack for corners
Watson, Ablett

Promising young players
Unsworth, Grant, Moore

Goal makers
Limpar, Hinchcliffe, Ferguson

LEEDS UNITED

COMMENTS

Premier League record

	Points gained	Goals scored	Goals conceded	Clean sheets
1994/45	73	59	38	17
1993/4	70	65	39	18

Club strengths

Solid defence
Stable management (Howard
Wilkinson since October 1988)
Classy midfield
Yeboah

Club weaknesses

Failure to bring through younger
players

New Players

None at time of going to print, but
there are plenty of rumours

Top goal scorers

1994/5		1993/4	
13(1)	Yeboah	17(0)	Wallace (Rod)
9(1)	Deane	11(1)	Deane
7	Whelan	10(2)	Speed
6	McAllister	8(0)	McAllister
5(4)	Masinga	5(1)	White

Who takes

**Attacking Penalties? Corners?
free kicks?**

1)	McAllister	McAllister McAllister
2)		Dorigo Dorigo
3)		Speed

Attacking midfielders	**Attacking defenders**
1) McAllister	Dorigo
2) Speed	Kelly
3) Palmer	Wetherall
4) White	

**Defenders who join
the attack for corners**

Wetherall, Pemberton

Promising young players

Whelan, Sharp, Couzens

Goal makers

McAllister, Dean

Throughout the 1994/5 season Leeds maintained a healthy league position, always in the top eight, but never challenging for the top spot. An impressive run-in of nine games unbeaten, assured them of fifth position and a guaranteed place in Europe, irrespective of the result of the Cup Final. Most of the glory during the period from February to the end of the season centred around Tony Yeboah, who scored 13 goals from only 16 starts. The Ghanaian, who scored 61 goals in 109 Bundesliga games for Eintracht Frankfurt, signed for a record £3.4 million in January (completed in late May), and completely changed the confidence and performance of the Leeds team. With a solid defence, on which to build, and a reliable midfield, Leeds fans are looking forward to a run in Europe and a genuine chance of winning the FA Carling Premier League Championship.

The introduction of Yeboah has meant that Brian Deane has been able to take a wider role, to the benefit of the team. The introduction of Pemberton alongside Wetherall at the heart of the defence released the leggy, somewhat ungainly Carlton Palmer into midfield where he did much more damage with his boundless energy and enthusiasm. Finally, the return of Tony Dorigo, after a number of injuries, strengthened the left hand side of defence.

What about selections for fantasy teams? The obvious and outstanding contender is the exciting Tony Yeboah. He outscored Alan Shearer during the tail-end of the season and he has a proven track record in Germany. He is not just a big striker. His first touch, skill in the box and uncanny eye for goal make him a real world class striker. He may not be quite as expensive as Shearer in some of the newspapers, but he is likely to get almost as many fantasy points. He will almost certainly be in the author's fantasy teams.

Who will be with him up front is less certain. Lanky youngster, Noel Whelan has the best goalscoring record (7 goals from his 18 starts last season) and at only 20, his best days lie ahead. If he regains his place in the first team, he may surprise fans with an even better goal return, with defenders having to pay special attention to Yeboah. Furthermore, he may not be too expensive. However, he will face serious competition for the second striking spot from Masinga and particularly Deane.

All of the defenders will score good fantasy points, but they will be expensive. None are goalscorers and for the money that you would have to pay, you would probably do better to look elsewhere, unless you think that Leeds are going to be the defensive team of 1995/6. Bowman Couzens and Sharpe are all cheaper young defenders who are on the verge of the first team and if any of them win a place, probably as a result of injury, you may pick up a bargain.

In midfield, Speed, McAllister, Wallace, Palmer and White can all be relied upon to score a few goals and assist in a few others, but the evidence of the past two seasons is that none are likely to give you a good return for the high price that you will undoubtedly have to pay for them.

1995/6 may well be the year in which Leeds win the Championship, and Tony Yeboah may help you to win your own particular fantasy league.

LIVERPOOL

COMMENTS

For most fans, a season where your club finished fourth in the Premiership, won the Coca Cola League Cup and the right to play in Europe, would have been a highly successful one. Whilst fans are not complaining after a few barren seasons, the glut of trophies which they have won in the recent past leaves them very much like Oliver Twist: they want more.

This was Roy Evans' first full season as manager and it has set the right foundation from which to build a team which can compete for the League Championship, which is their ultimate objective. Some of his decisions were inspirational. His purchase of Babb and Scales and his decision to play three central defenders, with two wide defenders getting forward, not only bolstered the defence, but also gave it a more balanced look and a base from which to attack. It also proved to be an innovation which a number of other Premiership teams copied. Liverpool Football Club and their fans enjoy being trendsetters and they approve of the new approach which proved to be so successful, after a few weeks of settling down.

Another inspired move was to give Steve McManaman a "free" midfield role. His contribution was enormous and he has played his way into the full England squad as a result. In fact, each of Liverpool's recognised first team players is now either an established international, or on the fringes.

In a team of stars, where every one is a first rate performer, where does one look for fantasy team players? In the 1994/5 season, many spotted that it was possible to buy the new signings, Babb and Scales, along with two other Liverpool defenders. Usually Bjornebye was cheap and proved to be an excellent buy. Because of their mediocre defensive record the previous season, the price of their defenders was not usually terribly high and those who followed this approach were very well rewarded. Liverpool ended the season with 17 clean sheets, a figure bettered only by Manchester United. Do not expect the defenders to be so cheap this year!

In attack, Robbie Fowler had an excellent season, scoring 25 Premiership goals, second only to Alan Shearer. And he is still only 20 years old. His is a unique talent for scoring goals from all angles and distances. One fan describes his potential as "breathtaking". He can only get better and better and it is impossible to predict just how many times he will hit the back of the net in the coming season, except that it will be a great many. Doubtless his price will rise to astronomical proportions in most fantasy games. The introduction of Stan Collymore alongside him gives Liverpool a frightening front-line. The potential is huge, and either (or both) of them could top thirty goals in the coming season. You have to consider each of them even more so now that they have paired up in this awesome attack.

The young talent in midfield is surely the envy of every other club. McManaman, Redknapp and now Kennedy form the future midfield basis of Liverpool's team. In addition, there is Dominic Matteo, a strong athletic, coltish player who can play in a number of positions. He may become the midfield holding player. In addition, there are John Barnes, Jan Molby, Paul Stewart, Michael Thomas and Mark Walters. It is unlikely that there will be room for all of them at the club and one or two may move on. Any of the first three are potential high point scorers in fantasy leagues, with McManaman being the best bet. However, each of them is likely to be expensive and you may have to look elsewhere.

MANCHESTER CITY

FACTS

Key players
Uwe Rösler, Garry Flitcroft, Paul Lake

Premier League record

	Points gained	Goals scored	Goals conceded	Clean sheets
1994/45	49	53	64	10
1993/4	45	38	49	12

Club strengths
Considerably improved goalscoring record
Great potential in the youth team

Club weaknesses
Defensive structure has deteriorated badly
Very unlucky with injuries, again!
Lack of strength in depth in the squad

New Players
None at time of going to print

Top goal scorers

1994/5	1993/4
15(7) Rösler	6(0) Sheron
12(3) Walsh	5(0) Rösler
8(2) Quinn	5(1) Quinn
5 Flitcroft	4(0) Walsh
	4(0) Griffiths

Who takes

Attacking free kicks?	Penalties?	Corners?
1) Curle	Beagrie	Beagrie
2)	Summerbee	Flitcroft
3)		Simpson
4)		

Attacking midfielders	Attacking defenders
1) Gaudino	Phelan
2) Flitcroft	Vonk
3) Beagrie	Brightwell (Ian)

Defenders who join the attack for corners
Kerhaghan, Vonk, Curle

Promising young players
Edghill, Thomas

Goal makers
Beagrie, Summerbee, Quinn

COMMENTS

Brian Horton made it to the end of the season as the manager at Maine Road, just about. It was almost inevitable that he would not survive, not only because the season was such a disappointment to fans as the team struggled to avoid relegation, but also because there were times when it appeared that he did not know what his best team was. The way in which he switched his strikers around was disturbing and did nothing to establish an understanding among them.

It is perfectly true that, after a very promising start to the season, injuries to key players played a significant part. However, this type of thing is always likely to happen and top teams must be able to overcome. Unfortunately, the injury to Steve Lomas was of particular significance. He was the main ballwinner, and with playmakers such as Gaudino and Beagrie in midfield, City struggled to win the ball.

This was a great pity because at the start of the season they seemed able to score at will and by the end of November they had risen to seventh place in the league. The rot really set in after defeating Ipswich at Portman Road on 3rd December. They did not win another game until they played Ipswich again on 22nd February. By this time they had dropped to 15th position, and the battle against relegation had begun.

Another place where injuries caused problems was in defence, where on a number of occasions, centre backs were playing in both full back positions. This, together with the extra pressure mentioned earlier, contributed to a far worse defensive record than they had had in the previous season. Whereas in 1993/4 the defence had looked very solid and had conceded only 49 goals, last season an alarming 64 were let in.

One area of promise is with the youth team. They reached the semi final of the FA Youth Cup with 6 first year apprentices and the future certainly looks bright there. However, that will not affect the new manager's immediate future, only the medium-to-long term.

In terms of fantasy football players, there are few who will feature in your team. Unless you are prepared to gamble that Alan Ball will make a tremendous difference to the defensive record, it would be foolish to include City defenders in any of your teams. In midfield the most likely star fantasy player is Gary Flitcroft. He contributes going forward and regularly scores about five goals per season. If you are prepared to take a really big gamble you might just strike lucky by selecting Paul Lake. Paul is the midfield player whom City fans rave about. He has scored 27 goals in 106 first team appearances, but has been out of action through horrific injuries for about four years.

In attack, it is likely that Niall Quinn will have left Maine Road by the start of the new season. That may make life easier for Alan Ball in terms of selecting his first choice strikers. However, it will badly affect his attacking back-up. The main attraction to fantasy football managers will be Uwe Rösler. He scored 15 league goals (plus 7 in the Cup) in 26 games and became a great favourite with the fans. In a full season he might be expected to score 25 goals, not as many as a Shearer or a Fowler, but there again, he will not cost as much. Check his price and be prepared to include this natural goalscorer if it seems reasonable.

One thing is sure. City will not be challenging United as the top team in Manchester. They are hoping to establish a side which can attain a mid-table position, however, if Alan Ball can get it right, the footballing world may just be surprised by what City achieve. With a natural striker like Rösler, anything is possible!

MANCHESTER UNITED

COMMENTS

At the end of a season when they won nothing, far from being depressed, United's fans blamed bad luck, injuries etc (none actually blamed the Selhurst Park incident) for them collecting no silverware. They were full of praise for Alex Ferguson and Brian Kidd and they are confident that, next season, the trophies will return to Old Trafford.

Let us try to analyse, as independent observers, their performance. What was that little extra which meant the difference between winning the League, and finishing second? Anyone who saw the frustrating scoreless draw against Chelsea in April or the 1-1 draw at Upton Park in the final league match, or indeed the FA Cup Final, will have little doubt. Most football pundits will point to the man who was out of the team, not through injury, but because of his uncontrollable Gallic temperament. Surely, if Cantona had been in the team for the run-in, the Championship would not have gone to Ewood Park.

One very pleasing sight was the development of the talented youngsters who are coming off the Old Trafford production line. The list seems endless: Gary Neville, Nicky Butt, Paul Scholes, David Beckham, Phil Neville, Simon Davies, Chris Casper, John O'Kane, Kevin Pilkington, Ben Thornley, Craig Dean and so on. Virtually all made an appearance in the United first team, some as substitutes, while others are fully-fledged members of the first team squad. Not all will make it to the very top, but Alex Ferguson should be congratulated that he has given youth a chance.

We have just commended Ferguson on his youth policy. However, many are disturbed to see the level of support that he gives to players who are blatantly out of line. It may not be right to kick a man when he is down (nor for that matter, when he is standing up!), but surely when one of his players has flouted the laws of the game, or even those of the land, a manager should let it be known that he disapproves strongly. He has a responsibility to thousands of young followers of United to say clearly that such behaviour is not good enough and will not be tolerated.

As we go to print, there is much speculation about Paul Ince; will he join Inter Milan or not? It was interesting to hear the comments of one Reds' supporter, on the radio, despairing over the proposed move. In his opinion, Paul was irreplaceable. He believed that even Cantona could be replaced, but not Ince. We believe that his replacement is already signed on, available, young and proven at the top level; his name is Nicky Butt. We believe that Nicky will prove to be as good as Paul Ince, and has a better temperament.

You could look anywhere for fantasy points in the United set-up, particularly in defence. Irwin and Pallister are the most likely to gain attacking points in addition to the guaranteed haul from defensive clean sheets. But they will be very expensive and may not be good value for money. In midfield, apart from the less expensive Butt, if Kanchelskis sorts out his problems and gains a regular place in the team, he is a great source of points. His speed and attacking flair were a revelation last season. Even if he moves, you should buy him.

In attack, you may find that this is the year of Andy Cole. With the supply line provided by Cantona, plus a better understanding with his new team-mates, he could again score 30-plus goals. The real fantasy bargain at Old Trafford could come from the young attacker Paul Scholes. He is a prolific goalscorer in junior and reserve team football and has found the net five times from six starts in the first team. Given a chance, he could score an abundance of goals, at a very cheap price.

FACTS

Key players
Peter Schmeichel, Denis Irwin, Andrei Kanchelskis, Gary Pallister, Andy Cole, Nicky Butt, Paul Scholes

Premier League record

	Points gained	Goals scored	Goals conceded	Clean sheets
1994/45	88	77	28	24
1993/4	92	80	38	17

Club strengths
Outstanding skill and committment in every position
Progressive management
Arguably the best supporters in the world
Almost embarrassingly sound financially

Club weaknesses
Excessive management loyalty
Lack of opportunity for younger players

New Players
None at time of going to print

Top goal scorers

1994/5		1993/4	
14(1)	Kanchelskis	18(7)	Cantona
12(2)	Cantona	13(4)	Giggs
12	Cole	12(10)	Hughes
8(4)	Hughes	9(2)	Sharpe
5(1)	Ince	8(0)	Ince
5(3)	McClair	6(4)	Kanchelskis
5(2)	Scholes	5(3)	Keane

Who takes

	Penalties?	Corners?	Attacking free kicks?
1)	Irwin	Giggs	Irwin
2)	Cantona	Sharpe	Giggs
3)		Irwin	Cantona

Attacking midfielders	Attacking defenders
1) Ince	Irwin
2) McClair	Neville
3) Giggs	Bruce
4) Keane	Pallister

Defenders who join the attack for corners
Bruce, Pallister and occasionally Schmeichel!

Promising young players
Neville, Butt, Beckham, Scholes, P Nevill

Goal makers
Cantona, Sharpe, Ince, McClair, Hughes, Giggs

MIDDLESBROUGH

FACTS

Key players

Nigel Pearson, Steve Vickers, Alan Miller, Neil Cox, Craig Hignett, Alan Moore, Jamie Pollock, Jan Aage Fjortoft

Premier League record

	Points gained	Goals scored	Goals conceded	Clean sheets
1994/45	82	67	40	18
1993/4	67	66	54	13

Club strengths

Excellent defence
High potential management team
Several young stars
Good financial backing

Club weaknesses

A few top class squad mebers needed

New Players

Phil Whelan, a utility defender from Ipswich

Top goal scorers

1994/5		1993/4	
15(2)	Hendrie	16(4)	Wilkinson
9	Fuchs	14(6)	Hendrie
8(1)	Hignett	10(1)	Moore
6(3)	Wilkinson	9	Pollock
5(1)	Pollock	5(5)	Hignett

Who takes

Attacking Penalties? Corners? free kicks?

	Penalties?	Corners?
1)	Hignett	Moore Blackmore
2)		Blackmore Hignett
3)	Wilkinson	

Attacking midfielders	Attacking defenders
1) Pollock	Pearson
2) Moore	Fleming
3) Mustoe	

Defenders who join the attack for corners

Whyte, Vickers, Pearson

Promising young players

Pollock, Moore, Moreno, Freestone

Goal makers

Moore, Hendrie, Robson

COMMENTS

1994/5 has been an incredible year for Middlesbrough. Bryan Robson arrived as manager in only May 1994, yet with wise investment and excellent motivation he has brought them into the Premiership, as Champions, at his first attempt. The new season starts in a splendid new stadium and there is a totally justified optimism that the coming season will hold even more good things than the past one. With the inspiration of Robson, the financial backing of the Chairman, Steve Gibson and the enthusiasm of the Teesside fans, it would be a brave man who would suggest that they will not get into Europe.

Robson's approach has been interesting. He has tried to produce a blend of experienced quality players with talented and enthusiastic youngsters. He has bought Clayton Blackmore, Jan Aage Fjortoft, Nigel Pearson and of course himself who fit into the former category and signed Neil Cox to join the likes of Jamie Pollock, Alan Moore and Jaime Moreno who are in the latter. Add to these 'Boro stalwarts like John Hendrie, Derek Whyte and Curtis Fleming, and you have a recipe for success.

Middlesbrough's style has begun to resemble that of Robbo's old club Manchester United with the team not afraid to pass the ball around, looking for the moment to prise open the opposition defence. This approach has worked well for United and it should stand 'Boro in good stead, even though their players may not be up to quite the same standard.

So how will Middlesbrough fare? Defensively, they have the best record among promoted teams over the past few seasons, having conceded only 40 goals in the whole of the season, an excellent performance. However their goals scored was only 67 compared with 73, 74 and 72 in the previous year by Crystal Palace, Nottingham Forest and Leicester City respectively. Bryan Robson has obviously realised that his attack would be lacking in the top league and has bought in Jan Aage Fjortoft who has a proven goalscoring record in the Premiership, for Swindon, even when they were relegated. All the signs are that, with a few more millions to spend, Robbo will lead 'Boro forward into another excellent season.

In attack Fjortoft may be priced reasonably and will more or less guarantee a fair supply of goals. Hendrie's record is not too far behind him. He has scored 18 goals in 87 games in the Premier League and old Division 1 for Middlesbrough, Newcastle and Leeds. In midfield the obvious name to think of is 21 year old Jamie Pollock who is a star of the future. His goalscoring record is adequate, but no better than that, 5 in 40 games last year. By far the highest scorer among the midfield players is Craig Hignett who scored 8 goals from only 26 league games. He takes a mean penalty and would be an ideal fantasy player, if only you could guarantee him being in the team.

Defenders of promoted teams are rarely expensive in fantasy leagues and we should pick up some bargains there. All of the indications are that Middlesbrough will run a very mean defence. Pearson and Vickers each scored 3 goals last season. Curtis Fleming gets forward well but never scores any goals. Any of these plus Alan Miller and Neil Cox are likely to get you plenty of defensive points and a few from their attacking.

You may well find that you may share the delight of Middlesbrough's first season back in the big time by using some of their stars.

NEWCASTLE UNITED

COMMENTS

One thing about Kevin Keegan is that he is unpredictable. One event overshadows the rest of this most eventful season at St James' Park, the sale of Andy Cole to Championship rivals Manchester United. It could be said that, neither was the winner. Cole was not replaced and Newcastle fell away as the season progressed. Meanwhile, the plan to play Cole alongside Cantona was thwarted by a little incident at Selhurst Park and Cole's introduction into the United team did not result in the expected Premier League title. Maybe Blackburn Rovers were the only beneficiaries of the Cole move!

Newcastle's season had started so brilliantly, going 17 games without defeat, averaging almost 3 goals per game and topping the League from the start of the season through to the end of October. After that point their away form deteriorated and they won only one more game away from home during the remainder of the season, against Ipswich. Only 'Fortress St James' form kept them in a reasonable league position, but even so, their final placing of sixth was a huge disappointment.

Most fans put down the reason for their decline as the injuries to their key players Philippe Albert and Scott Sellars. Lengthy absences by other influential players, viz Venison, Beresford and Lee did not help. That certainly played a big part, but with a squad the size and quality of that at Newcastle, there must be more to it than that. Others say that Kevin Keegan was wrong, not in selling Cole, but in failing to replace him immediately with a ready made, experienced striker.

Now Les Ferdinand has been signed as the replacement and Newcastle will continue to play attacking football. That is what Keegan wants and that is what the fanatical fans demand. With the service provided by players such as Beardsley, Fox, Albert, Gillespie, Lee and Sellars, expect Ferdinand to score a hatful of goals.

There is one outstanding fantasy candidate in Philippe (Prince) Albert. He joined Newcastle as a central defender but was soon transferred to a midfield role. In his 25 appearances he scored three goals and would have got more, had he not picked up an injury which kept him out of action from Christmas onwards. It is possible that he will again be classified as a defender and if so, he must be in your team. He would be the very first name that the author would write in in his fantasy team. One defender who may be cheaper than the rest is Robbie Elliott. He was challenging for Beresford's place at left full back when he too was injured. At 21, he is an outstanding prospect if he can keep clear of further injuries.

In midfield, Fox will almost certainly be the most expensive, and may play a few games as a striker. Lee began last season in dynamic goalscoring mood, but faded rapidly in that capacity. If he can reproduce that early season form he would be a bargain at almost any price. Sellars will lay on many chances, but will not score many goals. Gillespie is not renowned as a goalscorer, but will certainly contribute with assists. Beardsley plays between midfield and attack but is usually classified as a striker. As such, he is not a particularly good buy, although Kevin Keegan would probably have him in any team of his!! Overall, the expensive midfielders are likely to be less attractive to fantasy managers than are defenders mentioned above.

Finally of course, there is Les Ferdinand. He has always been an accomplished goalscorer and you can expect plenty of goals, with such an inventive and powerful supply line as the one which will be supporting him. Check the price and sign him on if he looks good value.

FACTS

Key players
Philippe Albert!, Robbie Elliott, Les Ferdinand, Robert Lee, Ruel Fox

Premier League record

	Points gained	Goals scored	Goals conceded	Clean sheets
1994/45	72	67	47	15
1993/4	77	82	41	14

Club strengths
Excellent financial support
Brilliant management
Outstanding squad
Incredibla supporters

Club weaknesses
Keegan's plan to change style of play may present problems

New Players
Warren Barton from Wimbledon for £4 million
Les Ferdinand from Queen's Par Rangers for £6 million

Top goal scorers

1994/5		1993/4	
13(2)	Beardsley	34(7)	Cole
10(2)	Fox	21(3)	Beardsley
9(6)	Cole	7(1)	Lee
9(5)	Lee	5(2)	Allen
8(4)	Kitson		

Who takes

	Penalties?	Corners?	Attacking free kicks?
1)	Beardsley	Gillespie	Albert
2)	Fox	Sellars	Beardsley
3)		Fox	Fox
4)		Clark	Hottiger

Attacking midfielders	Attacking defenders
1) Lee	Beresford
2) Fox	Albert
3) Sellars	Hottiger
4) Clark	

Defenders who join the attack for corners
Albert, Peacock, Howey

Promising young players
Watson, Elliott, Gillespie, Brayson

Goal makers
Beardsley, Sellars, Gillespie, Fox

NOTTINGHAM FOREST

FACTS

Key players
Bryan Roy, Stuart Pearce, Alf Inge Haagland, Steve Stone, Ian Woan, Lars Bohinen

Premier League record

	Points gained	Goals scored	Goals conceded	Clean sheets
1994/45	77	72	43	13
1993/4	83	74	49	15

(Endsleigh Div 1)

Club strengths
A prolific pair of goalscorers in Stan Collymore and Brian Roy
A defence which was surprisingly solid
Excellent management

Club weaknesses
Potential problem resulting from the almost certain loss of Collymore
Possible change of style of play may affect results

New Players
None at time of going to print

Top goal scorers

1993/4		1992/3	
22(3)	Collymore	19(6)	Collymore
13(1)	Roy	8(2)	Gemmill
8(2)	Pearce	7(2)	Cooper
6(1)	Bohinen	6(0)	Pearce
5	Woan	5(1)	Glover
5	Stone	5(0)	Woan
		5(0)	Stone

Who takes

Penalties?	Corners?	Attacking free kicks?
1) Pearce	Roy	Pearce
2) Collymore	Bohinen	Cooper
3)	Woan	Phillips
4)	Gemmill	

Attacking midfielders / Attacking defenders

Attacking midfielders	Attacking defenders
1) Bohinen	Pearce
2) Woan	Cooper
3) Stone	Lyttle

Defenders who join the attack for corners
Cooper, Chettle, Pearce

Promising young players
McGregor, Warner, Armstrong

Goal makers
Bohinen, Gemmill, Stone, Woan, Rosario

COMMENTS

Nottingham Forest surprised many football pundits with their performance during the 1994/5 season. Not so surprised were many of the supporters who knew that the team was good enough to do well, although perhaps not quite as well as finishing third.

Frank Clark gets the plaudits of the fans, not only for the way in which he has guided and motivated the players through the long season, but also for the way in which he has handled the Collymore saga; "like a seasoned diplomat," says one fan. He has managed to keep his players' feet firmly on the floor, at the same time building their confidence, and has made Forest into one of the most entertaining teams in the Premiership. The team is built on a solid defence and quick, incisive breaks forward, ideal for the speed and sharpshooting ability of Collymore and Roy. He must take the credit for the inspired signing of Bryan Roy, which was one of the coups of the season. He fitted in perfectly to the playing strategy which Clark planned to adopt.

The team settled into the Premiership as though they had never been away and the good start set the tone for the season. They were never out of the top five and when the pressure was on for European places in the run-in at the end of the season, they finished far more strongly than any of their competitors. In the last ten games, they gained five points on Leeds, seven on Manchester United, nine on Blackburn, ten on Liverpool and fourteen on Newcastle. To qualify for Europe was a great achievement, and to finish third was remarkable.

So what of the season ahead? Will Frank Clark strengthen his squad? Will Forest do well in Europe? Perhaps more importantly, will the team be able to mount a serious challenge for the League title?

An area that must not be overlooked is the strength in depth (or lack of it) of the squad. Forest were fortunate that they had an almost injury-free season among their first choice players. A few players missed the odd game, but the usual first team choice of Crossley, Lyttle, Pearce, Cooper, Chettle, Stone, Phillips, Bohinen, Woan, Roy and Collymore remained more or less fixed throughout the season. A few others such as Alf Inge Haaland, Scot Gemmill, Kingsley Black, Carl Tiler and Jason Lee were called in from time to time, but this was necessary only rarely.

Where should you look for players who will serve you well in fantasy football? Last year we recommended that you should buy Bryan Roy, as a midfielder, on the basis of his 14 goals for Foggia in the Italian Serie A league. If you did so, you would have been more than adequately rewarded. Only Matt Le Tissier and possibly Andre Kanchelskis (depending upon the method of scoring) among midfielders, exceeded his points total. We believe that there is even better to come, but his price is certain to rise. You cannot afford to ignore him, so check out how much he would cost and make your decision.

Stone and Woan each scored five league goals last season (as they did the year before) and either of them might improve in 1995/6. You should check their prices.

Last season there were some bargains to be picked up in the Forest defence. That is less likely to be the case in 1995/6. Haaland may force his way into the team and if so, he may be the cheapest. Of course, the incredible Stuart Pearce must be considered because of his regular goal supply, however, we expect that his price will rocket this season. You may have to give the defenders a miss this year.

QUEENS PARK RANGERS

COMMENTS

1994/5 was quite a season at Loftus Road. It was not a place to visit, nor were QPR a team to support, if you had a weak heart. They scored 61 goals and conceded 59, and only Southampton and Spurs could compete with that sort of entertainment. The message from the fans is that when they attacked, everyone wanted to get in on the act, and every time the opposition did so, it looked as though they were going to score. QPR having conceded 25 goals in 14 games by the middle of November, it is perhaps surprising that Alan Sugar saw in Gerry Francis the manager to sort out exactly the same type of defensive problem at White Hart Lane. Nevertheless he did and Gerry departed, giving Ray Wilkins (why doesn't anyone call him "Butch" any more?) the opportunity to start his managerial career. He had a big task to hold the team together after Gerry left and he is to be congratulated on the way in which he did it. By the end of the season, even though the defence still gets the jitters, it did not appear as though they were going to concede a goal every time the opposition attacked.

Another achievement was to manage to hold on to Les Ferdinand until the end of the season, when the vultures moved in and whisked him away. At least there was one winner among the even smaller clubs, with Hayes picking up a reported £600,000 windfall which should meet their needs for a few months. With the balance of £5.4 million safely in the bank, QPR should also manage to keep the bailiffs away.

In Kevin Gallen they have a rich talent, described by one zealous fan as "the best young hope in the country". After scoring lots of goals in youth and reserve matches, he burst onto the Premiership scene with 10 league goals in 36 games and made a huge impact in the way in which he set up chances for Ferdinand. They also have Daniele Dichio, Gallen's partner in the youth and reserve teams, who is ready to follow in his partner's footsteps. In addition, there are the experienced Gary Penrice, Bradley Allen and Dennis Bailey, each of whom can score goals.

With the talents of Holloway, Barker, Impey and Sinclair in midfield, there is plenty of attacking flair, but they need a ball-winner who will also strengthen their defensive resolve. They are all good with assists, but the midfield scores very few goals. The one possibility here is Michael Meaker who can be a match-winner and is a favourite with some of the crowd. He played only a few games last year and will certainly be a cheap buy if he stays at Loftus Road. With Bardsley at Right Full back and Wilson or the promising Brevett on the left, there appear to be no problems at Full back. There is possibly a need for a good central defender to partner Alan McDonald. Yates, Maddix and Ready have all been used in that capacity, yet none has the position permanently.

In goal, Tony Roberts won back his place from Sieb Dykstra at Christmas, having been replaced by him earlier in the season. There is healthy competition between the two good keepers.

Fans are uncertain, yet optimistic about the prospects for 1995/6. It is hard to see them winning any trophies or getting into Europe, but they may set the basis for doing so the following season.

The outstanding candidate has to be Gallen. He may not be too expensive and his goalscoring potential is great. Be ready to snap him up. Dichio also did well, scoring twice after coming on as substitute and once in his six starts.

FACTS

Key players
Kevin Gallen, Michael Meaker, Daniele Dichio

Premier League record

	Points gained	Goals scored	Goals conceded	Clean sheets
1994/45	60	61	59	10
1993/4	60	62	61	10

Club strengths
Good strike potential, even without Ferdinand
Some very good young players

Club weaknesses
A very fragile defence
The club's financial situation means that they will always have to sell their star players

New Players
None at time of going to print

Top goal scorers

1993/4		1992/3	
24(2)	Ferdinand	16(2)	Ferdinand
10(2)	Gallen	8(0)	Penrice
4(1)	Sinclair	7(3)	Allen
4	Barker	7(0)	White
		5(3)	Barker

Who takes

	Penalties?	Corners?	Attacking free kicks?
1)	Wilson	Penrice	Bardsley
2)	Barker	Holloway	Ferdinand
3)			Wilson

Attacking midfielders	Attacking defenders
1) Impey	Bardsley
2) Sinclair	Wilson
3)	Brevett

Defenders who join the attack for corners
McDonald, Ready, Maddix

Promising young players
Gallen, Brevett, Dichio

Goal makers
Gallen, Sinclair, Ferdinand, Impey

SHEFFIELD WEDNESDAY

FACTS

Key players
Peter Atherton, Ian Nolan, Andy Pearce, Chris Woods, Chris Bart-Williams, Klas Ingesson, Steve Howey

Premier League record

	Points gained	Goals scored	Goals conceded	Clean sheets
1994/45	51	49	57	14
1993/4	64	76	54	10

Club strengths
Consistent defence
Talented and creative midfield

Club weaknesses
Uncertainty of new managerial situation
Dramatic drop in the number of goals scored

New Players
None at time of writing, until the managerial situation is sorted out

Top goal scorers

1993/4		1992/3	
11(2)	Bright	19(4)	Bright
9	Whittingham	12(2)	Watson
5	Hyde	8(2)	Bart-Williams
		6(1)	Jones
		5(2)	Palmer
		5(1)	Jemson

Who takes

Attacking Penalties?	Corners?	free kicks?
1) Bright	Waddle	Sheridan
2) Sheridan	Sinton	Waddle
3)	Bart-Williams	
4)		

Attacking midfielders / Attacking defenders

Attacking midfielders	Attacking defenders
1) Bart-Williams	Nolan
2) Ingesson	Atherton
3) Jones	Petrescu

Defenders who join the attack for corners
Pearce

Promising young players
Briscoe, Key

Goal makers
Bart-Williams, Sinton, Waddle

COMMENTS

1994/5 proved to be a very disappointing season for Sheffield Wednesday, promising so much, but delivering so little. The Owls always get off to a bad start and last season was no exception. Trevor Francis had spent over £6 million to strengthen the defence and midfield, yet there was no striker bought. That proved to be very costly as the goalscoring dried up and the team lost confidence. At the outset, even the defence looked very vulnerable, conceding four goals to Spurs, three to QPR and four to Nottingham Forest in the first five games. One fan says that against QPR it looked "all over the place" and "like our U-10s defence". However, excluding those three games, which might justifiably be described as being in the settling-down period, the defence conceded only 46 goals in the remaining 43 matches and kept 14 clean sheets; a very commendable record.

As we go to press, we hear that David Pleat is taking over as manager. This seems to us an inspired choice that would give Wednesday the impetus to become a power in the Premiership. David has always produced good footballing sides, usually playing attractive one-touch football which pleases the crowds and often (but not always) gets results.

Because we say that he likes his sides to play football does not mean that he does not employ a big striker, such as Whittingham. Readers may recall that one of his most successful sides at Luton included big Mick Harford playing alongside Brian Stein. He brought the best out of that pairing and who is to say that he will not do the same with skilful front players such as Bright, Hirst and Whittingham.

After another season of injuries, the jury must be out on talented attacker, David Hirst. Bright's goal tally dropped from 19 to 11 last season and Whittingham's 9 from 16 starts has not convinced Owls' fans that he is the long-term answer to their problems. However, it is worth noting that in the first 19 games before he joined them at Christmas, Wednesday had scored just 19 goals, whereas in the 16 games in which he played, they scored 23 times.

At the start of the season, Bart-Williams appeared to be the midfielder most likely to score well in fantasy leagues but, although he contributed well with a number of assists, he scored only twice, compared with five times the previous season. Trevor Francis thought very highly of him and now that he is gone Bart-Williams may have greater problems keeping his place, if indeed he stays at Hillsborough. The highly talented but injury-prone Chris Waddle scored four league goals from only 19 starts and if he could be guaranteed to survive a full season, he would be in many fantasy managers' teams.

It is from the defence that you are most likely to collect fantasy points. Not only is the team's defensive record good, but there are players who make significant contributions in attack. Peter Atherton is probably the number one choice, because, even though he scored only one goal, he contributes with a number of assists. He is a very important member of the defence, as is indicated by the fact that the one league match which he missed was the 7 - 1 drubbing at home by Nottingham Forest. Ian Nolan scored three times but his distribution is poor and so does not gain many points for assists. Andy Pearce also helps in attack, particularly in going forward for corners. He failed to score last season, whereas in 1993/4 he had found the net three times. Any of these, plus goalkeeper Chris Woods, would gain you points, if you can afford them.

SOUTHAMPTON

COMMENTS

Southampton fans did not want the 1994/5 season to end. At the end of March they were in 19th position in the Premiership and the usual relegation battle seemed to be in full swing again. Yet in their last eleven league matches they picked up no less than 21 points and climbed to finish in 10th place, their highest of the season.. That was more like championship form than relegation.

Once again the name of Matt Le Tissier is being hailed as the genius of Southampton, yet not of England. It seems that Terry Venables has written him off, even though he continues to produce outstanding form season after season. It is little wonder that the Saints' fans are so frustrated. Last season he managed only 20 goals compared with 25 the season before, but he scored an amazing 10 cup goals in only 8 matches, including four against unlucky Huddersfield. It must be a second division team's nightmare to be drawn against "Le Matt".

The fans are full of admiration for the job done by Alan Ball and are very dissappointed that he has moved on.

He introduced a new pair of strikers, 20-year-old Neil Shipperley from Chelsea who joined them in January, followed in March by 24-year-old Gordon Watson from Sheffield Wednesday which means that Southampton must have one of the youngest attacks in the Premiership. "Flash", as he was called at Hillsborough, is a real hustler who has taken the pressure off young Shipperley and found the net three times in his twelve games. You will note that the good run which we mentioned earlier started just as Watson arrived at The Dell. His style may not look pretty, but he is an all-action, old-fashioned centre-forward who hits the net regularly. It would seem that his chance has come and he may just cause quite a stir. The combination of Shipperley picking up the scraps and Watson doing the hustling has already started to work and might become quite a potent force.

So where do we look for players for our fantasy team? Obviously, number one consideration is Le Tissier. He is regularly the top midfield points scorer in those games which classify him as such. In midfield, apart from Le Tissier, Jim Magilton, the club's playmaker, was also the second highest scorer with six goals. He may benefit from the new attack and might possibly improve slightly. He has always been a reasonable goalscorer and the new set-up might be to his liking. Neil Maddison usually gets more than the three goals which he managed last season.

You cannot consider any of the defenders, even though Richard Hall enjoys attacking and scored four goals. Defenders of any team which regularly concedes over 60 goals per season have to be avoided like the plague. They conceded nine goals more than Norwich and fourteen more than Crystal Palace, both of whom were relegated!

Paul McDonald is a left winger who has scored 15 goals in 33 games for the reserves (quite a strike rate!) and he has been given a couple of run-outs in the first team, as sub. If he gets a chance, he is the type to go for in fantasy football and he will be cheap. Unfortunately, even if he gets in the team, he is unlikely to be listed among your paper's fantasy players.

You might give one of the new strikers some thought. Of the two, Watson has the better scoring record, but Shipperley is the younger and he has never had the type of service which he will get from Watson and Le Tissier. Take your choice, but do not ignore them.

FACTS

Key players
Matt Le Tissier, Gordon Watson, Neil Shipperley, Jim Magilton, Neil Maddison, Paul McDonald

Premier League record

	Points gained	Goals scored	Goals conceded	Clean sheets
1994/45	54	61	63	9
1993/4	43	35	66	6

Club strengths
A constructive attacking midfield
Still the youngest Premiership team
An interesting policy – they do not buy anyone over 26
MATT LE TISSIER

Club weaknesses
Every year, a very poor defence
Too dependent upon one man

New Players
Alan Neilson, a Welsh centre back from Newcastle United

Top goal scorers

1993/4		1992/3	
20(10)	Le Tissier	25(0)	Le Tissier
6(1)	Magilton	7(0)	Maddison
5	Dowie	5(1)	Dowie
5	Eklund		

Who takes

Penalties?	Corners?	Attacking free kicks?
1) Le Tissier	Le Tissier	Le Tissier

Attacking midfielders	Attacking defenders
1) Le Tissier	Hall
2) Maddison	
3) Magilton	

Defenders who join the attack for corners
Monkou, Hall

Promising young players
Neil Shipperley, David Hughes, Paul Tisdale

Goal makers
Le Tissier, Magilton

TOTTENHAM HOTSPUR

FACTS

Key players
Darren Caskey, Jason Dozzell

Premier League record

	Points gained	Goals scored	Goals conceded	Clean sheets
1994/45	62	66	58	11
1993/4	45	54	59	7

Club strengths
Excellent youth policy
Attractive attacking play
Creative midfield

Club weaknesses
Leaky defence
Minus Klinsmann, too dependent
upon Sheringham for goals

New Players
Chris Armstrong, striker from Crystal Palace

Top goal scorers

1993/4		1992/3	
20(9)	Klinsmann	13(2)	
	Sheringham		
18(5)	Sheringham	8(1)	Dozzell
9(2)	Barmby	6(0)	Sedgley
5(2)	Anderton	6(0)	Anderton
4(1)	Dumitrescu	5(2)	Barmby
		4(1)	Caskey

Who takes

Penalties?	Corners?	Attacking free kicks?
1) Klinsmann	Anderton	Anderton
2) Sheringham		
Sheringham		
3)		Klinsmann

Attacking midfielders	Attacking defenders
1) Anderton	Popescu
2) Dumitrescu	Edinburgh
3)	Austin
4)	Kerslake

Defenders who join the attack for corners
Calderwood, Mabbutt

Promising young players
Carr, Hill, Turner, Caskey

Goal makers
Anderton, Barmby, Sheringham

COMMENTS

In view of how things stood at the outset of the season, Spurs fans can feel pretty pleased with the final results. From a situation where they had a twelve point deduction and an FA Cup ban hovering, to end the season in seventh place in the league, having reached the semi final of the FA Cup, was quite an achievement. However, they will probably look back, thinking that it could have been so much better.

So much of their success, and indeed the enjoyment provided in their performances, originated in the brilliance of the German superstar, Jurgen Klinsmann. He won over, not only Spurs fans, but the English football pundits generally, with his incisive skills in both scoring goals and laying on chances for his team-mates. Not only Alan Sugar is disappointed that his visit lasted for only one season.

Another arrival at White Hart Lane was Gerry Francis, who made the somewhat shorter journey, from Loftus Road. Gerry's first and crucial act was to bring in David Howells as a midfield anchor man, to introduce a defensive aspect to the midfield. This did not work instantly, but when he followed it by restoring Calderwod and Mabbutt to the heart of the defence, the required stability was achieved, shown by a run of six clean sheets, spanning the New Year. It meant that one member of the attack-minded midfield had to go and the victim was the unfortunate Dumitrescu, who had contributed five goals in his 13 games. Of one thing you can be sure; you should not select Spurs' defenders in your team, unless you enjoy playing Russian roulette.

Fans are wondering whether Chris Armstrong will provide the necessary level of fire-power needed in the Spurs attack. Certainly, with the likes of Darren Anderton and Teddy Sheringham laying on chances, he will get a better service than he has ever experienced at Crystal Palace. He has the misfortune of having to step into Klinsmann's shoes and he is certainly not of that ability. He scored only eight league goals in the 1994/5 season, compared with 23 the previous year in the Endsleigh League and one has to question whether he cannot perform against the defences of Premiership quality.

The emergence of Anderton during last season as a player of genuine international class was the best news at White Hart Lane for some time. He can only improve and he must be one of the few Spurs players who are front-runners for selection for your fantasy team. He guarantees good points for a midfielder, but are you able to afford him?

Teddy Sheringham always scores his share of goals and this season he did so without the benefit of being the penalty taker. After being so reliable in previous seasons, he had a bad spell at the start of the season and lost the job to first Dumitrescu, and then Klinsmann. Surely the task will return to Sheringham in the coming season, which should boost his tally a little. He is a borderline choice for consideration for your team.

The area where you may pick up good points cheaply is by watching what is likely to happen to a couple of players who finished the season in the reserves. Dozzell and Caskey are good fantasy team players, both goalscoring midfielders. Because they have been out of favour, they are likely to be cheap. A few games as substitute for Caskey and an appearance by Dozzell (again as substitute) may mean that they are not written off and that there may be places in the first team for one or both. They may be the means of good points to be collected cheaply. Keep watch at the start of the season.

WEST HAM UNITED

COMMENTS

The 1994/5 season has been "more of the same" in that, once again West Ham have finished mid-table (14th compared with 13th the previous season), once again scoring goals has been a problem (44 compared with 47 in 1993/4) and once again there have been no big name signings. However, the most important change is that the defence seems to have tightened up; last season they conceded only 48 goals compared with 58 in the previous season. Also, the introduction of Don Hutchison has given a much-needed goalscoring boost to the midfield. The re-introduction of Tony Cottee into the attack has given it a regular supply of goals.

It is necessary to put their achievements into perspective. Although they finished in 14th position, they were only two points ahead of Aston Villa in 18th. Of course, one point or even one goal is often the difference between survival and relegation or between winning the championship and finishing runners-up, but West Ham fans would be foolish to read too much into the position in which they finished in the table.

Apart from the injury to Alvin Martin, the Hammers have been able to field a very settled defensive line-up. Miklosko and Potts have been ever-present, Rieper has deputised for Martin very successfully and without a break, and Breacker and Dicks (since he arrived) have missed only the odd game or two. Having a settled defence is always a recipe for improved performance, since they get to know one another's play.

The second cause for optimism is the form in the end of season run-in. During the last ten games of the season, their record in both defence and attack was very impressive. They kept five clean sheets, a record bettered by only Manchester United and Everton (with 6) and conceded only five goals, the lowest of anyone in the Premiership. Since the opponents during these last ten games included six of the top eight goalscoring clubs in the Premiership, that performance was nothing short of outstanding! Meanwhile, in attack they were scoring 14 goals and picking up 17. That sort of form throughout the season would have meant that they would have been challenging for a place in Europe rather than battling against relegation.

The reason for the relative success that has been achieved is closely tied to four signings during the past twelve months. The return of Cottee and Dicks to their roots, and the arrival of Moncur and Hutchison, has formed the basis on which to build a team which is capable of doing battle in the top half of the table rather than the bottom.

So far as fantasy football games are concerned, the main question revolves around whether you believe that West Ham really have sorted out an effective defence which can keep 17 or 18 clean sheets in a season. If so, then a goalscorer such as Julian Dicks or an attacking full back such as Tim Breacker, who lays on plenty of chances for the forwards, would give excellent returns. Martin and Rieper also go forward for set pieces and might contribute the odd goal. You may well find a few bargains in this area.

The one outstanding fantasy prospect is Don Hutchison. Those who bought him last year (as the author did) got him as a Liverpool reserve, and paid that sort of price. If so, you had a bargain. He might be a bargain again this year, for a different reason. Towards the end of last season Harry Redknapp played Don as a striker and he was rewarded with five goals in his last seven games. Unfortunately, the run was interrupted by an injury. If he is again categorised as a midfielder yet plays as a striker, you simply cannot afford to leave him out.

The other midfielder who should be considered is the classy John Moncur, although you may find that his price makes him unattractive.

FACTS

Key players
Julian Dicks, Tim Breacker, Don Hutchison, John Moncur

Premier League record

	Points gained	Goals scored	Goals conceded	Clean sheets
1994/45	50	44	48	13
1993/4	52	47	58	14

Club strengths
A well-balanced side

Club weaknesses
Lack of goals
Limited financial resources

New Players
None at time of going to print

Top goal scorers

1993/4		1992/3	
12(2)	Cottee	13(3)	Morley
9(2)	Hutchison	7(4)	Chapman
7	Boere	7(2)	Allen M
5	Dicks		

Who takes

	Penalties?	Corners?	Attacking free kicks?
1)	Dicks	Moncur	Dicks
2)	Hutchison	Holmes	Allen

Attacking midfielders	Attacking defenders
1) Moncur	Breacker
2) Allen	Dicks

Defenders who join the attack for corners
Martin, Rieper, Dicks

Promising young players
Williamson, Shipp, Moors

Goal makers
Moncur, Holmes

WIMBLEDON

FACTS

Key players
Robbie Earle, Marcus Gayle, Oyvind Leonhardsen

Premier League record

	Points gained	Goals scored	Goals conceded	Clean sheets
1994/45	56	48	65	12
1993/4	65	56	53	12

Club strengths
Energetic all-action approach
Good youth policy

Club weaknesses
Poor attendances mean on-going financial struggle
Best players frequently have to be sold

New Players
None at time of going to print

Top goal scorers

1993/4		1992/3	
9	Ekoku	17(7)	Holdsworth
7(1)	Holdsworth	11(1)	Fashanu
6(2)	Harford	9(3)	Earle
4(1)	Leonhardsen		
4	Goodman		

Who takes

Penalties?	Corners?	Attacking free kicks?
1) Holdsworth	Elkins	Barton
2)	Ardley	Elkins

Attacking midfielders	Attacking defenders
1) Leonhardsen	Barton
2) Earle	Reeves
3) Gayle	Elkins
4) Castledine	

Defenders who join the attack for corners
Elkins, Reeves, Thorn

Promising young players
Perry, Fear, Castledine

Goal makers
Holdsworth, Jones

COMMENTS

Once again, Wimbledon finished in the top half of the table, in ninth position, albeit, last season their results were not as impressive as in 1993/4. Their points tally dropped from 65 down to 56 along with their goalscoring which fell from 56 to 48. At the same time, their defence became less secure, conceding 65 goals compared with 53 the previous season. Somewhat surprisingly, they managed the same number of clean sheets, twelve. Nevertheless, with average home attendances over the season of only 10,230, leading to continual financial pressures, it is amazing that they manage to exist amongst the likes of Manchester United, Newcastle, Blackburn, Liverpool, etc with the millions of pounds which they seem to have available to spend. It is a tribute indeed, to the shrewd housekeeping and youth policy of Wimbledon, in general, and Joe Kinnear, in particular.

Once again, it has been necessary to provide a stream of top-class players for other Premiership clubs, in order to balance the books. At the start of the season John Scales went to Liverpool for £3.5 million and at the close, Warren Barton broke the English record for a defender, when he signed for Newcastle United for £4 million.

They started the season very badly defensively and in the first seventeen games conceded 31 goals. They also allowed Aston Villa to knock in seven in one game in February. It appears that every time Alan Kimble does not play, the defence falls to pieces. In the 16 games which he missed, for one reason or another, they conceded 34 goals. By the end of the season, the defence was settled once again and in the last eleven matches they kept six clean sheets, a record which could be compared with even Manchester United. Now, of course, as the season ends, Warren Barton has moved on and so the defence will have to be looked at again, although, for much of the season, he moved to he right side of midfield, and Cunningham and Kimble filled the full back positions.

Possibly an even greater cause for concern has been the sudden lack of goalscoring from both attack and midfield. Holdsworth scored only seven league goals compared with the 17 in 1993/4. Robbie Earle missed much of the season through injury and in the few games which he played, he failed to find the net. With Fashanu gone (he had scored 11 times in 1993/4), the whole goalscoring machine dried up.

Kinnear's selection policy could not have helped. It seemed that he did not know what was his best strike force was. He appeared to shuffle his deck of strikers and randomly deal out whichever two came to hand from Holdsworth (27 games), Ekoku (24), Harford (17), Goodman (13) and Clarke (8). The results were unimpressive and if Wimbledon are to score more goals next season, some stability must be achieved.

It is in midfield that we must look for potential fantasy purchases. Robbie Earle's price is likely to drop from last season and a regular goalscorer such as he can never be ignored in fantasy games. He is the ideal type of player and may be a real bargain for 1995/6. Oyvind Leonhardsen has already shown his sharpness in the penalty area. If he stays at Selhurst Park, he will continue to find the net regularly, and if he is not too expensive, he is another good points scorer in fantasy games.

Finally, we will give the benefit of the doubt to Marcus Gayle. Now that he has found his feet in the Premiership, perhaps he will begin to fulfil the progress which was expected of him. Once again, he is likely to be inexpensive and if you are looking for a cheap midfield player, consider him.

THE PLAYERS

This section gives pen pictures of more than 475 players who are with 1995/6 Premiership clubs. Not all of them will appear in fantasy team listings, but the vast majority of those who are listed will be in the book.

If you are uncertain about where to find a particular player, there are two indexes at the end of the section to help you. The players are first listed in alphabetical order, and then by club. So even if you only know the player's name, you will be able to find your way through to his pen picture.

There is one important point which you must note. Normally a clear recommendation has been given in respect of each midfield player or striker. We say whether or not, in our opinion, you should consider them for selection in your team. However, we do not do that for defenders, because they are selected more on the performance of their team than their own individual capabilities. It would not be practical to comment on each individual in that way. It is better to refer initially to their Club in Section 2, and then look at the comments on the individual.

When you eventually come to selecting your shortlists, you will find in Section 4 that, adjacent to the work sheets, there are lists of the individual players whom you should check on. These are categorised by position and by rating, 'Star', 'Medium priced' or 'Budget'.

The selection rating will help you to decide which players to consider and which to ignore for this season. The rating is based on the player's likelihood to score valuable points for you and upon his probable price range in the fantasy football games. It is not a general comment on his ability as a football player. A rating of ✪✪✪ means you could not choose a better player; ✪✪ mean that he is worth consideration and ✪ indicates that he is a borderline consideration for the coming season.

In the statistics relating to appearances, the number of games where a player started the match as a substitute, but came on during the match, is shown in brackets. Thus 25(7) indicates that he started 25 games and came on as substitute in 7.

GOALKEEPERS

Vince Bartram Goalkeeper

Club ARSENAL

Date of birth 7.8.68

	Appearances (as substitute)		Goals		Clean sheets	
	League	Cups	League	Cups	League	Cups
1994/5	11	0	0	0	2	0

Playing strength
Good shot-stopper

Pen picture
Signed from Bournemouth for £300,000 during the summer of 1994, where he had been the first team keeper for three years. Fans consider Vince to be an adequate deputy based on his appearances when Seaman was injured. However he appears to lack a little confidence on crosses and certainly will not challenge the player whom Arsenal fans consider to be England's number one goalkeeper.

David Seaman Goalkeeper ✪✪
RECOMMENDED

Club ARSENAL

Date of birth 19.9.63

	Appearances (as substitute)		Goals		Clean sheets	
	League	Cups	League	Cups	League	Cups
1994/5	31	19	0	0	11	9
1993/4	39	17	0	0		

Playing strength
Consistent international goalkeeper
He is excellent on crosses and has brilliant reflexes

Pen picture
1994/5 has not been such a good season for any of the Arsenal defenders and that is certainly the case with Seaman. He has had to pick the ball out of the back of the net much more often than last season, he has lost his place in the England team and then there was his major blunder in the European Cup Winners' Cup in Paris. But he did get Arsenal to the Final with some outstanding penalty saves and no-one could say that the poor season was down to him. He may well have a stormer in the coming season. You should consider him if the price is right.

Mark Bosnich Goalkeeper

Club ASTON VILLA

Date of birth 13.1.72

	Appearances (as substitute)		Goals		Clean sheets	
	League	Cups	League	Cups	League	Cups
1994/5	30	4	0	0	6	2
1993/4	28	12(1)	0	0		

Playing strength
Specialist penalty saver
Great shot-stopper

Pen picture
Mark is the heart-throb of the Villa female fans and is rated, not only by them, as the best young goalkeeper in the world. He is certainly among the top few in the country and his remarkable reflexes enable him to make some outstanding saves, including penalties. He has a tremendous future, his only weaknesses being a possible over-confidence and his kicking, which could be better.

Michael Oakes Goalkeeper

Club ASTON VILLA

Date of birth 30.10.73

	Appearances (as substitute)		Goals		Clean sheets	
	League	Cups	League	Cups	League	Cups
1994/5	0	1	0	0	0	1

Playing strength
Very promising, young, all-round keeper

Pen picture
Michael is the son of Alan Oakes, the former Manchester City favourite, and has made his way through the youth side to win his place in the England U-21 team. He has not yet made an impact on the first team and has strong opposition in Bosnich and the veteran, Spink. It is unlikely that he will get too many games.

Nigel Spink Goalkeeper

Club ASTON VILLA

Date of birth 8.8.58

	Appearances (as substitute)		Goals		Clean sheets	
	League	Cups	League	Cups	League	Cups
1994/5	12(1)	5	0	0	5	3
1993/4	14(1)	3	0	0		

Playing strength
Very good reflexes
Vast experience

Pen picture
Now 37, Nigel has been a great servant for the club and ambassador for the game over many years. Now at the tail end of his career, he is still a very able deputy for Mark Bosnich. It will soon be time for Michael Oakes to take over as the number two.

Tim Flowers Goalkeeper ⊙

RECOMMENDED

Club BLACKBURN ROVERS

Date of birth 3.2.67

	Appearances (as substitute)		Goals		Clean sheets	
	League	Cups	League	Cups	League	Cups
1994/5	39	9	0	0	16	2
1993/4	28	4	0	0		
1993/4 (for Southampton)	12	2	0	0		

Playing strength
Outstanding shot-stopper
All-round goalkeeping strength

Pen picture
An England international goalkeeper, Tim showed this season why he is Britain's most expensive keeper. In outstanding form for club and country, he looks like being in or on the fringe of the England team for years ahead. In a very solid Blackburn defence, he is an ideal fantasy team member. His price will present the only problem. A good investment, if you can afford him.

Bobby Mimms Goalkeeper

Club BLACKBURN ROVERS

Date of birth 12.10.63

	Appearances (as substitute)		Goals		Clean sheets	
	League	Cups	League	Cups	League	Cups
1994/5	3(1)	0	0	0	0	0
1993/4	13	5	0	0		

Playing strength
Good shot-stopper
Excellent deputy

Pen picture
Rovers have a very good deputy goalkeeper in Bobby. An ever-present for the club in the 1992/3 season, he played only 3 games last season and will not get very many more in the coming one unless Flowers is injured. If he is, you may get a bargain point-scoring goalkeeper.

Keith Branagan Goalkeeper ⊙⊙

RECOMMENDED

Club BOLTON WANDERERS

Date of birth 10.7.66

	Appearances (as substitute)		Goals		Clean sheets	
	League	Cups	League	Cups	League	Cups
1994/5	43	9	0	0	19	3

Playing strength
Confident with crosses
Good shot-stopper
Distributes quickly

Pen picture
Keith is an Irish International keeper, who has been extremely consistent since joining Bolton in 1992. He is a good all-round goalkeeper who has no obvious weakness and who gives confidence to his defence. His shot-stopping is well known, including saving penalties. The one which he saved in the play-off against Reading almost certainly kept their hopes alive, enabling the dramatic recovery. Any of the Bolton defence might be selected and Keith is guaranteed his position between the posts, so why not choose him?

Aidan Davison Goalkeeper

Club BOLTON WANDERERS

Date of birth 11.5.68

	Appearances (as substitute)		Goals		Clean sheets	
	League	Cups	League	Cups	League	Cups
1994/5	3(1)	0	0	0	0	0

Playing strength
Good shot-stopper

Pen picture
Aidan Davison is the understudy to Branagan and the fans are agreed that that is how it should be. Although he is a good shot stopper, he is often hesitant to come off his line, and his general positional sense is not as good as that of Branagan. Nevertheless, he is a competent keeper who will not let the side down.

Peter Shilton Goalkeeper

Club BOLTON WANDERERS

Date of birth 18.9.49

	Appearances (as substitute)		Goals		Clean sheets	
	League	Cups	League	Cups	League	Cups
1994/5	(1)	0	0	0	0	0

Playing strength
Outstanding experience
Helpful from a coaching point of view

Pen picture
I understand that there is no truth in the rumour which some Bolton fans were spreading around, that Peter was coming in as Financial Advisor. He will mainly operate as Goalkeeping Coach, but has already been called on in an emergency. In terms of reading the game, he is still as alert as ever, but he is obviously out of condition. He is only likely to play in a dire emergency.

Kevin Hitchcock Goalkeeper

Club CHELSEA

Date of birth 5.10.62

	Appearances (as substitute)		Goals		Clean sheets	
	League	Cups	League	Cups	League	Cups
1994/5	11(1)	4	0	0	2	1
1993/4	2	0	0	0		

Playing strength
Athletic
Motivator
Good with crosses despite lack of height

Pen picture
Although number two to Kharine, Kevin had his chance through injury and played so well that, for a time, he hung onto the goalkeeping spot. It is likely that he will be back to number two at the outset of the season and so you should not consider him for your team.

Dmitri Kharine Goalkeeper

Club CHELSEA

Date of birth 16.8.68

	Appearances (as substitute)		Goals		Clean sheets	
	League	Cups	League	Cups	League	Cups
1994/5	31	10	0	0	11	5
1993/4	40	12	0	0		

Playing strength
Reliable international goalkeeper
Two-footed and ambidextrous
A great shot-stopper
Very mobile with excellent reactions

Pen picture
After a season when Dmitri has suffered badly with injuries, he has re-established himself as the first choice keeper. As his playing strengths above show, he is a goalkeeper who seems to have absolutely everything. In addition to those areas mentioned, he is a superb penalty-stopper and he is good in the air. The only fault we could get from the Bridge faithful is that he does not communicate as well as he might. Well, I ask you, when a Russian goalkeeper is asked to play behind a multi-national defence such as has been assembled at Chelsea (including a few Scots!), who can blame him? Maybe the fact that they do not understand one another has something to do with the problems they sometimes have. You should avoid Chelsea defenders.

John Filan Goalkeeper

Club COVENTRY CITY

Date of birth 8.2.70

	Appearances (as substitute)		Goals		Clean sheets	
	League	Cups	League	Cups	League	Cups
1994/5	2	0	0	0	1	0

Pen picture

John is an Australian goalkeeper bought from Cambridge for £200,000. He is obviously intended to provide a challenge to Gould when Ogrizovic eventually calls it a day. Fans agree that he looks to have all the qualities to make him a top-class keeper.

Jonathan Gould Goalkeeper

Club COVENTRY CITY

Date of birth 18.7.68

	Appearances (as substitute)		Goals		Clean sheets	
	League	Cups	League	Cups	League	Cups
1994/5	7	0	0	0	2	0
1993/4	9	0	0	0		

Playing strength

Very agile

Good shot-stopper

Confident handling

Pen picture

Jonathan is a very good deputy, but suffers from the brilliant form of Ogrizovic. He is most unlikely to break into the first team whilst the latter is so outstanding and so he cannot be considered for your team.

Steve Ogrizovic Goalkeeper

Club COVENTRY CITY

Date of birth 12.9.57

	Appearances (as substitute)		Goals		Clean sheets	
	League	Cups	League	Cups	League	Cups
1994/5	33	7	0	0	11	1
1993/4	33	4	0	0		

Playing strength

Good shot-stopper

Clean handling

Pen picture

Steve is a loyal professional who is now 37 years old and still going strong. There must come a time when he is no longer able to produce the same high level of performance, but there are no signs of reaching that point at the moment. The only aspect of his game which fans can see their way to criticising is his kicking; he rarely reaches the halfway line.

Jason Kearton Goalkeeper

Club EVERTON

Date of birth 9.7.69

	Appearances (as substitute)		Goals		Clean sheets	
	League	Cups	League	Cups	League	Cups
1994/5	1	0	0	0	1	0
1993/4	0	1	0	0		

Playing strength

Good shot-stopper

Pen picture

Jason has been deputy to Neville Southall since October 1988 and, not surprisingly, he has had only a handful of first team opportunities. He is a reliable stand in on the rare occasions when he plays .

Neville Southall Goalkeeper

Club EVERTON

Date of birth 16.9.58

	Appearances (as substitute)		Goals		Clean sheets	
	League	Cups	League	Cups	League	Cups
1994/5	41	8	0	0	13	5
1993/4	42	6	0	0		

Playing strength

Great shot stopper

Organises his defence well

Excellent positional play

Pen picture

Neville has been an outstanding servant of the club since joining them in July 1981. Likewise he has served Wales admirably. He is an outstanding motivator and his reflex saves are outstanding, which cannot be said for his appearance. The fans will forgive him for being called "the scruffiest keeper in the Premiership" if he continues to turn in the same level of performance that he has attained for so long. At the moment he has another year to go on his contract and coming up to 37 years of age, you would think that there cannot be many more left. As a result of Everton's good defensive form last season, his price may put him out of your range.

Mark Beeney Goalkeeper

Club LEEDS UNITED

Date of birth 30.12.67

	Appearances (as substitute)		Goals		Clean sheets	
	League	Cups	League	Cups	League	Cups
1994/5	0	0	0	0	0	0
1993/4	22	5	0	0		

Playing strength

Reliable performer

The rumour is that Mark enjoys running, but unfortunately he does most of it keeping himself warm as John Lukic's substitute. He has had no opportunity this year due to John's fine form.

John Lukic Goalkeeper

Club LEEDS UNITED

Date of birth 11.12.60

	Appearances (as substitute)		Goals		Clean sheets	
	League	Cups	League	Cups	League	Cups
1994/5	42	6	0	0	17	1
1993/4	20	0	0	0		

Playing strength
Spectacular
Consistent

Pen picture
Last season was probably John's best at Elland Road. In the past he has always pulled off outstanding saves, but, on occasions has been at fault through lack of concentration. This year he has been at his very best, combining spectacular saves with a consistency which has kept Leeds in games which they might otherwise have lost. This consistent Leeds defence is always a guaranteed point-scorer in fantasy football games, but they will all be expensive. John will be no exception. If you can afford him, he will not let you down.

David James Goalkeeper

Club LIVERPOOL

Date of birth 1.8.70

	Appearances (as substitute)		Goals		Clean sheets	
	League	Cups	League	Cups	League	Cups
1994/5	42	15	0	0	17	8
1993/4	13(1)	0	0	0		

Playing strength
Good shot-stopper with excellent reflexes
Extremely agile

Pen picture
David is a tall athletic goalkeeper who dominates his area well. He has grown in confidence and in the level of his performances which have been quite outstanding. Expect Liverpool defenders to be very expensive this year; you will be forced to ignore them.

Michael Stensgaard Goalkeeper

Club LIVERPOOL

Date of birth 1.9.74

	Appearances (as substitute)		Goals		Clean sheets	
	League	Cups	League	Cups	League	Cups
1994/5	0	0	0	0	0	0

Playing strength
Agile

Pen picture
Michael is the Danish U-21 Goalkeeper, but as yet has had no opportunity to show his abilities at the top level due to the excellent form of David James. He is still learning, but has great potential. He was very unlucky with injuries last season.

Tony Coton Goalkeeper

Club MANCHESTER CITY

Date of birth 19.5.61

	Appearances (as substitute)		Goals		Clean sheets	
	League	Cups	League	Cups	League	Cups
1994/5	21(1)	2	0	0	6	1
1993/4	31	6	0	0		

Playing strength
Good on crosses
Great reflexes and a good shot-stopper

Pen picture
Fans do not blame Tony for the poor defensive record. He had a nightmare season trying to make up for the way in which the defence left him exposed. Despite his great goalkeeping ability, behind a defence like that, you do not want him in your team.

Andy Dibble Goalkeeper

Club MANCHESTER CITY

Date of birth 8.5.65

	Appearances (as substitute)		Goals		Clean sheets	
	League	Cups	League	Cups	League	Cups
1994/5	15	8	0	0	4	1
1993/4	11	1(1)	0	0		

Playing strength
Good shot-stopper

Pen picture
According to fans, Andy is a great shot-stopper, but sometimes panics on crosses and back passes and lets in the occasional howler. Once again, the Manchester City defence will not have any representatives in my fantasy teams.

Martyn Margetson Goalkeeper

Club MANCHESTER CITY

Date of birth 8.9.71

	Appearances (as substitute)		Goals		Clean sheets	
	League	Cups	League	Cups	League	Cups
1994/5	0	0	0	0	0	0
1993/4	0	0	0	0	0	0

Playing strength
Safe hands

Pen picture
Under Brian Horton he was third choice, but with a new manager he could well rise to second. He is a first-class keeper in all aspects except obeying the back pass rule. He may well get a few first team games this season.

Peter Schmeichel Goalkeeper

Club MANCHESTER UNITED

Date of birth 18.11.63

	Appearances (as substitute)		Goals		Clean sheets	
	League	Cups	League	Cups	League	Cups
1994/5	32	14	0	0	21	4
1993/4	40	18	0	0		

Playing strength
Dominant in the box
Excellent distribution
First-class communication with defenders

Pen picture
Peter is a Danish international who joined United in August 1991 and has helped to make the Manchester United defence arguably the best in the country. Apart from all of the general goalkeeping skills which all top-class keepers should exhibit, Peter demonstrates three others in which he is outstanding, if not unique. Firstly, at 6'4" Peter is a truly dominant figure in his penalty area. His height is invaluable in dealing with dangerous crosses. Secondly, when he spreads himself in front of an oncoming striker, it seems almost impossible to pass him, and thirdly, his speedy distribution of the ball, showing his total awareness of the situation, is second to none. Unfortunately he will probably be too expensive for most fantasy managers.

Gary Walsh Goalkeeper

Club MANCHESTER UNITED

Date of birth 21.3.68

	Appearances (as substitute)		Goals		Clean sheets	
	League	Cups	League	Cups	League	Cups
1994/5	10	6	0	0	3	2

Playing strength
Reliability
A good all-round goalkeeper

Pen picture
Gary has the unenviable task of having to play second fiddle to one of the finest goalkeepers in the world. He rarely gets a first team game, and when he does, everyone's eyes are on him, looking for a mistake. Gary could probably play in the Premiership for a number of other clubs, but he stays, waiting for the occasional chance at Old Trafford. He will not get many, likewise you will not get many points if you select him.

Alan Miller Goalkeeper ◉◉

RECOMMENDED

Club MIDDLESBROUGH

Date of birth 29.3.70

	Appearances (as substitute)		Goals		Clean sheets	
	League	Cups	League	Cups	League	Cups
1994/5	41	5	0	0	16	2

Playing strength
Organises his defence well
Good shot stopper

Pen picture
Alan joined Middlesbrough from Arsenal at the start of the season and the fans are not sure about him. He makes good saves but they are concerned that he is not always confident and tends to stay on his line. He may well be a relatively cheap keeper and behind Boro's solid defence, he is well worth buying.

Steve Pears Goalkeeper

Club MIDDLESBROUGH

Date of birth 22.1.62

	Appearances (as substitute)		Goals		Clean sheets	
	League	Cups	League	Cups	League	Cups
1994/5	5	3	0	0	2	0

Playing strength
Good shot-stopper
Lightning reflexes

Pen picture
Steve is Boro's longest-serving player, having played over 400 matches for them. Some say that he is arguably their greatest-ever goalkeeper. He has had few opportunities of late, having been kept out for most of this season by Alan Miller. He is still a class goalkeeper and some of the old faithful are finding it difficult to get used to a new face.

Ben Roberts Goalkeeper

Club MIDDLESBROUGH

Date of birth 22.6.75

	Appearances (as substitute)		Goals		Clean sheets	
	League	Cups	League	Cups	League	Cups
1994/5	0	1	0	0	0	0

Playing strength
Very aware
Good reflexes

Pen picture
Ben is a promising young keeper of whom we are likely to see more in the coming season. He is unlikely to get the number one spot for a little while yet.

Mike Hooper Goalkeeper

Club NEWCASTLE UNITED

Date of birth 10.2.64

	Appearances (as substitute)		Goals		Clean sheets	
	League	Cups	League	Cups	League	Cups
1994/5	4(2)	0	0	0	1	0
1993/4	19	5	0	0		

Playing strength
Consistent all-round goalkeeper

Pen picture
Mike is highly thought of by Kevin Keegan, but not so by many of the fans. Having held the first team slot for much of the *1993/4* season, he has been unable to cope with the challenge of Pavel Srnicek. With all of the money spent by the manager over the close season, some of the fans wonder why there has not been a change of deputy goalkeeper.

Pavel Srnicek Goalkeeper

Club NEWCASTLE UNITED

Date of birth 10.3.68

	Appearances (as substitute)		Goals		Clean sheets	
	League	Cups	League	Cups	League	Cups
1994/5	37	14	0	0	14	4
1993/4	21	1	0	0		

Playing strength
Excellent shot-stopper
Good positional play

Pen picture
For many, Pavel was their Player of the Season, becoming a firm favourite with the fans at St James' Park. "Pavel is a Geordie" has always been an outstanding shot-stopper, but has now added to his game excellent positioning and an ability to deal with crosses. There is little likelihood of anyone replacing him and so you can invest in him without hesitation, if you can afford him.

Mark Crossley Goalkeeper

Club NOTTINGHAM FOREST

Date of birth 16.6.69

	Appearances (as substitute)		Goals		Clean sheets	
	League	Cups	League	Cups	League	Cups
1994/5	42	6	0	0	13	2
1993/4	36(1)	9	0	0		
(Endsleigh League Div 1)						

Playing strength
Great shot-stopper

The fans are agreed that there has been a remarkable improvement in Mark's performances in the past two seasons. He has always been a great shot-stopper, but his ability to deal with crosses has improved out of all recognition. They are even talking about him as a possible challenger for the England spot. He may be too expensive for your team.

Tommy Wright Goalkeeper

Club NOTTINGHAM FOREST

Date of birth 29.8.63

	Appearances (as substitute)		Goals		Clean sheets	
	League	Cups	League	Cups	League	Cups
1994/5	0	0	0	0	0	0
1993/4	10	2	0	0		

(Endsleigh League Div 1)

Playing strength
Reliable, solid goalkeeper

Pen picture
Probably the biggest contribution made by Tommy over the past two years has been that he has provided a very real challenge to Crossley, forcing him to raise the level of his game. In the meantime, he has had a run of injury problems which have kept him out of the game for much of the time. For 1995/6, he cannot expect to start as anything other than number two, but if he turns in the usual reliable performances, he will be ready to mount a challenge, if the opportunity occurs. Not one for your team.

Sieb Dykstra Goalkeeper

Club QUEEN'S PARK RANGERS

Date of birth 20.10.66

	Appearances (as substitute)		Goals		Clean sheets	
	League	Cups	League	Cups	League	Cups
1994/5	11	1	0	0	3	0

Playing strength
A consistent, reliable keeper

Pen picture
In October, Dutchman Sieb, a £250,000 signing from Motherwell, took the goalkeeping position from Tony Roberts, but lost it again at Christmas. He is a good reliable keeper, but has not been able to compete with the high standards being set by Roberts. It looks as though he will certainly be number two for next season.

Tony Roberts Goalkeeper

Club QUEEN'S PARK RANGERS

Date of birth 4.8.69

	Appearances (as substitute)		Goals		Clean sheets	
	League	Cups	League	Cups	League	Cups
1994/5	31	6	0	0	7	5
1993/4	16(1)	0	0	0		

Playing strength
Reliable and consistent

Pen picture
Tony is the number two goalkeeper for Wales and for each of the past two seasons he has lost his place in the QPR team for part of the season. In *1993/4* it was to Jan Steyskal and last season to Sieb Dykstra. On both occasions he won it back before the end of the season. His form this season has been very good and it is unlikely that he will lose his place again unless it falls away considerably. The QPR defence is far too generous to consider any of its members for your fantasy team.

Kevin Pressman Goalkeeper

Club SHEFFIELD WEDNESDAY

Date of birth 6.11.67

	Appearances (as substitute)		Goals		Clean sheets	
	League	Cups	League	Cups	League	Cups
1994/5	34	3	0	0	9	2
1993/4	32	10	0	0		

Playing strength
Excellent all round keeper
Marshals his defence well

Pen picture
Kevin began last season as the number one choice and kept that position almost until the end of the season. He is an excellent keeper, with particularly good reflexes and distribution. However, he is uncertain with crosses and has an unnerving habit of dribbling round opposition forwards. He has twice been sent off this season. He will start the new season as the number two keeper, but it will be interesting to see what ideas David Pleat has on the subject. Watch the teamsheets and if he is getting in the team, he might be a cheap keeper within a good defence.

Chris Woods Goalkeeper

Club SHEFFIELD WEDNESDAY

Date of birth 14.11.59

	Appearances (as substitute)		Goals		Clean sheets	
	League	Cups	League	Cups	League	Cups
1994/5	8(1)	0	0	0	5	0
1993/4	10	2	0	0		

Playing strength
A great shot stopper
Positive when dealing with corners

Pen picture
During the last two months of the season, Chris won back his place in the first team from Kevin Pressman. Although he is excellent in coming out for crosses, he can sometimes be faulted for being slow to come off his line in normal play. However, he is a good talker, getting the best out of his defenders and he always shows confidence. There is a suspicion among fans that he might be a little overweight. If you are confident that Chris will keep his place in the team and that the defensive improvement shown by Wednesday at the end of last season will continue, it may be worth investing in him.

Dave Beasant Goalkeeper

Club SOUTHAMPTON

Date of birth 20.3.59

	Appearances (as substitute)		Goals		Clean sheets	
	League	Cups	League	Cups	League	Cups
1994/5	12(1)	0	0	0	4	0
1993/4	25	2	0	0		

Playing strength
A good shot-stopper
Vast experience
Tall and commanding

Pen picture
Dave is 6'4" tall and played very well after regaining his place towards the end of the season. With a commanding reach, he dominates his area, but is still prone to the occasional silly mistake. You should not consider anyone from the generous Southampton defence.

Bruce Grobbelaar Goalkeeper

Club SOUTHAMPTON

Date of birth 6.10.57

	Appearances (as substitute)		Goals		Clean sheets	
	League	Cups	League	Cups	League	Cups
1994/5	30	8	0	0	5	4
1993/4 (for Liverpool)	29	7	0	0		

Playing strength
Vast experience
Crowd entertainer

Pen picture
Bruce was the first choice for much of the season. However, with all of the activity surrounding the bribery allegations, for whatever reasons, he lost his place. At nearly 38, one wonders whether he will come back. If not, it will be goodbye to a real crowd entertainer.

Erik Thorstvedt Goalkeeper

Club TOTTENHAM HOTSPUR

Date of birth 28.10.62

	Appearances (as substitute)		Goals		Clean sheets	
	League	Cups	League	Cups	League	Cups
1994/5	1	1	0	0	0	0
1993/4	32	5	0	0		

Playing strength
An all-round reliable goalkeeper.
Inspires confidence in the defence with his total reliability
A good organiser

Pen picture
A Norwegian international who played in Germany and Sweden before joining Tottenham in 1988 for £400,000. He lost his place to Walker and has played only two games this year. With Walker's fine form, there does not seem to be any way back for Erik.

Ian Walker Goalkeeper

Club TOTTENHAM HOTSPUR

Date of birth 31.10.71

	Appearances (as substitute)		Goals		Clean sheets	
	League	Cups	League	Cups	League	Cups
1994/5	41	8	0	0	11	1
1993/4	11(1)	2	0	0		

Playing strength
Great reactions
Superb saver of penalties.

Pen picture
Still only 23, Ian has made the first team spot his own this year with a succession of great performances. His reaction saves are brilliant and he virtually always at least gets his hands to penalties. With the very dodgy Spurs defence, there will be no call-up for Ian into our fantasy team.

Ian Feuer Goalkeeper

Club WEST HAM UNITED

Date of birth 20.5.70

	Appearances (as substitute)		Goals		Clean sheets	
	League	Cups	League	Cups	League	Cups
1994/5	0	0	0	0	0	

Playing strength
Very tall

Pen picture
This giant American keeper, who joined the Hammers 12 months ago, has not yet been able to win the first team slot from Miklosko. He has now returned to Upton Park after a successful loan spell with Peterborough United and will continue the struggle in the new season. You should not consider him for your team.

Ludo Miklosko Goalkeeper

Club WEST HAM UNITED

Date of birth 9.12.61

	Appearances (as substitute)		Goals		Clean sheets	
	League	Cups	League	Cups	League	Cups
1994/5	42	6	0	0	13	3
1993/4	42	8	0	0		

Playing strength
An excellent shot-stopper
Can be outstanding

Pen picture
Ludek (known as Ludo) is established as the no. 1 goalkeeper and did not miss a game in either of the last two seasons. He is normally a most reliable goalie and then, out of the blue, he has an atrocious match. He is an outstanding shot-stopper but tends to flap at crosses. If you are convinced that the noticeable improvement of the Hammers' defensive form at the end of last season (see club write-up) is here to stay, you may wish to buy him; you may get a bargain.

Les Sealey Goalkeeper

Club WEST HAM UNITED

Date of birth 29.9.57

	Appearances (as substitute)		Goals		Clean sheets	
	League	Cups	League	Cups	League	Cups
1994/5	0	0	0	0	0	0

Playing strength
Vast experience

Pen picture
The much-travelled Sealey came back to his roots to join the Hammers, but it is unlikely that he will make any contribution other than act as cover for Miklosko.

Hans Segers Goalkeeper

Club WIMBLEDON

Date of birth 30.10.61

	Appearances (as substitute)		Goals		Clean sheets	
	League	Cups	League	Cups	League	Cups
1994/5	31(1)	7	0	0	6	4
1993/4	41	9	0	0		

Playing strength
Consistent, reliable performer

Pen picture
Hans is a Dutch goalkeeper who has spent most of his footballing career in the UK with Nottingham Forest and Wimbledon (plus loan periods elsewhere). He has played approximately 300 games for Wimbledon, but has recently lost his place to Neil Sullivan shortly after allegations of bribery were made. The two may or may not be related, but in any case, the future looks uncertain and we cannot recommend that you select him.

Neil Sullivan Goalkeeper

Club WIMBLEDON

Date of birth 24.2.70

	Appearances (as substitute)		Goals		Clean sheets	
	League	Cups	League	Cups	League	Cups
1994/5	11	0	0	0	6	0
1993/4	1(1)	0	0	0		

Playing strength
Consistent performer

Pen picture
Neil is a loyal club man who, until this season, has had only occasional opportunities in the first team. He won his place in March and held it until the end of the season. We cannot recommend that you take players from the very average Wimbledon defence.

FULL BACKS

Lee Dixon Right Full back ⦿
RECOMMENDED

Club ARSENAL

Date of birth 17.3.64

	Appearances (as substitute)		Goals		Clean sheets	
	League	Cups	League	Cups	League	Cups
1994/5	39	18	1	0	12	8
1993/4	32(1)	15	0	0		

Playing strength
Extremely consistent
Good positional play
Fast and likes to attack

Pen picture
Lee is an international right full back who is an integral part of the usually reliable Arsenal defence. Fans say that he was the most consistent player last season and that he always gives 100%. He enjoys attacking down the right wing, but he scores only rarely. He is a good crosser of the ball with either foot. Worthy of consideration.

Gavin McGowan Left Full back

Club ARSENAL

Date of birth 16.1.76

	Appearances (as substitute)		Goals		Clean sheets	
	League	Cups	League	Cups	League	Cups
1994/5	1	0	0	0	0	0

Playing strength
Very promising youngster
Good distribution

Pen picture

Gavin played in the final match of the season against Chelsea and acquitted himself well. It could be that he is being groomed to take over from Nigel Winterburn when he retires, but with Morrow and Keown around as potential stand-ins at left back and with new management taking over, who can tell what will happen. Keep your eye on this one!

Nigel Winterburn Left Full back ⦿
RECOMMENDED

Club ARSENAL

Date of birth 11.12.63

	Appearances (as substitute)		Goals		Clean sheets	
	League	Cups	League	Cups	League	Cups
1994/5	39	18	0	0	12	8
1993/4	34	16	0	0		

Playing strength
Totally reliable defender
Good left foot

Pen picture
Nigel is a regular first team member, a good defender who does not advance up the left wing as much as he used to, nor does he score many goals. He is going to be expensive but probably less so than other members of the Arsenal defence. Check out his price, you may get a bargain.

Gary Charles Right Full back

Club ASTON VILLA

Date of birth 13.4.70

	Appearances (as substitute)		Goals		Clean sheets	
	League	Cups	League	Cups	League	Cups
1994/5	14(2)	0	0	0	4	0

Playing strength
Attacking Full back
Good pace
Impressive distribution

Pen picture
Gary is an England international who joined Villa from Derby in January. He has settled in well and is able to use his pace and attacking ability because of the freedom allowed by the three man central defence which Brian Little favours. It is not out of the question that the reconstituted Villa defence will be much tighter this season and if so, Gary might produce a few bonus points.

Phil King Left Full back

Club ASTON VILLA

Date of birth 28.12.67

Alternative position Left Midfield

	Appearances (as substitute)		Goals		Clean sheets	
	League	Cups	League	Cups	League	Cups
1994/5	13(2)	7	0	0	3	3
1993/4	7(3)	2	0	0		
(for Sheffield Wednesday)						

Playing strength
Good attacking capabilities

Pen picture
Phil was signed by Ron Atkinson at the start of the season, which he began in the first team. However, after the arrival of Brian Little he lost his place at Christmas and now is very much second choice to Alan Wright. Even if he is injured, it is likely that Steve Staunton would switch to full back and so the future does not look too bright for Phil. He makes good runs down the left wing, but needs to be more consistent defensively to have any chance of regaining the place which he lost.

Bryan Small Full back

Club ASTON VILLA

Date of birth 15.11.71

	Appearances (as substitute)		Goals		Clean sheets	
	League	Cups	League	Cups	League	Cups
1994/5	5	0	0	0	1	0
1993/4	8(1)	3	0	0		

Playing strength
Very fast
Excellent man-marker

Pen picture
You might imagine that a player named Bryan Small would get on well with a manager called Brian Little, but it does not seem to have worked out. This speedy, left-footed player, who was once an England U-21 team member, has never realised the full potential which he showed as a young player and he may have to move on to become a first team regular.

Steve Staunton Full back ⦿⦿⦿
RECOMMENDED

Club ASTON VILLA

Date of birth 19.1.69

Alternative Position Midfield

	Appearances (as substitute)		Goals		Clean sheets	
	League	Cups	League	Cups	League	Cups
1994/5	34(1)	8	5	0	10	5
1993/4	24	9	3	0		

Playing strength
Tough tackler
Man-marker
Likes to go forward
Takes penalties

Pen picture
Steve is a very experienced professional who is still only 26 years old. He has played at left back for much of his time at Villa but last season reverted to midfield, where he plays for Ireland. Steve could be a must for your fantasy team if he is classified as a full back. He scores goals, particularly from set pieces, and he may also pick up defensive points from a reconstituted Villa defence which looks as though it could be much more solid in 1995/6 than it has been in the past. If he is categorised as a full back, buy him at all costs!!

Alan Wright Left Full back

Club ASTON VILLA

Date of birth 28.9.71

	Appearances (as substitute)		Goals		Clean sheets	
	League	Cups	League	Cups	League	Cups
1994/5	8	0	0	0	3	0
1994/5 (for Blackburn)	4(1)	0(1)	0	0	1	0
1993/4 (for Blackburn)	6(5)	2	0	0		

Playing strength
Very skilful
Enjoys attacking
Tenacious

Pen picture
Alan joined Villa from Blackburn Rovers for £900,000 in March and his attacking style suits their system of having three central defenders. Despite his lack of inches, (at 5' 4" he must be one of the smallest Premiership players around), he has established his place in the first team. He does not score very many goals, but will contribute with assists. However, there will probably be better defensive bargains around.

Henning Berg Full back

Club BLACKBURN ROVERS

Date of birth 1.9.69

Alternative Position Centre back

	Appearances (as substitute)		Goals		Clean sheets	
	League	Cups	League	Cups	League	Cups
1994/5	40	9	1	0	15	2
1993/4	37(3)	7	0	0		

Playing strength
Strong tackler
Excellent distribution
Good when he joins the attack

Pen picture
Henning is a very classy, Norwegian international right back. He played for his country in the 1994 World Cup. A first-class defender, he shows that he is much more than a stopper, by the very skilful use of the ball from defence. He enjoys joining the attack down the right wing and crosses the ball well. He is an ideal choice for your fantasy team, if you can afford him.

Jeff Kenna Right Full back

Club BLACKBURN ROVERS

Date of birth 27.8.70

Alternative Position Left Full back

	Appearances (as substitute)		Goals		Clean sheets	
	League	Cups	League	Cups	League	Cups
1994/5	9	0	1	0	2	0
1994/5 (for Southampton)	28	7	0	0	5	3
1993/4 (for Southampton)	40(1)	3	2	0		

Playing strength
A good defender
Enjoys making positive forward runs
Versatile

Pen picture
Jeff is an Irish international at right back. Bought for his versatility, he has played in four positions in his nine games. He is a strong tackler who is comfortable on the ball. He scores the odd goal, but his frequent positive runs are more likely to result in a punishing cross rather than a direct shot. It is not certain that he will hold a regular place when all of the Blackburn squad are fit and so we cannot recommend him for your team.

Graeme Le Saux Full back ⦿⦿⦿

RECOMMENDED

Club BLACKBURN ROVERS

Date of birth 7.10.68

Alternative Position Left Midfield

	Appearances (as substitute)		Goals		Clean sheets	
	League	Cups	League	Cups	League	Cups
1994/5	39	9	3	0	15	2
1993/4	39(1)	8	2	0		

Playing strength
Good in defence and attack
Very fast
Good crosser of the ball
Dead ball specialist

Pen picture

Pen picture
Graeme is now the regular England left back although he has also been used on the left hand side of midfield for both club and country. Although he loves to attack, he has never scored many goals, although that may change as he plays more often in midfield. Also, he contributes with a large number of assists. He is the ideal full back for you and he will rightly be very expensive, however; if he plays in midfield, you will not be able to afford to leave him out.

John Dreyer   Left Full back

Club BOLTON WANDERERS

Date of birth 11.6.63

Alternative Position Centre back

	Appearances (as substitute)		Goals		Clean sheets	
	League	Cups	League	Cups	League	Cups
1994/5	1(1)	0	0	0	0	0

Playing strength
Positive in the air
Strong tackler
Good distribution

Pen picture
John was with Bolton on loan from Stoke at the end of the season. Whether this will be made permanent is unknown at the time of writing. John impressed as a strong, hard stopper, but also by the way in which he carried the ball out of defence into attack. There is limited evidence upon which to base judgement, but what has been seen is positive.

Scott Green   Right Full back   ◉◉

RECOMMENDED

Club BOLTON WANDERERS

Date of birth 15.1.70

Alternative Position Right Midfield

	Appearances (as substitute)		Goals		Clean sheets	
	League	Cups	League	Cups	League	Cups
1994/5	26(5)	7	1	0	12	1

Playing strength
Tough tackler
Versatile
Good distribution

Pen picture
Scott is likely to play in the first team, but the question is, "Where?". Much of the season he has played at Right back, and he may well start there, but it is quite likely that he will move to midfield. He can beat defenders, pass and cross well and he is cool when under pressure. If he is categorised as a defender, he will be a very good buy, because the likelihood is that he will play further forward at some time, and even if he does play at Right back, he gets forward a great deal. Scott is well worth an investment.

Jimmy Phillips   Left Full back

Club BOLTON WANDERERS

Date of birth 8.2.66

	Appearances (as substitute)		Goals		Clean sheets	
	League	Cups	League	Cups	League	Cups
1994/5	46	9	1	0	19	3

Playing strength
Good attacking Left Full back

Pen picture
It is surprising that the one player who was an ever-present, is the one that all of my small sample of fans say will probably be replaced. They are full of praise for his attacking capabilities, for how he gets forward and for his crosses, but the message is that he does not have the pace to get back and that he might struggle in the Premiership. If he does keep his place, in view of his attacking instincts, he is an ideal defender to buy.

Nicky Spooner   Right Full back

Club BOLTON WANDERERS

Date of birth 5.6.71

	Appearances (as substitute)		Goals		Clean sheets	
	League	Cups	League	Cups	League	Cups
1994/5	1	1	0	0	0	1

Playing strength
Brave defender
Good tackler

Pen picture
Nicky is the reserve Right back who is a good, reliable defender, but who has been dogged by injury. Apparently he is on the transfer list and there have been enquiries about him. He is not for consideration for your fantasy team.

Darren Barnard   Full back

Club CHELSEA

Date of birth 30.11.71

Alternative Position Midfield

	Appearances (as substitute)		Goals		Clean sheets	
	League	Cups	League	Cups	League	Cups
1994/5	0	0	0	0		
1993/4	9(3)	2(1)	1	0		

Playing strength
Score great individual goals

Pen picture
Although he normally operates on the left hand side of midfield, he was categorised in some of the newspapers as a Full back. In a defence which was more secure than Chelsea's, that could have been an invitation to pick up points. Unfortunately it is not and although Darren has scored 7 goals in thirty appearances in the reserves, he has not played in the first team in 1994/5. He may be moving on.

Anthony Barness Right Full back

Club CHELSEA

Date of birth 25.3.72

Alternative Position Right Midfield

	Appearances (as substitute)		Goals		Clean sheets	
	League	Cups	League	Cups	League	Cups
1994/5	10(2)	3(1)	0	0	4	0
1993/4	2	0	0	0		

Playing strength

Versatile defender/midfielder

Comfortable on the ball

Pen picture

Anthony has played a number of times this season because of the injury situation at the tail-end of 1994. He has not won a regular place, but showed confidence and ability when he was called upon and there are likely to be more opportunities in the future. As with other Chelsea defenders, you should ignore him.

Steve Clarke Right Full back

Club CHELSEA

Date of birth 29.8.63

	Appearances (as substitute)		Goals		Clean sheets	
	League	Cups	League	Cups	League	Cups
1994/5	29	10	0	0	7	6
1993/4	39	11	0	0		

Playing strength

Reliable defensive full back

Strong tackler

Good going forward

Pen picture

Steve is the longest-serving first team player, a Scotland international, and continues to show good form. He times his tackles well, not diving in, and his experience helps him to read the game. He also makes a good contribution going forward, where his distribution is impressive. He rarely scores goals and even if he was in a more solid defence than Chelsea's, we could not recommend him for your fantasy teams.

Andy Dow Left Full back

Club CHELSEA

Date of birth 7.2.73

Alternative Position Left Midfield

	Appearances (as substitute)		Goals		Clean sheets	
	League	Cups	League	Cups	League	Cups
1994/5	0	0	0	0	0	0
1993/4	13(1)	3	0	0		

Playing strength

A steady defender

Pen picture

Andy is only 22 and it is early to say that time is running out for him. However, after a reasonable number of games in *1993/4*, he was not called upon in 1994/5. Considering the problems that Chelsea have had at left back, that makes his future at Stamford Bridge rather dubious.

Gareth Hall Right Full back

Club CHELSEA

Date of birth 20.3.69

Alternative Position Centre back

	Appearances (as substitute)		Goals		Clean sheets	
	League	Cups	League	Cups	League	Cups
1994/5	4(2)	2(1)	0	0	2	0
1993/4	4(3)	0(1)	0	0		

Playing strength

Utility defensive player

Good tackler

Pen picture

Even with all of the injury problems, Glenn Hoddle was obviously reluctant to play Gareth at Right back. Only two years ago he was the first choice in that position, so maybe now is time for a move.

Scott Minto Left Full back

Club CHELSEA

Date of birth 6.8.71

	Appearances (as substitute)		Goals		Clean sheets	
	League	Cups	League	Cups	League	Cups
1994/5	19	8(1)	0	0	5	1
1993/4	N/A	N/A	N/A	N/A		

Playing strength

Good going forward

Fast

Excellent timing

Pen picture

For some of the fans Scott has not lived up to the high expectations of him. At Charlton he was spoken of as a future England player, but his defensive form has not reached to those high claims. In attack he looks very impressive and he undoubtedly has the support of Glenn Hoddle. Fans hope that 1995/6 will be a better year.

Andy Myers Left Full back

Club CHELSEA

Date of birth 3.11.73

Alternative Position Left Midfield

	Appearances (as substitute)		Goals		Clean sheets	
	League	Cups	League	Cups	League	Cups
1994/5	9(1)	2	0	0	1	0
1993/4	6	4	0	0		
1992/3	3	1	0	0		

Playing strength
Fast
Determined
Confident with the ball

Pen picture
At only 21, Andy has a good footballing career ahead. Fans like him for his composure on the ball and his speed and ability to deliver a good cross. There is a great deal of competition at full back, but Andy has time on his side. Maybe this season will be his opportunity to establish a permanent place in the team.

Brian Borrows Right Full back
Club COVENTRY CITY
Date of birth 20.12.60
Alternative Position Centre back

	Appearances (as substitute)		Goals		Clean sheets	
	League	Cups	League	Cups	League	Cups
1994/5	33(2)	5	0	0	12	1
1993/4	29	2	0	0		

Playing strength
Very fit defender
Excellent tackler

Pen picture
At 34 years of age, Brian seems to be as fit as ever. Although he is normally a Full back, he has been playing in the centre of defence and, as a result, is less likely to do any attacking. Maybe that is his first concession to his age! He has been the most consistent player, but even so with his lack of involvement in attack, coupled with Coventry's leaky defence, you should ignore him.

David Burrows Left Full back
Club COVENTRY CITY
Date of birth 25.10.68

	Appearances (as substitute)		Goals		Clean sheets	
	League	Cups	League	Cups	League	Cups
1994/5	11	0	0	0	4	0
1993/4	25	5	1	1		

Playing strength
Hard tackling defender
Powerful shot

Pen picture
Wingers know when they have had a game against David Burrows, and they do not usually like it. He tackles hard and plays a tight marking game. He has a lethal shot which has not brought him as many goals as one would have expected. He must watch a rather fiery temperament which can get him into trouble. He is not for your fantasy teams.

Marcus Hall Left back
Club COVENTRY CITY
Date of birth 24.3.76

	Appearances (as substitute)		Goals		Clean sheets	
	League	Cups	League	Cups	League	Cups
1994/5	2(3)	0	0	0	0	0

Playing strength
Composure
Skill on the ball

Pen picture
Marcus shows great composure for someone of his tender years. He may need a little more time and a little more weight, but watch out for him in a year or so's time. It is obviously too early to select him yet.

Steve Morgan Full back
Club COVENTRY CITY
Date of birth 19.9.68

	Appearances (as substitute)		Goals		Clean sheets	
	League	Cups	League	Cups	League	Cups
1994/5	26(2)	6	0	0	9	1
1993/4	39	4	2	3		

Playing strength
Excellent tackler
Powerful left foot, takes attacking free kicks

Pen picture
Since the arrival of David Burrows, Steve has lost his first team place, which some fans think, was rather hard on him since he had turned in solid and reliable performances. In any case the leaky defence will not encourage fantasy managers to invest in the Coventry back five.

Ally Pickering Full back
Club COVENTRY CITY
Date of birth 22.6.67
Alternative Position Midfield

	Appearances (as substitute)		Goals		Clean sheets	
	League	Cups	League	Cups	League	Cups
1994/5	27(3)	5	0	0	8	1
1993/4	1(3)	0	0	0		

Playing strength
Skilful player
Good awareness

Pen picture

Despite his high level of skill, fans feel that Ally has not made the progress expected of him. This has affected his confidence which, together with something of a speed problem, has meant that his performances are not to the level that the fans (and no doubt the manager) would like.

Gary Ablett Left back ⊙
RECOMMENDED

Club EVERTON

Date of birth 19.11.65

Alternative Position Centre back

	Appearances (as substitute)		Goals		Clean sheets	
	League	*Cups*	*League*	*Cups*	*League*	*Cups*
1994/5	26	4	3	0	11	3
1993/4	32	7	1	0		

Playing strength

Strong in the tackle

Good in the air

Reads the game well

Pen picture

Gary had an excellent season for Everton. His consistent performance and vast experience make him an essential part of the well-drilled defence. He may not be expensive, and worth consideration for your team.

Earl Barrett Right Full back

Club EVERTON

Date of birth 28.4.67

Alternative Position Centre back

	Appearances (as substitute)		Goals		Clean sheets	
	League	*Cups*	*League*	*Cups*	*League*	*Cups*
1994/5	17	0	0	0	7	0
1994/5 (for Aston Villa)	24(1)	9	0	0	7	4
1993/4 (for Aston Villa)	39	13	0	1		

Playing strength

Versatile

Very fast

Pen picture

Earl is yet to convince many of the Everton fans that Joe Royle was right to buy him. They question his positional play and his first touch. Surprisingly they did not mention his shooting, (8 goals in more than 250 games) for which he has something of a reputation! Perhaps that is because he gets forward less frequently these days and so they have had less opportunity to witness it. However, he seems to have convinced Joe and is now a regular in the team. In view of his lack of goals or attacking inclination, he should not be in yours.

Andy Hinchcliffe Left Full back ⊙⊙
RECOMMENDED

Club EVERTON

Date of birth 5.2.69

Alternative Position Left Midfield

	Appearances (as substitute)		Goals		Clean sheets	
	League	*Cups*	*League*	*Cups*	*League*	*Cups*
1994/5	28(1)	7	2	1		
1993/4	25(1)	5	0	0		

Playing strength

Outstanding dead-ball artist

Hard tackler

Good distribution

Pen picture

Andy was a revelation last season. He started the season as a substitute left Full back, won his place there and then moved to play in midfield. Fans say that he has been Everton's most consistent player this season and, of course, his free kicks and corners have become legendary. His place in the team is now guaranteed and if he is again classified as a Full back, he should also be in yours. That is probably too much to hope for and he will almost certainly be categorised as a midfielder. Even so, he is worth your consideration.

Paul Holmes Right Full back

Club EVERTON

Date of birth 18.2.68

Alternative Position Centre back

	Appearances (as substitute)		Goals		Clean sheets	
	League	*Cups*	*League*	*Cups*	*League*	*Cups*
1994/5	1	0	0	0	0	0
1993/4	15	5	0	0		

Playing strength

Fast

Strong tackler

Pen picture

Paul is now the third choice right back behind Barrett and Jackson and as there would appear to be little future for him at Goodison Park. There is no future for you including him in your fantasy team.

Matthew Jackson Right Full back ⊙
RECOMMENDED

Club EVERTON

Date of birth 19.10.71

Alternative Position Centre back

	Appearances (as substitute)		Goals		Clean sheets	
	League	*Cups*	*League*	*Cups*	*League*	*Cups*
1994/5	26	6	0	0	9	5
1993/4	37(1)	6	0	0		

Playing strength

Very fast and enjoys attacking

Tough tackler

Pen picture

Matthew is a very bright, young prospect at right back whom the fans feel has been unlucky to lose his place to Earl Barrett. If he stays with Everton, he may just win back his place and prove to be a cheap defender in a side which turns in solid defensive performances. Monitor the situation carefully.

Neil Moore Full back

Club EVERTON

Date of birth 21.9.72

Alternative Position Various

	Appearances (as substitute)		Goals		Clean sheets	
	League	Cups	League	Cups	League	Cups
1994/5	0	0	0	0		0
01993/4	4(1)	0(1)	0	0		

Playing strength

Reliable young defender

Pen picture

Neil has a great deal of potential and is unfortunate to have had no opportunity in the first team this season. He can play in a number of positions and fans believe that he will start more games next year. It is too much of a gamble for you to consider him.

Gary Rowett Full back

Club EVERTON

Date of birth

Alternative Position Centre back

	Appearances (as substitute)		Goals		Clean sheets	
	League	Cups	League	Cups	League	Cups
1994/5	2	0	0	0	0	0
1993/4	0(2)	0	0	0		

Playing strength

Versatile

Pen picture

Gary is a versatile twenty-one-year-old who, in his career has played in virtually every position from Full back to Striker. He had only two games last season and it is difficult to see where he would fit into the team. You should not consider him.

Tony Dorigo Left Full back

Club LEEDS UNITED

Date of birth 31.12.65

	Appearances (as substitute)		Goals		Clean sheets	
	League	Cups	League	Cups	League	Cups
1994/5	28	1(1)	0	0	10	0
1993/4	37	5	0	0		

Playing strength

A speedy full back who likes to attack.

Dead-ball specialist

Pen picture

There is something of a mystery about Tony. He is known as a speedy full back who loves to move up the wing to join the attack. He is also known to have a very hard shot. Yet in three years he has scored only one goal in the Premiership. One of these years he is going to hit the jackpot and have a bonanza, but it is too much of a gamble to bank on it. Despite his excellent form in the league last year (inspite of the injury which affected his season), you cannot afford to have a non-scorer in your team.

Gary Kelly Right Full back

Club LEEDS UNITED

Date of birth 9.7.74

	Appearances (as substitute)		Goals		Clean sheets	
	League	Cups	League	Cups	League	Cups
1994/5	42	6	0	0	17	1
1993/4	42	5	0	0		

Playing strength

Very fast

Strong tackler

Reads the game well

Pen picture

Gary has not missed a league or cup game in two seasons, which is not bad for a player who is just 21 and had never played a top class game before. However, he is still to score his first goal. His season was not quite up to the standard of his previous one when he really took the footballing world by storm, but even so he is established as the number one right back. Once again, he will be more expensive than you are able to justify.

Kevin Sharp   Left Full back   ⊙⊙
RECOMMENDED

Club LEEDS UNITED
Date of birth 9.9.74
Alternative Position Left Midfield

	Appearances (as substitute)		Goals		Clean sheets	
	League	Cups	League	Cups	League	Cups
1994/5	(2)		0	0	0	0
1993/4	7(3)		0	0		

Playing strength
Versatile, equally at home at full back or in midfield
He is showing signs of good defensive capabilities.
Strong tackler

Pen picture
Kevin is a favourite with the Leeds fans and just may be of interest to you. Still only 20 now, in *1993/4* he deputised for Tony Dorigo at Left Back. However, the two substitute appearances he made for Leeds at the tail end of last season, he came on to replace Rod Wallace. If he does win a place in the Leeds team, he may well be categorised as a defender. If so, you will really have struck gold, because he will certainly be inexpensive and you will be picking up defensive points for the solid Leeds defence, plus any attacking points he may gain. Definitely one to check out.

Nigel Worthington   Left Full back

Club LEEDS UNITED
Date of birth 4.11.61
Alternative Position Left Midfield

	Appearances (as substitute)		Goals		Clean sheets	
	League	Cups	League	Cups	League	Cups
1994/5	21(6)	5(1)	1	0	7	1
1993/4	30(1)	4	1	0		

Playing strength
Good attacking full back
Versatile
A calming influence

Pen picture
Nigel played in a run of games at the start of the season when Dorigo was injured, and again in the New Year. He also made a few appearances in midfield. He is a reliable deputy who will not let the side down when he plays. However, he is now at the veteran stage and his contribution will probably be mainly as a substitute. He is not one for your team.

Stig Bjornebye   Left Full back

Club LIVERPOOL
Date of birth 11.12.69

	Appearances (as substitute)		Goals		Clean sheets	
	League	Cups	League	Cups	League	Cups
1994/5	31	12(1)	0	0	13	6
1993/4	6(3)	0(1)	0	0		

Playing strength
Excellent crosser of the ball with a very good left foot

Pen picture
Stig is a Norwegian international who had a very impressive season at left back. His main strength is his crossing ability; he is a corner-kick specialist. His season was curtailed when he broke his leg at the beginning of April. He was frequently substituted and some fans wonder whether he will be replaced by a big name signing during the close season. In some fantasy games last season, he was one of the big bargains, he certainly will not be this year. You probably cannot afford to consider him.

Steve Harkness   Left Full back

Club LIVERPOOL
Date of birth 27.8.71
Alternative Position Centre back

	Appearances (as substitute)		Goals		Clean sheets	
	League	Cups	League	Cups	League	Cups
1994/5	8	0	1	0	4	0
1993/4	10(1)	3(1)	0	0		

Playing strength
Strong tackler
Competitive
Good left foot

Pen picture
Steve is a useful squad player whose versatility is appreciated by the fans. He stood in as an emergency Centre back in four games at the end of the season, although his normal position is Left back. He is a gutsy player, liked by the fans, with a great future. However, some of the fantasy games wrongly classified him as a midfielder. You should certainly not touch him.

Rob Jones Right Full back

Club LIVERPOOL

Date of birth 5.11.71

	Appearances (as substitute)		Goals		Clean sheets	
	League	Cups	League	Cups	League	Cups
1994/5	31	15	0	0	12	8
1993/4	38	7	0	0		

Playing strength

Good anticipation and distribution

Very speedy

Pen picture

Rob is a cultured footballer who combines pace, anticipation and vision. An established international at right back at the age of 23, he has a great future ahead. One fan comments "This player has it all, apart from a shot that hits the back of the net." . Another says "Surely he must score soon!". That is one reason why you should not have him for a fantasy team. Another is his price, which will be high.

Dominic Matteo Left Full back

Club LIVERPOOL

Date of birth 28.4.74

Alternative Position Left Midfield

	Appearances (as substitute)		Goals		Clean sheets	
	League	Cups	League	Cups	League	Cups
1994/5	2(5)	1	0	0	0	0
1993/4	11	2	0	0		

Playing strength

Powerful

A great deal of stamina

Pen picture

Dominic is a true athlete, strong, good pace and very determined. He did not make the anticipated break through into the first team last season, but his tine will come. However, he is not an ideal fantasy team member. His strengths lie in a defensive midfield role and so he does not score many goals.

Ian Brightwell Full back

Club MANCHESTER CITY

Date of birth 9.4.68

Alternative Position Midfield

	Appearances (as substitute)		Goals		Clean sheets	
	League	Cups	League	Cups	League	Cups
1994/5	29	9	0	0	6	2
1993/4	6(1)	0	0	0		

Playing strength

Energetic chaser

Good control and distribution

Pen picture

Ian usually plays in midfield, but some of the fantasy games had him as a full back. In the City defence, that is quite an indictment. He missed the tail-end of last season as a result of a double hernia operation. Do not buy him, it could cost you points.

Richard Edghill Right Full back

Club MANCHESTER CITY

Date of birth 23.9.74

Alternative Position Centre back

	Appearances (as substitute)		Goals		Clean sheets	
	League	Cups	League	Cups	League	Cups
1994/5	14	3	0	0	2	0
1993/4	22	5	0	0		

Playing strength

Very fast and good on the ground

Good timing with his tackles

Pen picture

Last season Richard suffered from injury and lack of confidence. When he is in form, he likes to overlap and get in centres. If he struggles however, the opposition half is out of bounds. Another City defender to avoid.

Andy Hill Right Full back

Club MANCHESTER CITY

Date of birth 20.1.65

Alternative Position Centre back

	Appearances (as substitute)		Goals		Clean sheets	
	League	Cups	League	Cups	League	Cups
1994/5	10(3)	3	0	0	3	0
1993/4	15(2)	0	0	0		

Playing strength

Good in the air - goes up for corners

Strong tackler

Pen picture

It seems likely that Andy will get fewer games next year as younger defenders take a firmer grip. Whether or not that is so, you still do not buy a member of the City defence.

Terry Phelan Left Full back

Club MANCHESTER CITY

Date of birth 16.3.67

	Appearances (as substitute)		Goals		Clean sheets	
	League	Cups	League	Cups	League	Cups
1994/5	26(1)	4	0	0	6	0

Playing strength
Strong tackler
Good on overlap

Pen picture
This was not a good season for Terry. Fans gained the impression that he was not particularly interested, as a result of which, he was made the scapegoat for the bad results. Hopefully the new manager will sort the problem out.

Denis Irwin Left Full back ◉
RECOMMENDED

Club MANCHESTER UNITED
Date of birth 31.10.65

	Appearances (as substitute)		Goals		Clean sheets	
	League	Cups	League	Cups	League	Cups
1994/5	40	13	1	4	23	4
1993/4	42	18(1)	2	2		

Playing strength
Excellent defender
Great dead ball kicker
Very calm under pressure

Pen picture
Denis is a true professional and greatly appreciated by his team mates and the fans. In addition to his defensive abilities, playing at left back, you can rely on him to score a few goals per season from set-pieces or from open play. His outstanding work rate and total commitment put him in a class which most other full backs dream about. He will be very expensive to buy for your team.

Gary Neville Right Full back
Club MANCHESTER UNITED
Date of birth 18.2.75
Alternative Position Centre back

	Appearances (as substitute)		Goals		Clean sheets	
	League	Cups	League	Cups	League	Cups
1994/5	16(2)	6(2)	0	0	10	3
1993/4	1	0(1)	0	0		

Playing strength
A penetrating long throw
A steady, versatile, young defender

Pen picture
The progress that this young man has made during the last year is absolutely phenomenal. This time last year, he was hardly known (unless you had read this book and had seen all of our positive comments about him!). Indeed, most of the fantasy games did not include him or many of the other young United players. Now he has forced his way into the United first team and even played for England. He is remarkably cool for a youngster and obviously has a great future ahead. If he is reasonably priced, you could invest wisely here, however we think that he will cost more than you can afford.

Philip Neville Left Full back
Club MANCHESTER UNITED
Date of birth 21.1.77
Alternative Position Left Centre Back

	Appearances (as substitute)		Goals		Clean sheets	
	League	Cups	League	Cups	League	Cups
1994/5	1(1)	1	0	0	1	0

Playing strength
Good vision
Good Passer

Pen picture
Philip is the younger brother of Gary and is captain of the Youth side. He is an assured player who shows composure on the ball, good vision and excellent passing ability. He will undoubtedly figure in United teams of the future, but it is too early for him to figure in your fantasy team for 1995/6.

Paul Parker Full back
Club MANCHESTER UNITED
Date of birth 4.4.64
Alternative Position Centre back

	Appearances (as substitute)		Goals		Clean sheets	
	League	Cups	League	Cups	League	Cups
1994/5	1(1)	2(1)	0	0	0	0
1993/4	39(1)	16	0	0		

Playing strength
Versatile
Determined
Reliable

Pen picture
Paul has missed almost the whole of the season through injury and the mass of young United talent has come through. If all of the defenders are fit, who on earth would get the Right Full back position? I think that there is too much doubt and so I will steer clear of the contenders when I am choosing my fantasy teams.

Neil Cox Right Full back ◉◉
RECOMMENDED

Club MIDDLESBROUGH
Date of birth 8.10.71

	Appearances (as substitute)		Goals		Clean sheets	
	League	Cups	League	Cups	League	Cups
1994/5	40	5	1	0	15	1

Playing strength
Strong tackler
Joins the attack

Pen picture
Neil has had a promising first season, unfortunately interrupted by injury. He is not afraid to get forward, but sometimes gets caught out of position as a result. You should check his price and consider him as a member of this solid defence.

Curtis Fleming Left Full back
Club MIDDLESBROUGH
Date of birth 8.10.68

	Appearances (as substitute)		Goals		Clean sheets	
	League	Cups	League	Cups	League	Cups
1994/5	21	6	0	0	12	1

Playing strength
He has everything
Hard tackler
Good passer
Battles well for the ball
Gets forward

Pen picture
One of our contributors describes Curtis as "Ireland's great undiscovered left back". You will see from that that he is very highly thought of on Teesside. We have to leave this hero out of our list of recommendations because he has never scored a goal for Boro at any level.

Chris Morris Right Full back
Club MIDDLESBROUGH
Date of birth 24.12.63
Alternative Position Left Full back

	Appearances (as substitute)		Goals		Clean sheets	
	League	Cups	League	Cups	League	Cups
1994/5	15	6	0	1	6	1

Playing strength
Much experience
Good runs down the wing

Pen picture
Chris is a dependable Full back who provides support down the flanks, to the midfielders. In the past he has been known to take penalties, but that is less likely now. He is normally the first reserve for the Full back and is unlikely to be the first choice.

Warren Barton Right Full back
Club NEWCASTLE UNITED
Date of birth 19.3.69

	Appearances (as substitute)		Goals		Clean sheets	
	League	Cups	League	Cups	League	Cups
1994/5 (for Wimbledon)	40	6	2	0	11	3
1993/4 (for Wimbledon)	37	8	2	1		

Playing strength
Has great pace
Loves to attack
Frequently takes shots at goal from free-kicks

Pen picture
Warren is an all-round, effective attacking right back for whom the 1994/5 season was a thoroughly successful one. Although his recognised position is at Full back, he has in fact played for Wimbledon on the right hand side of midfield for much of the past season. He had a full season in the first team and played some of the best football of his career. The move to St James' Park gives him the chance to operate within one of the really large clubs and it is unlikely to overawe him. Upon signing, he said on radio "When I heard that it was Newcastle who wanted to sign me, that was it. As I said, I'd go to China to play for them." In view of his record transfer fee for a defender, we assume that his football is better than his geography. You can expect his fantasy price to rise, but he may still be worth considering. You are certain to gain good points, but can you afford him? If he plays in midfield, it will make him of particular interest.

John Beresford Left Full back
Club NEWCASTLE UNITED
Date of birth 4.9.66
Alternative Position Left Midfield

	Appearances (as substitute)		Goals		Clean sheets	
	League	Cups	League	Cups	League	Cups
1994/5	32	13	0	1	12	3
1993/4	34	6	0	0		

Playing strength
Makes good attacking runs
Good in the air for a small player

Pen picture
At his best, John is an exciting player, with his attacking forward runs. Unfortunately, last season those were restricted due to the absence of Scott Sellars. The fans expect him to be seriously challenged for the Left Full back position this year by Robbie Elliott, with their vote going to Elliott. They were saying much the same sort of things last year, and John survived. However, it is too uncertain a situation for you to risk selecting him.

Robbie Elliott Left Full back ⊙⊙⊙
RECOMMENDED

Club NEWCASTLE UNITED
Date of birth 25.12.73
Alternative Position Midfield

	Appearances (as substitute)		Goals		Clean sheets	
	League	Cups	League	Cups	League	Cups
1994/5	10(4)	3(1)	2	0	3	1
1993/4	13(2)	2	0	0		

Playing strength
A competitive and reliable young full back
A strong shot

Pen picture
You could possibly cash in here! Watch what is happening at the start of the season at Newcastle. It could well be that Robbie takes over the Left Full back position from John Beresford. He is likely to be less expensive and he is likely to score more goals than him. Therefore, be ready to pick up lots of defensive and attacking points from this young man. At St James' Park they talk about him being ready for an England cap, assuming that he gets no recurral of his injury problems. Robbie is a really high potential footballer, both real and fantasy!

Stuart Elliott Full back
Club NEWCASTLE UNITED
Date of birth 27.8.77

	Appearances (as substitute)		Goals		Clean sheets	
	League	Cups	League	Cups	League	Cups
1994/5	0	0	0	0	0	0

Playing strength
Good defender
Great header
Thunderous shot

Pen picture
Not to be confused with Robbie Elliott, above. This young man has not yet made it into the first team, but our sources tell us that he is the best header of the ball at the club, has a thunderous shot, and is a great prospect. With all of the full back talent at the club, he may not make it this year, but look out for the name in future.

Marc Hottiger Right Full back
Club NEWCASTLE UNITED
Date of birth 7.11.67
Alternative Position Right Midfield

	Appearances (as substitute)		Goals		Clean sheets	
	League	Cups	League	Cups	League	Cups
1994/5	37	13	1	1	12	4

Playing strength
Inventive attacking Full back

Pen picture
Before Warren Barton was signed, fans were already questioning the defensive capabilities of the Swiss international. He is excellent going forward, but does sometimes get caught out at the back. Presumably he will lose his place to Barton and, although he can play on the right hand side of midfield, the competition for places in the Newcastle midfield is likely to be terribly intense. He will probably have to be satisfied with being a squad member, getting only the occasional game, therefore you should not select him either.

Craig Armstrong Left Full back
Club NOTTINGHAM FOREST
Date of birth 23.5.75

	Appearances (as substitute)		Goals		Clean sheets	
	League	Cups	League	Cups	League	Cups
1994/5	0	0	0	0	0	0
1993/4	0	0	0	0		

(Endsleigh League Div 1)

Playing strength
Strong tackler
Composed on the ball when going forward

Pen picture
It is unlikely that Craig will feature in the fantasy league in 1995/6, but look out for him in the future. He is a young left back with a great deal of potential, both in defence and going forward. However, with Stuart Pearce around for a few more years, there is no chance of him breaking into the team.

Alf Inge Haaland Right back ⊙
RECOMMENDED

Club NOTTINGHAM FOREST
Date of birth 23.11.72
Alternative Position Centre back or Midfield

	Appearances (as substitute)		Goals		Clean sheets	
	League	Cups	League	Cups	League	Cups
1994/5	18(2)	1(1)	1	0	5	1
1993/4	3	0	0	0		

(Endsleigh League Div 1)

Playing strength
Good header
Tough tackler
Utility player

Pen picture
Alf Inge has not been a first choice for the Forest team, but his versatility makes him an automatic choice as a short-term injury replacement. He is a very tenacious tackler who normally plays on the right hand side of the defence or midfield, but has stood in for Pearce on the left. We have categorised him as a Full back,

because this is the classification given in some of the newspapers, although he has sometimes played in midfield as a ball-winner. He is likely to be cheaper than others in the Forest defence and it is worth checking up on whether he wins a place in the team at the start of the season. He may prove to be a bargain buy.

Des Lyttle Right Full back

Club NOTTINGHAM FOREST

Date of birth 24.9.71

	Appearances (as substitute)		Goals		Clean sheets	
	League	Cups	League	Cups	League	Cups
1994/5	38	6	0	0	11	2
1993/4	37	10	1	0		

(Endsleigh League Div 1)

Playing strength
Clean tackler
Keen and committed

Pen picture
Des surprised many with the way in which he adapted to life in the Premiership. He is undoubtedly Forest's most improved player. His strength is his defensive capability. There are mixed reports about the other part of his game, some saying that he rarely goes forward, whilst others say that he is confident going forward. Well, I suppose that both comments could be right. Last season, in most fantasy games, he was a cheap defender. That will probably change for the coming season.

Stuart Pearce Full back

RECOMMENDED

Club NOTTINGHAM FOREST

Date of birth 24.4.62

	Appearances (as substitute)		Goals		Clean sheets	
	League	Cups	League	Cups	League	Cups
1994/5	36	4	8	(2)	12	2
1993/4	42	9	6	0		

(Endsleigh League Div 1)

Playing strength
Inspirational leader
Tremendous left foot shot
Ferocious tackler
Goal scorer

Pen picture
There is not much more to be said about Stuart Pearce. All Forest fans agree that he is still the best Full back in the country and it seems that he may have resurrected his England career at the age of 33. He is an inspirational captain and his influence undoubtedly played a major role in the outstanding season which Nottingham Forest enjoyed. Since he scored an amazing 10 goals (8 in the league), he is also an ideal player in your fantasy team, if you can afford him. Do not expect him to be cheap, but you cannot ignore him!

David Bardsley Right Full back

Club QUEEN'S PARK RANGERS

Date of birth 11.9.64

Alternative Position Centre back

	Appearances (as substitute)		Goals		Clean sheets	
	League	Cups	League	Cups	League	Cups
1994/5	30	7	0	0	6	5
1993/4	32	5	0	0		

Playing strength
Very good pace
Crosses the ball well

Pen picture
David Bardsley has good pace and attacking flair and his forward runs and effective crosses have helped to provide goals for the attackers. He is also steady in his defensive role, although sometimes his tackles get him into trouble and he has missed a number of games through suspension this season. The QPR defence is not one of the most dependable and so we cannot recommend him to you.

Rufus Brevett Right Full back

Club QUEEN'S PARK RANGERS

Date of birth 24.9.69

Alternative Position Centre Back

	Appearances (as substitute)		Goals		Clean sheets	
	League	Cups	League	Cups	League	Cups
1994/5	17(2)	1	0	0	4	0
1993/4	4	0(1)	0	0		

Playing strength
Versatile
Good pace

Pen picture

Rufus is a reliable deputy who comes into the side in place of Full backs or Centre backs when they are injured. He is a strong, committed player who never lets the side down and who enjoys contributing in attack when the opportunity occurs. He is unlikely to be a regular and so you should not consider him.

Clive Wilson Full back

Club QUEEN'S PARK RANGERS

Date of birth 13.11.61

| | Appearances (as substitute) | | Goals | | Clean sheets | |
	League	Cups	League	Cups	League	Cups
1994/5	36	6	2	(2)	9	4
1993/4	42	5	3	0		

Playing strength

Consistent

Reads the game well

A reliable taker of penalties

Pen picture

Clive is a model professional who is very highly regarded by both the management and the fans at Loftus Road. He is an experienced professional (age 33) who has good vision and who loves to attack. He is also a specialist spot-kicker. In a side which was more consistent in defence, he would be an ideal choice for a fantasy team, however, QPR concede far too many goals and therefore you must ignore him.

Peter Atherton Full back ◉◉

RECOMMENDED

Club SHEFFIELD WEDNESDAY

Date of birth 6.4.70

Alternative Position Centre back

| | Appearances (as substitute) | | Goals | | Clean sheets | |
	League	Cups	League	Cups	League	Cups
1994/5	41(1)	7	0	0	14	2
1993/4	39(1)	3	0	0		
(for Coventry)						

Playing strength

Reliable, solid defender

Versatile

Very quick

Pen picture

Peter was signed from Coventry City a year ago and in his first year at Hillsborough, for many he was the player of the year. He can play anywhere across the back four and has an excellent positional sense. He goes on the overlap at the right time and his distribution is superb. Some indication of how badly Wednesday miss him is possibly to be gained from the fact that the one game that he missed (against Nottingham Forest), they lost 7-1! He does not score many goals, but he contributes with assists and

should be considered very seriously in view of the club's improved defensive record.

Brian Linighan Right Full back

Club SHEFFIELD WEDNESDAY

Date of birth 2.11.73

| | Appearances (as substitute) | | Goals | | Clean sheets | |
	League	Cups	League	Cups	League	Cups
1994/5	0	0	0	0	0	0
1993/4	1	2	0	0		

Playing strength

Good young deputy

Pen picture

Brian was the deputy twelve months ago, but with an abundance of talented right backs (Atherton, Petrescu and Nolan, who plays left back but is right-footed), his prospects look bleak. He may be moved on when David Pleat has a clear-out after reviewing his playing staff. You should steer clear of him.

Ian Nolan Left Full back

RECOMMENDED ◉◉

Club SHEFFIELD WEDNESDAY

Date of birth 9.7.70

Alternative Position Right Full back

| | Appearances (as substitute) | | Goals | | Clean sheets | |
	League	Cups	League	Cups	League	Cups
1994/5	42	7	3	0	14	2

Playing strength

Very quick

Covers well

Good overlapping

Pen picture

Ian joined Wednesday from Tranmere at the start of the 1994/5 season and has been an ever-present. He is right-footed yet plays left back, presumably to accommodate Atherton at Right back. He has a superb attitude and every aspect of his game is first-rate apart from his distribution, which could be improved.

Dan Petrescu Right Full back

Club SHEFFIELD WEDNESDAY

Date of birth 22.12.67

Alternative Position Right Midfield

| | Appearances (as substitute) | | Goals | | Clean sheets | |
	League	Cups	League	Cups	League	Cups
1994/5	20(9)	2(2)	3	0	6	0

Playing strength
Very quick
Superb positional sense
Breaks forward really well

Pen picture
Dan took a little time to settle after he joined the Owls from Genoa for £1.3m during the 1994 close season. He has become a favourite of the fans who love his breaks into attack. He is less impressive defensively due to weakness in the tackle, but his excellent positional sense makes up for many of the problems. He scores a few goals, but not enough to warrant selection for your team.

Francis Benali Left Full back

Club SOUTHAMPTON

Date of birth 10.12.68

Alternative Position Centre back

| | Appearances (as substitute) | | Goals | | Clean sheets | |
	League	Cups	League	Cups	League	Cups
1994/5	32(3)	7	0	0	8	3
1993/4	34(3)	3	0	0		

Playing strength
Tough tackling
Committed professional

Pen picture
Francis played at left back at the start of the season, but was switched to Centre back from time to time. He is a fearsome tackler and he has great speed. Once again we have to say that we cannot recommend Southampton defenders.

Simon Charlton Left Full back

Club SOUTHAMPTON

Date of birth 25.10.71

Alternative Position Midfield

| | Appearances (as substitute) | | Goals | | Clean sheets | |
	League	Cups	League	Cups	League	Cups
1994/5	25	3(1)	1	0	5	2
1993/4	29(4)	2	1	0		

Playing strength
Very pacey
Good crosser
Likes to attack

Pen picture
Simon normally plays at left back and frequently joins the attack and crosses the ball well, but, he rarely scores. However, he enjoyed one of those rare moments in the penultimate game of the season at Old Trafford. He will not do it anywhere near often enough to make us recommend him.

Jason Dodd Right Full back

Club SOUTHAMPTON

Date of birth 2.11.70

Alternative Position Midfield

| | Appearances (as substitute) | | Goals | | Clean sheets | |
	League	Cups	League	Cups	League	Cups
1994/5	23(2)	4	2	0	6	3
1993/4	5(5)	2	0	0		

Playing strength
Solid defender
Good distribution and crosses

Pen picture
Jason is a sound, reliable defender who has taken over the Right back spot since Kenna was transferred to Blackburn Rovers. He is an adventurous player going forward and puts his runs to good use with an accurate pass or cross. Having lost his place through injury the previous season, this ex-England U-21 international now has a chance to re-establish a regular place in the side.

Dean Austin Left Full back

Club TOTTENHAM HOTSPUR

Date of birth 26.4.70

Alternative Position Right Full back

| | Appearances (as substitute) | | Goals | | Clean sheets | |
	League	Cups	League	Cups	League	Cups
1994/5	23(1)	6(1)	0	0	11	1
1993/4	21(3)	2(1)	0	0		

Playing strength
A solid defender who is very strong in the tackle.
He loves to attack

Pen picture
Dean is a hard-tackling, no-nonsense type of player, who contributes to the attack, but rarely scores. His forward runs usually end with a telling pass rather than a shot on goal. Although he played in only 23 league games, he was in all eleven in which Spurs kept a clean sheet. That must mean something!

Sol Campbell Left/Right Full back

Club TOTTENHAM HOTSPUR

Date of birth 18.9.74

Alternative Position Centre back

| | Appearances (as substitute) | | Goals | | Clean sheets | |
	League	Cups	League	Cups	League	Cups
1994/5	29(1)	6	0	0	6	1
1993/4	27(7)	6(2)	0	1		

Playing strength
A utility player who is comfortable in any position.
Strong tackler

Still only 20, Sol has broken through into the first team and is now a regular member of the defence which, although it has its bad times, showed signs from time to time, of having found stability. Sol is very mature for his years, and reads the game well. However, he rarely scores and that, together with the club's poor goals-against record, means that you should not select him.

Stephen Carr Left Full-back
Club TOTTENHAM HOTSPUR

Date of birth 29.8.76

Alternative Position Midfield

	Appearances (as substitute)		Goals		Clean sheets	
	League	Cups	League	Cups	League	Cups
1994/5	0	0	0	0	0	0
1993/4	1	1	0	0		

Playing strength
Constructive goalmaker, both in open play and from free-kicks.

Pen picture
A good all-round player, attacking or defensive. He played two games in *1993/4*, but did not get a chance last season. Maybe this year, will be his opportunity; time is still on his side, as he is only 18.

Justin Edinburgh Left/Right Full back
Club TOTTENHAM HOTSPUR

Date of birth 18.12.69

	Appearances (as substitute)		Goals		Clean sheets	
	League	Cups	League	Cups	League	Cups
1994/5	29(2)	6	0	0	5	0
1993/4	23	6	0	0		

Playing strength
Strong tackler
Contributes well to the attack.

Pen picture
Justin has played almost 150 games for Tottenham in their ever-changing defence. He is more impressive going forward than he is in a more defensive role. As with the other Spurs defenders, you should not consider him for your fantasy team and in any case, he rarely scores a goal.

David Kerslake Full back
Club TOTTENHAM HOTSPUR

Date of birth 19.6.66

Alternative Position Midfield

	Appearances (as substitute)		Goals		Clean sheets	
	League	Cups	League	Cups	League	Cups
1994/5	16(2)	2	0	0	0	0
1993/4	16(1)	4(1)	0	0		

Playing strength
A player who always gives 100%
Good going forward

Pen picture
David joined Spurs two years ago and although he is more at home going forward than defending, he is still to score his first goal. In his sixteen games last season, Spurs never kept a clean sheet. You should not consider him for your team.

Tim Breacker Right Full back ⊙

Club WEST HAM UNITED

Date of birth 2.7.65

	Appearances (as substitute)		Goals		Clean sheets	
	League	Cups	League	Cups	League	Cups
1994/5	33	5	0	0	12	3
1993/4	40	7	3	0		

Playing strength
Speedy
Strong
Loves to attack

Pen picture
Tim joined West Ham from Luton in October 1990 and is the first choice right back. In his defensive role, he is a solid tackler, but he loves to get forward into attacking positions. He possesses a good shot however he does not score very often; he is more likely to create chances for others. He will gain reasonable points and you may decide to risk it and buy him.

Ken Brown Right Full back
Club WEST HAM UNITED

Date of birth 11.7.67

	Appearances (as substitute)		Goals		Clean sheets	
	League	Cups	League	Cups	League	Cups
1994/5	8(1)	1(2)	0	1	0	0
1993/4	6(3)	2(1)	0	0		

Playing strength
Reliable utility player

Pen picture
Ken joined the Hammers from Plymouth in the summer of 1991, but has not secured a regular first team position. He never lets the side down when he plays, but he usually has to wait for calls from the substitute's bench or as a stand-in for an injured player.

Julian Dicks Left Full back ⊙

RECOMMENDED

Club WEST HAM UNITED

Date of birth 8.8.68

	Appearances (as substitute)		Goals		Clean sheets	
	League	Cups	League	Cups	League	Cups
1994/5	29	4	5	0	9	2
1993/4	24	4	3	0		
(for Liverpool)						

Playing strength
Tough tackler
Aggressive style
A powerful left-foot shot
Excellent penalty taker

Pen picture
Julian joined Liverpool from West Ham in September 1993 and returned to Upton Park just over a year later. He never settled at Anfield and is happy to have returned home where he is a hero. The fans love his approach to the game, which is raw and aggressive. Also, he has a thunderbolt left-foot shot. If the West Ham defence really has improved, this is the man to pick, since he is certain to get at least 5 or 6 goals a season minimum at Upton Park where he takes penalties and free-kicks. Make your mind up about the defence (see club write-up).

Keith Rowland Left Full back

Club WEST HAM UNITED

Date of birth 1.9.71

Alternative Position Midfield

	Appearances (as substitute)		Goals		Clean sheets	
	League	Cups	League	Cups	League	Cups
1994/5	11(1)	2	0	0	3	1
1993/4	16(7)	5	0	0		

Playing strength
Versatile
Good left-footed player

Pen picture
Keith is a Left Full back who also played in midfield on the left hand side. In some ways, although Full back is his recognised position, he sometimes looks more comfortable in a wide midfield role. He does not play regularly and you should not select him.

Ken Cunningham Full back

Club WIMBLEDON

Date of birth 28.6.71

	Appearances (as substitute)		Goals		Clean sheets	
	League	Cups	League	Cups	League	Cups
1994/5	28	4	0	0	9	2

Playing strength
Good all-round defender

Pen picture
He joined Wimbledon from Millwall in November and established his place in the first team immediately. He is a Republic of Ireland U-21 international and his future at Wimbledon looks secure.

Gary Elkins Left Full back

Club WIMBLEDON

Date of birth 4.5.66

Alternative Position Left Midfield

	Appearances (as substitute)		Goals		Clean sheets	
	League	Cups	League	Cups	League	Cups
1994/5	33(3)	4	1	0	12	3
1993/4	18	4	1	0		

Playing strength
A very solid reliable defender
Takes attacking free kicks

Pen picture
Gary has been a regular fixture in the team this season, playing usually in Midfield or at Left Full back where he is classified in most fantasy games. He likes to be involved in attack and goes forward for corners and sometimes is involved in dead-ball situations. If you are going to go for a Wimbledon defender, he may well pay the best dividends, (if he is still classified as one), but we would not recommend it.

Alan Kimble Full back

Club WIMBLEDON

Date of birth 6.8.66

	Appearances (as substitute)		Goals		Clean sheets	
	League	Cups	League	Cups	League	Cups
1994/5	26	5	0	0	9	3
1993/4	14	3	0	0		

Playing strength
A good defensive record at lower levels

Pen picture
Alan joined Wimbledon from Cambridge United, where he had played more than 300 games, for £175,000, in the summer of 1993 . He is a solid defender who has established his place in the first team this season, but do not expect to pick up too many attacking points.

CENTRE BACKS

Tony Adams Centre back
RECOMMENDED

Club ARSENAL
Date of birth 10.10.66
Alternative Position

	Appearances (as substitute)		Goals		Clean sheets	
	League	Cups	League	Cups	League	Cups
1994/5	27	14	3	1	8	7
1993/4	35	13	0	4		

Playing strength
Strong team captain and international
Hard tackler
Good in the air
Joins the attack for corners and scores goals

Pen picture
Tony is the captain and inspirational leader of the Arsenal, and a regular member of the England back four. He is tough and temprementally sound, holding and leading the defensive line. He always gives 100% and enjoys getting forward at set-pieces. One would expect more goals from him than other Arsenal defenders.

Steve Bould Centre back
RECOMMENDED

Club ARSENAL
Date of birth 16.11.62

	Appearances (as substitute)		Goals		Clean sheets	
	League	Cups	League	Cups	League	Cups
1994/5	30(1)	13(1)	0	2	9	5
1993/4	23(2)	11(1)	1	0		

Playing strength
Reliable defender
Good in the air
Joins the attack for corners, especially good at flick-ons

Pen picture
He is certainly the best partner for Tony Adams. For a big man, he is skilful on the floor and dominant in the air. He joins the attack for corners and free-kicks, but usually to flick the ball on rather than to attempt a header at goal. At 32 he has not too many years to go. Will Bruce Rioch be looking to replace him with Alan Stubbs?

Martin Keown Centre back

Club ARSENAL
Date of birth 24.7.66
Alternative Position Midfield

	Appearances (as substitute)		Goals		Clean sheets	
	League	Cups	League	Cups	League	Cups
1994/5	24(7)	4	1	0	8	4
1993/4	23(10)	9(4)	0	0		

Playing strength
Excellent man-to-man marker
Extremely versatile
Strong Player

Pen picture
Although Martin has been unable to find a regular place in the Arsenal team, he is a very valuable utility player in the squad. Although his normal position is centre back, he stands in as either full back or in midfield and has frequently been given a man-to-man marking role, (particularly in European matches), at which he is superb. Probably not regular enough to be in your team.

Andy Linighan Centre back

Club ARSENAL
Date of birth 18.6.62

	Appearances (as substitute)		Goals		Clean sheets	
	League	Cups	League	Cups	League	Cups
1994/5						
1993/4						

Playing strength
Good in the air
Uncompromising

Pen picture

Andy is a strong determined defender who is stronger in the air than on the ground. No longer a regular in the first team, Andy is nevertheless very reliable when called upon. He will probably find it difficult to win back a first team place and in any case he is not one for a fantasy team as he does very little attacking.

Scott Marshall Centre back

Club ARSENAL

Date of birth 1.5.73

	Appearances (as substitute)		Goals		Clean sheets	
	League	Cups	League	Cups	League	Cups
1994/5	0	0	0	0	0	0
1993/4	0	0	0	0		

Playing strength

Young and promising

Good in the air

Strong tackler

Pen picture

After making two appearances during the 1992/3 season, Scott has found the opposition too strong for him since. He has good potential, but, fifth in line behind Adams, Bould, Keown and Linighan for his position, he is unlikely to see much action. He is one for the future, but probably not for your fantasy team this season.

Ugo Ehiogu Centre back ⊙

RECOMMENDED

Club ASTON VILLA

Date of birth 3.11.72

	Appearances (as substitute)		Goals		Clean sheets	
	League	Cups	League	Cups	League	Cups
1994/5	38(1)	9	3	1	11	4
1993/4	14(3)	0(2)	0	0		

Playing strength

Good in the air

Strong tackler

Pen picture

Ugo has great potential and having established his place firmly in the first team at only 22, the best is yet to come. He is a former England Under-21 captain (he was tipped by Ron Atkinson as a future full England captain) and is good in every area of the game. He comes forward for corners and scored 3 league goals last season. If the Villa defence improves, as seems likely, this season, Ugo could be a very high points scorer in various fantasy leagues. Check him out.

Paul McGrath Centre back

Club ASTON VILLA

Date of birth 4.12.59

	Appearances (as substitute)		Goals		Clean sheets	
	League	Cups	League	Cups	League	Cups
1994/5						
1993/4						

Playing strength

Great tackler

Excellent positional sense

Good in the air

Pen picture

Paul McGrath continues to astound the footballing world. At 35, with dodgy knees which prevent him from doing much training, our contacts at Villa Park are agreed that Paul is still the master craftsman and probably the best in the country. The fans rave about him. He may have lost half a yard of pace, but he is still in a different class to ther defenders; ask the strikers. He has signed for another year, but is too old to do much attacking, so avoid him for your fantasy selection.

Shaun Teale Centre back

Club ASTON VILLA

Date of birth 10.3.64

	Appearances (as substitute)		Goals		Clean sheets	
	League	Cups	League	Cups	League	Cups
1994/5	28	4	0	0	9	3
1993/4	37(1)	13	1	1		

Playing strength

Excellent tackler

Good in the air

Always gives 100%

Pen picture

Shaun joined Villa from Bournemouth in 1991, and with McGrath and Ehiogu forms a formidable defensive wall. He is a traditional English stopper centre half, who also goes forward for set-pieces and scores the occasional goal. He is an excellent defender, but hos right foot is weak and his distribution could be better. You will find better buys for your fantasy team.

Colin Hendry Centre back ⊙⊙

RECOMMENDED

Club BLACKBURN ROVERS

Date of birth 7.12.65

	Appearances (as substitute)		Goals		Clean sheets	
	League	Cups	League	Cups	League	Cups
1994/5	38	9	4	0	14	2
1993/4	21(1)	7				

Playing strength
Dominant in the air
A great tackler

Pen picture
Colin has had a tremendous season at the heart of the defence. He always gives 100% and is a dominant and, with his long blond hair, a distinctive figure. He also contributed with four goals which was a new aspect of his game. He will play a big part in Blackburn's defence of the championship and if you buy him he could make a big contribution to your fantasy points total.

Nick Marker Centre back

Club BLACKBURN ROVERS

Date of birth 3.5.65

Alternative Position Centre Midfield

	Appearances (as substitute)		Goals		Clean sheets	
	League	Cups	League	Cups	League	Cups
1994/5	0	0	0	0	0	0
1993/4	16(7)	5	0	0		

Playing strength
Versatile
Strong tackler

Pen picture
When he is fit, Nicky provides the cover in virtually any of the defensive positions. He can also play in a defensive, man-marking midfield role. He missed out on virtually the whole of last season because of cruciate ligament problems, but he is well on the way to recovery. At the right price he could be a good buy if his injury does not recur, and if he forces his way back into the team.

Ian Pearce Centre back

Club BLACKBURN ROVERS

Date of birth 7.5.74

	Appearances (as substitute)		Goals		Clean sheets	
	League	Cups	League	Cups	League	Cups
1994/5	22	6	0	0	8	2

Playing strength
Strong tackler
Good in the air

Pen picture
Ian is described by one fan as the most improved player at Ewood Park in 1994/5. He obviously benefited from playing alongside the dominant Colin Hendry. Ian needs to improve on his positional play, but it would appear that he will have every opportunity of doing so, as he appears to have made the position in the centre of defence his own. Although he should pick up plenty of defensive fantasy points, he will be quite expensive and there will be others who will score more goals, so avoid him.

Gudni Bergsson Centre back

Club BOLTON WANDERERS

Date of birth 21.7.65

Alternative Position Right Full back

	Appearances (as substitute)		Goals		Clean sheets	
	League	Cups	League	Cups	League	Cups
1994/5	8	(1)	0	0	4	0

Playing strength
Hard tackler
Strong in the air
Good covering player

Pen picture
Gudni impressed with his performance after arriving in March. Fans are questioning whether he will be in the side at the start of the season. They suggest that Coleman will replace him in the centre, to partner Stubbs, if he is still with Bolton. Gudni might then move to take over the Right back position. They would like there to be a place for him.

Simon Coleman Centre back ⦿⦿
RECOMMENDED

Club BOLTON WANDERES

Date of birth 13.3.68

	Appearances (as substitute)		Goals		Clean sheets	
	League	Cups	League	Cups	League	Cups
1994/5	22	5	4	0	8	1

Playing strength
Strong in the tackle
Good positional sense

Pen picture
Simon joined Bolton from Sheffield Wednesday for £350,000, where he had been for only one season (he was originally with Derby County). He brought stability to the centre of the defence with Stubbs, but he was unfortunate to break his leg at Derby in February. This kept him out for the remainder of the season, but he should be ready for the start of 1995/6. He is a very useful defender to have since he gets goals as well as amassing points for the failry solid Bolton defence. You should try to sign him.

Mark Seagraves Centre back

Club BOLTON WANDERERS

Date of birth 22.10.66

	Appearances (as substitute)		Goals		Clean sheets	
	League	Cups	League	Cups	League	Cups
1994/5	13	2	0	0	7	0

Playing strength
Very good in the air

Pen picture
Mark was Alan Stubbs' partner at the centre of the defence until he had a broken ankle. Coleman was brought in and it is unlikely now that Mark will win back his place. He may just play a few games as a stand-in. You should not buy him.

Alan Stubbs Centre back ◉◉

RECOMMENDED

Club BOLTON WANDERERS

Date of birth 6.10.71

	Appearances (as substitute)		Goals		Clean sheets	
	League	Cups	League	Cups	League	Cups
1994/5	37(2)	7	1	1	15	2

Playing strength
The complete defender
(Awareness, distribution, timing, good in the air, solid tackler, etc)

Pen picture
The fans are agreed, Alan Stubbs is the greatest defender around. They are all running out of superlatives to describe him. What a pity that it looks as though he is leaving them. If he stays, he will probably be more expensive than the other defenders and he may not get more attacking points. We have to recommend him, but shop around.

Michael Duberry Centre back

Club CHELSEA

Date of birth 14.10.75

	Appearances (as substitute)		Goals		Clean sheets	
	League	Cups	League	Cups	League	Cups
1994/5	0	0	0	0	0	0
1993/4	1	0	0	0		

Playing strength
Fast
Strong

Pen picture
A young, 19-year-old, described by our Stamford Bridge contacts as 'in the Paul Elliott mould'. He played regularly in the reserves and was impressive, but he did not get a chance in the first team this year. Certainly one to look out for in the future, but not for this year's fantasy league.

Ruud Gullit Centre back

Club CHELSEA

Date of birth 1.9.62

Alternative Position Anywhere

	Appearances (as substitute)		Goals		Clean sheets	
	League	Cups	League	Cups	League	Cups
1994/5						
1993/4						

Playing strength
World-class striker
All-round ability

Pen picture
Ruud played for Haarlem and Feyenoord in Holland before moving to PSV Eindhoven. In 1987 he was signed for a then-world record £6m. He scored twice in the 1989 European Cup Final victory. He made his debut for Holland in 1981 and captained his country to the European Chapionship triumph in 1988. He has had a string of knee injuries since 1989, but his recent form seems to have been as impressive as ever. For a world class star such as Ruud, you have to check out his price and the position in which he will play.

Erland Johnsen Centre back

Club CHELSEA

Date of birth 5.4.67

	Appearances (as substitute)		Goals		Clean sheets	
	League	Cups	League	Cups	League	Cups
1994/5	33	13	0	0	11	7
1993/4	27(1)	10	1	0		

Playing strength
Strong, determined tackler
Good in the air
Joins attack for corners

Pen picture
Erland has been with Chelsea since November 1989 and he is a very experienced centre back who makes up for his lack of pace with excellent positional sense. However, like other members of the Chelsea defence, he is unlikely to figure in your considerations. Apart from the team's defensive inadequacies, he has scored only one goal in over 130 appearances.

Jakob Kjeldberg Centre back
Club CHELSEA
Date of birth 21.10.96

	Appearances (as substitute)		Goals		Clean sheets	
	League	Cups	League	Cups	League	Cups
1994/5	23	6	1	0	9	5
1993/4	29	8(1)	1	0		

Playing strength
Good under pressure
Comfortable on the ball
Speedy

Pen picture
Jakob joined Chelsea from Silkeborg (Denmark) in August 1993 for £400,000 and is established in the side as a first choice central defender. He had a good season until he broke his collar bone at the end of January and did not return until into April. He has formed an effective partnership with Johnsen and his place is more or less guaranteed. However, we cannot recommend any Chelsea defenders.

David Lee Centre back
Club CHELSEA
Date of birth 26.11.69
Alternative Position Midfield

	Appearances (as substitute)		Goals		Clean sheets	
	League	Cups	League	Cups	League	Cups
1994/5	9(5)	2(3)	0	0	3	0
1993/4	3(4)	0(1)	1	0		

Playing strength
Excellent passer
Good shot from range

Pen picture
Since the arrival of Kjeldberg, David has been unable to reclaim his first team place. However, he is very popular with the Chelsea crowd and has played well on his few opportunities. Although basically a Centre back, he likes to attack and has played in a number of positions. He is not one that you should consider.

Frank Sinclair Centre back
Club CHELSEA
Date of birth 3.12.71
Alternative Position Full back

	Appearances (as substitute)		Goals		Clean sheets	
	League	Cups	League	Cups	League	Cups
1994/5	35	12	3	3	11	6
1993/4	34	10	0	0		

Playing strength
Good pace (probably the fastest at the club)
Good last-ditch saving tackles
Excellent spring makes up for lack of height
Most likely defender to score

Pen picture
Frank is a good defender, although at times he causes fans palpitations when he dives in. He looks clumsy on the ground (a Carlton Palmer type) but has great speed which makes up for any other inadequacies. He has scored more goals last season than in the rest of his career. Even so, you must not choose him.

Dave Busst Centre back
Club COVENTRY CITY
Date of birth 30.6.67

	Appearances (as substitute)		Goals		Clean sheets	
	League	Cups	League	Cups	League	Cups
1994/5	20	3	2	0	7	0
1993/4	1(1)	1	0	0		

Playing strength
Good heading ability
Good squad player

Pen picture
Dave took over the position which Phil Babb had filled before he went to liverpool, and he was making a success of it when he picked up an injury which has kept him out of action since Christmas. He is a reliable Centre back who will surely win back his place when he is fit. But Coventry defenders are not for you.

Steve Pressley Centre back
Club COVENTRY CITY
Date of birth 11.10.73

	Appearances (as substitute)		Goals		Clean sheets	
	League	Cups	League	Cups	League	Cups
1994/5	18(1)	3	1	0	8	1

Playing strength
Good in the air
Young and keen

Pen picture
Steve is young and raw, but with a great deal of potential. He is strong in the tackle and good in the air, but he can be rather impetuous, diving into tackles. One fan suggests that we watch for him giving away penalties. Well, you do not lose fantasy points for that, unless it's converted. We are continuing to ignore Coventry defenders.

David Unsworth Centre back

Club EVERTON

Date of birth 16.10.73

Alternative Position Midfield

	Appearances (as substitute)		Goals		Clean sheets	
	League	Cups	League	Cups	League	Cups
1994/5	37(1)	7	3	0	13	4
1993/4	7(1)	0	0	0		

Playing strength
Excellent all-round play
Good in the air
A strong tackler

Pen picture
We got it wrong last year. We extolled his virtues and predicted a great future for this young star, but we said that he might not get into the team in 1994/5. Well, we do not get them all right! He came from nowhere to become one of the best centre halves around and fans of the Toffees are predicting that he will be captain of both Everton and England. After seeing the way that he handled Mark Hughes in the Cup Final, who can argue with them? He gets one or two goals, but probably not enough to be considered for your team. Watch him prove us wrong again!

Dave Watson Centre back ◉◉

RECOMMENDED

Club EVERTON

Date of birth 20.11.61

	Appearances (as substitute)		Goals		Clean sheets	
	League	Cups	League	Cups	League	Cups
1994/5	38	8	2	2	13	5
1993/4	27(1)	3	1	3		

Playing strength
Leads by example
Strong in the tackle
Speedy
Good in the air

Pen picture
Dave's form has been awesome this year. He is deservedly captain and the team is built around him. He is strong in every area of the game and apart from his defensive duties, he loves to attack, getting occasional goals from set-pieces. It seems that he will go on for ever and certainly the coming season will

see him continuing his leading role. You could do much worse than have him in your team.

Robert Bowman Central Defence

Club LEEDS UNITED

Date of birth 21.11.75

Alternative Position Full back

	Appearances (as substitute)		Goals		Clean sheets	
	League	Cups	League	Cups	League	Cups
1994/5	0	0	0	0	0	0
1993/4	0	0	0	0		

Playing strength
A strong defensive player

Pen picture
Rob did not make any appearances although he did make three in 1992/3, and he is still only 19. One fan says that he was his Player of the Season in the reserve team. He is one to watch for the future, but probably not for this season.

Andrew Couzens Centre back

Club LEEDS UNITED

Date of birth 4.6.75

Alternative Position Full back

	Appearances (as substitute)		Goals		Clean sheets	
	League	Cups	League	Cups	League	Cups
1994/5	2(2)	0	0	0	1	0
1993/4	0	0	0	0		

Playing strength
Strong tackler
Cool under pressure
Excellent distribution

Pen picture
Andrew was converted from a Full back into a Centre back this season. He is rather small for that position but his firm tackling is some compensation. He is just 20 and undoubtedly has a good future in the game, but, he is not one for the fantasy games.

Chris Fairclough Central defence
Club LEEDS UNITED
Date of birth 12.4.64
Alternative Position Midfield

| | Appearances (as substitute) | | Goals | | Clean sheets | |
	League	Cups	League	Cups	League	Cups
1994/5	1(4)	2	0	0	1	1
1993/4	40	5	4	0		

Playing strength
Strong defender
Excellent man-marker
Enjoys attacking

Pen picture
During the previous season Chris was a fixture in the Leeds first team, but last season he made only one league appearance. He was kept out, partly by injury and partly by the excellent for of David Wetherall. There is a strong possibility that he will move on before the start of next season. He will strengthen the defence of the club he joins and might well score a few goals. Watch out for him and consider whether he is for you.

David O'Leary Central Defence
Club LEEDS UNITED
Date of birth 2.5.58

| | Appearances (as substitute) | | Goals | | Clean sheets | |
	League	Cups	League	Cups	League	Cups
1994/5	0	0	0	0	0	0
1993/4	10	0	0	0		

Playing strength
Vastly experienced, solid defender

Pen picture
Out of the team for most of the last two seasons due to injury. He keeps denying that he is going to retire, but it cannot be far off now. Surely if he is unable to start this season he will call it a day.

John Pemberton Central defence
Club LEEDS UNITED
Date of birth 18.11.64
Alternative Position Midfield

| | Appearances (as substitute) | | Goals | | Clean sheets | |
	League	Cups	League	Cups	League	Cups
1994/5	22(5)	4(1)	0	0	11	0
1993/4	5(3)	0	0	0		

Playing strength
A solid defender
Solid tackler
Great will to win

Pen picture
John won back his place for the second half of the season and the defence looked much stronger when he rejoined it. He is very populr with the fans for his never-say-die spirit. He is a great competitor, playing hard, but fair. He does not score goals and you should nnot consider him for your team.

Lucas Radebe Centre back
Club LEEDS UNITED
Date of birth 12.4.69
Alternative Position Midfield

| | Appearances (as substitute) | | Goals | | Clean sheets | |
	League	Cups	League	Cups	League	Cups
1994/5	9(3)	1(2)	0	0	0	0

Playing strength
Cultured defender or midfielder

Pen picture
His majestic style has been likened to that of Paul Madeley, which is praise indeed. A severe knee injury sustained in February kept him sidelined for the remainder of the season. He is a classy player who looks really good on the ball and will undoubtedly contribute in the future. Watch out for how he is classified and whether he plays in defenec or in midfield.

David Wetherall Central Defence
Club LEEDS UNITED
Date of birth 14.3.71

| | Appearances (as substitute) | | Goals | | Clean sheets | |
	League	Cups	League	Cups	League	Cups
1994/5	38	5	3	2	16	1
1993/4	31(1)	2(2)	1	1		

Playing strength
Solid defender
Good in the air
Joins the attack for corners

Pen picture
David was the most improved player in the team and Howard Wilkinson's Player of the Season. He is a strong tackler and combines well with John Pemberton at the centre of the defence. He also scored a few very important goals. The author, as a Walsall supporter, particularly remembers with horror, the one at Bescot Stadium, in the closing minutes, which kept Leeds in the Cup. If you go for a Leeds defender (other than Sharp), Wetherall is the one to go for.

Phil Babb Left Centre back

Club LIVERPOOL

Date of birth 30.11.70

	Appearances (as substitute)		Goals		Clean sheets	
	League	Cups	League	Cups	League	Cups
1994/5	33(1)	13	0	0	12	7
1993/4	41	4	3	1		

Playing strength
Very fast
Reads the game well
Strong tackler

Pen picture
Phil is a Republic of Ireland international who has settled in well to the Liverpool system of having three centre backs, after an uncertain start. His speed enables him to make up for the odd mistake that he might make. Once again, he will be too expensive for you to consider having in your team.

Neil Ruddock Centre back

Club LIVERPOOL

Date of birth 9.5.68

	Appearances (as substitute)		Goals		Clean sheets	
	League	Cups	League	Cups	League	Cups
1994/5	37	15	2	0	17	8
1993/4	39	7	3	1		

Playing strength
Good in the air
Powerful physical presence
Projects long accurate passes

Pen picture
He has injected aerial dominance and physical strength into the defence, and he is able to make long-range accurate passes. His defensive contribution is vital to Liverpool. It is interesting to note that on each occasion that Neil missed a match, Liverpool failed to keep a clean sheet! He is not just a defender, he loves to get forward for corners and he gets the occasional goal. Like the othe Liverpool defenders, he will also be too expensive.

John Scales Right Centre back

Club LIVERPOOL

Date of birth 4.7.66

	Appearances (as substitute)		Goals		Clean sheets	
	League	Cups	League	Cups	League	Cups
1994/5	35	14	2	1	14	8
1993/4	37	8	0	1		

Playing strength
Dominant central defender
Good in the air and goes forward for corners
Solid on the ground

Pen picture
Fans say that defensively he was Liverpool's strongest player. He has all of the necesary defensive qualities and he goes forward for corners. If you are going to have a Liverpool defender (and last year lots of fantasy managers were totally justified in doing so) John is probably the one to go for. However, like the others, he is going to be expensive.

Mark Wright Centre back

Club LIVERPOOL

Date of birth 1.8.63

	Appearances (as substitute)		Goals		Clean sheets	
	League	Cups	League	Cups	League	Cups
1994/5	6(2)	0	0	0	2	0
1993/4	31	5	1	0		

Playing strength
Good in the air
Stylish, cultured player

Pen picture
Mark eventually got a few games right at the end of the season to play an important role in the run-in. Some fans felt that he lacked pace and confidence, others that he would benefit from the three-man centre back system. He is not for your team.

David Brightwell Centre back

Club MANCHESTER CITY

Date of birth 7.1.71

Alternative Position Full back

	Appearances (as substitute)		Goals		Clean sheets	
	League	Cups	League	Cups	League	Cups
1994/5	9	4(2)	0	1	2	1
1993/4	19(3)	2				

Playing strength
Tall, thoughtful player

Pen picture
Although David is normally a Centre back, he played many games at Right Full back. He will struggle to keep his place next year and may possibly move on in order to find a first team place.

Keith Curle Centre back

Club MANCHESTER CITY

Date of birth 14.11.63

	Appearances (as substitute)		Goals		Clean sheets	
	League	Cups	League	Cups	League	Cups
1994/5	31	6	2	1	8	1
1993/4	29	6	1	0		

Playing strength
Very quick
Reads the game well

Pen picture
Keith is ideally suited to a sweeper role. His speed helps him to recover from unforseen problems, caused possibly by his far from perfect distribution. You might think that because he takes the penalties he is a good buy for your fantasy team. Not so; any member of the leaky City defence is likely to be a liability.

John Foster Centre back

Club MANCHESTER CITY

Date of birth 19.9.73

Alternative Position Full back

	Appearances (as substitute)		Goals		Clean sheets	
	League	Cups	League	Cups	League	Cups
1994/5	9(2)	2(2)	0	0	1	1
1993/4	1	1	0	0		

Playing strength
Solid defender

Pen picture
John is a good, reliable defender, who rarely crosses the halfway line and therefore is not suitable for a fantasy team.

Alan Kernaghan Centre back

Club MANCHESTER CITY

Date of birth 25.4.67

	Appearances (as substitute)		Goals		Clean sheets	
	League	Cups	League	Cups	League	Cups
1994/5	18(4)	5	1	0	5	1
1993/4	23(1)	7	0	1		

Playing strength
Solid defender
Good in the air

Pen picture
The former Middlesbrough defender has struggled with injury followed by a loss of confidence since arriving at Maine Road two years ago. Last season was a big improvement on the previous one and if his form continues to improve, expect to see more goals from him as he is quite a threat in the opposition box when he goes up for corners. Even so, the same rule applies as does for all the other City defenders; steer well clear.

Michael Vonk Centre back

Club MANCHESTER CITY

Date of birth 28.10.68

	Appearances (as substitute)		Goals		Clean sheets	
	League	Cups	League	Cups	League	Cups
1994/5	19(2)	2(1)	0	0	3	1
1993/4	34(1)	4(1)	1	1		

Playing strength
Very strong in the air
Goes up for corners
Solid on the ground

Pen picture
1994/5 was not a good season for Michael Vonk. He lost his place in the team for much of the season and according to rumour, he did not see eye to eye with Brian Horton. The coming season could hardly be worse, but it all depends upon whether he wins back his place in the centre of the defence. He is always a useful weapon in the opposition box at corners, where his threat in the air is considerable. Even so, like other City defenders, he is not recommended.

Steve Bruce Centre back

Club MANCHESTER UNITED

Date of birth 31.12.60

	Appearances (as substitute)		Goals		Clean sheets	
	League	Cups	League	Cups	League	Cups
1994/5	35	10(1)	2	2	19	5
1993/4	40(1)	19(1)	3	4		

Playing strength
Brilliant in the air
Leads (as captain) by example

Pen picture
Steve is a model professional who keeps cool and inspires his fellow players by his wholehearted approach. He is never afraid to go in where it hurts. His excellent heading ability means that he is always a threat at set-pieces in and around the opposition penalty box. He will probably be too expensive for you.

David May Centre back

Club MANCHESTER UNITED

Date of birth 24.6.70

Alternative Position Right back

	Appearances (as substitute)		Goals		Clean sheets	
	League	Cups	League	Cups	League	Cups
1994/5	15(4)	7	2	1	10	2
1993/4	40	6	1	2		
(for Blackburn)						

Playing strength
Versatile, fast and strong

Pen picture
David was bought twelve months ago to give more cover to the United squad. As it turned out, he was rarely used after the first two months of the campaign, Gary Neville or Roy Keane being preferred at right back. David came back strongly at the end of the season with a few good games at centre back (his best position) and maybe he will now be looked upon more favourably. He is powerful in the air, but is sometimes caught unawares on the ball. You should not buy him as he may struggle to keep his place in the team.

Gary Pallister Centre back ⊙

RECOMMENDED

Club MANCHESTER UNITED

Date of birth 30.6.65

	Appearances (as substitute)		Goals		Clean sheets	
	League	Cups	League	Cups	League	Cups
1994/5	42	14	2	2	24	6
1993/4	41	19	1	0		

Playing strength
Good in the air
Excellent skill on the ball

Pen picture
Gary is a highly consistent centre back who represents England as well as Manchester United. He is an all-round defender who is surprisingly quick for his size, 6'4". He makes forward runs and goes up for corners, but does not score as many goals as one would expect for the dominanace in the air that he shows when he is defending. He will rightly be very expensive and so you may not be able to afford him.

Viv Anderson Centre back

Club MIDDLESBROUGH

Date of birth 29.8.56

	Appearances (as substitute)		Goals		Clean sheets	
	League	Cups	League	Cups	League	Cups
1994/5	2	0	0	0	0	0

Playing strength
He is still very strong in the air and cool on the ball

Pen picture
Although Viv is primarily the Assistant Manager, he surprised the fans by signing a playing contract as well. Perhaps someone could explain to the author the "Private Boro joke" appended by our Ayresome Park (as it used to be) fan, "obvious liking for healthy foods for dinner a big weakness". Is there anything other than the obvious?

Michael Barron Centre back

Club MIDDLESBROUGH

Date of birth 22.12.74

Alternative Position

	Appearances (as substitute)		Goals		Clean sheets	
	League	Cups	League	Cups	League	Cups
1994/5	0	3	0	0	0	0

Playing strength
Strong in the tackle

Pen picture
Although only 20 and relatively lightweight, Michael has proved himself to be totally reliable when he has been called upon. Despite his lack of physical presence and his inexperience, he makes his presence known with his crunching tackles.

Nigel Pearson Centre back ⊙⊙⊙

RECOMMENDED

Club MIDDLESBROUGH

Date of birth 21.8.63

	Appearances (as substitute)		Goals		Clean sheets	
	League	Cups	League	Cups	League	Cups
1994/5	34	2	3	0	13	0

Playing strength
Powerful in the air
Brilliant awareness
Commanding

Pen picture
Nigel is the rock of Boro's defence. The former Sheffield Wednesday club captain is dominant in the air, commands the defence totally and uses his vast experience to good effect by being aware of what is going on. He also goes forward for the odd goal from set-pieces. Nigel is the perfect captain and the perfect choice for your fantasy team. We recommend him strongly.

Steve Vickers Centre back ⊙⊙⊙
RECOMMENDED

Club MIDDLESBROUGH

Date of birth 13.10.67

	Appearances (as substitute)		Goals		Clean sheets	
	League	Cups	League	Cups	League	Cups
1994/5	44	7	3	0	18	2

Playing strength
Strong tackler
Good pace

Pen picture
Steve is another solid defender with all-round ability. He tackles hard and has a good turn of speed. He also gets his share of goals from set-pieces.

Phil Whelan Centre back

Club MIDDLESBROUGH

Date of birth 7.8.72

Alternative Position Full back

Playing strength
Versatile

Pen picture
Phil has played for Ipswich alongside Wark and Linighan and he has also played at Right Full back. A horrific broken ankle at the end of the 1993/4 season kept him out at the start of last season. Playing in last season's Ipswich defence is not much of a recommendation, but Bryan Robson must rate him.

Derek Whyte Centre back

Club MIDDLESBROUGH

Date of birth 31.8.68

Alternative Position Full back

	Appearances (as substitute)		Goals		Clean sheets	
	League	Cups	League	Cups	League	Cups
1994/5	36	6	1	0	14	1

Playing strength
All-round consistency
Sets up goalscoring chances

Pen picture
After years of playing at Centre back, where he now stands in when Pearson is injured, he has adapted admirably to the Full back role, replacing the injured Curtis Fleming. He is the mainstay of the defence and although he does not score very often, he contributes to attacks with assists.

Philippe Albert Centre back ⊙⊙⊙
RECOMMENDED

Club NEWCASTLE UNITED

Date of birth 10.8.67

Alternative Position Midfield

	Appearances (as substitute)		Goals		Clean sheets	
	League	Cups	League	Cups	League	Cups
1994/5	17	8	2	1	5	3

Playing strength
Brilliant on the ball
Good in the air
Will score a few goals

Pen picture
"Prince Albert", as he is known, is simply in a different class. One rather biased contributor says "The best footballing defender in the league. 'Prince' makes Alan Hanson look poor." The big question concerns the position in which he will play. Supporters feel that his best position is at Centre back, although he was moved to midfield last season. If he is catagorised as a defender, but starts the season in midfield, his will be the first name to go on my fantasy team list. Numerous points from the solid Newcastle defence, plus lots of points for assists and strikes from Prince Albert are just too good to miss. Probably my number one fantasy player!!

Steve Howey Centre back ⊙
RECOMMENDED

Club NEWCASTLE UNITED

Date of birth 26.10.71

	Appearances (as substitute)		Goals		Clean sheets	
	League	Cups	League	Cups	League	Cups
1994/5	28(1)	10	1	0	10	3
1993/4	13(1)	3	0	0		

Playing strength

Tremendous pace

Good in the air

Highly rated all-round defender who likes to attack, not surprisingly as he is a converted striker.

Regularly joins the attack for corners

Pen picture

Last year one of our contributors tipped Steve for international honours, which was taken up by Terry Venables this year (Thank you Dave!). He is confident and strong in all aspects of the game, both defensively and attacking, and he should represent England many more times in the future. You should certainly have Steve in your team if you can afford him, but there are so many Newcastle contestants for your team, and you can only have two (in most fantasy games) so you may have to give him a miss.

Nathan Murray Centre back

Club NEWCASTLE UNITED

Date of birth 10.9.75

	Appearances (as substitute)		Goals		Clean sheets	
	League	Cups	League	Cups	League	Cups
1994/5	0	0	0	0	0	0

Playing strength

Extremely promising young defender

Pen picture

Nathan has yet to play for the first team and it is possible that he may be transferred. He has great potential, but injury has sapped his confidence and he may be released.

Darren Peacock Centre back

Club NEWCASTLE UNITED

Date of birth 3.2.68

	Appearances (as substitute)		Goals		Clean sheets	
	League	Cups	League	Cups	League	Cups
1994/5	33	13	0	0	13	4
1993/4	9	0	0	0		
1993/4 (for QPR)	30	5	3	0		

Playing strength

Excellent in the air

Contributes in attack, especially at set pieces

Very sound tackler

Pen picture

Darren had a rather mixed season, starting and finishing well, but having a poor spell in the middle. He seems to be forming a very good defensive partnership with Steve Howey, though what will happen when Albert returns is anybody's guess. In the solid Newcastle defence, everyone will be expensive and Darren would have to find the goalscoring form which he showed at QPR to justify

paying the large sum which will be asked. If you think that he will do so, go ahead and splash out!

Steve Chettle Centre back

Club NOTTINGHAM FOREST

Date of birth 27.9.68

	Appearances (as substitute)		Goals		Clean sheets	
	League	Cups	League	Cups	League	Cups
1994/5	41	6	0	0	13	2
1993/4	46	11	1	0		

(Endsleigh League Div 1)

Playing strength

Solid and consistent

Good positional play

Pen picture

Steve has formed an excellent partnership with Colin Cooper, which made a major contribution to the splendid performance of the Forest defence last season. There were few who at the start of the season would have rated Forest as having the fifth best defence in the Premiership, and the Centre back pair were a fundamental part of that success. Steve will be much more expensive this year and, as he rarely gets forward and his distribution is hardly the best area of his game, he is unlikely to pick up many attacking points. You had better leave him out of your team.

Colin Cooper Centre back

Club NOTTINGHAM FOREST

Date of birth 28.2.67

	Appearances (as substitute)		Goals		Clean sheets	
	League	Cups	League	Cups	League	Cups
1994/5	35	5	1	0	12	1
1993/4	36(1)	6	7	2		

(Endsleigh League Div 1)

Playing strength

Tough tackler

Good positional sense

Pen picture

Colin has formed a powerful defensive partnership with Steve Chettle which resulted in an excellent season for Forest and an England call-up for Colin. He is a tough, clean tackler and a great organiser of the defence. He captains the team in Pearce's absence and is not afraid to let the team know his views! He usually scores many more than the one goal that he scored in 1994/5, so expect something more like the nine that he picked up in 1993/4. He is worth serious consideration, if you can afford him.

Carl Tiler Centre back

Club NOTTINGHAM FOREST

Date of birth 11.2.70

Alternative Position Full back

	Appearances (as substitute)		Goals		Clean sheets	
	League	Cups	League	Cups	League	Cups
1994/5	3	1	0	0	1	0
1993/4	3	0	0	0		

(Endsleigh League Div 1)

Playing strength
Good in the air
Dependable

Pen picture
Carl is now the third choice Centre back behind Cooper and Chettle. He is very good in the air and he never lets the side down when he plays. His main problems are that he lacks pace and his distribution which is described by one contributor as being from "the Dave Bassett school of close-controlled passing!". You cannot expect him to play many Premiership games and therefore you have to ignore him.

Vance Warner Centre back

Club NOTTINGHAM FOREST

Date of birth 3.9.74

	Appearances (as substitute)		Goals		Clean sheets	
	League	Cups	League	Cups	League	Cups
1994/5	1	0	0	0	1	0
1993/4	1	1	0	0		

(Endsleigh League Div 1)

Playing strength
Exceptional pace
Good, clean tackler

Pen picture
Vance is described as "Out of the 'pre-Italy Des Walker' mould" by one of our contributors; that is praise indeed. He needs to improve his distribution before he will pose a threat to Cooper or Chettle, but he is young and has time on his side. Watch this space.

Alan McCarthy Centre back

Club QUEEN'S PARK RANGERS

Date of birth 11.1.72

Alternative Position Full back or Midfield

	Appearances (as substitute)		Goals		Clean sheets	
	League	Cups	League	Cups	League	Cups
1994/5	0(2)	0	0	0	0	0
1993/4	4	0	0	0		

Playing strength
Versatile

Pen picture
It rather looks as though Alan is not likely to gain a place in the first team. He first played in the senior team when he was only 17 and unfortunately has failed to live up to his early promise. You should ignore him.

Alan McDonald Centre back

Club QUEEN'S PARK RANGERS

Date of birth 12.10.63

	Appearances (as substitute)		Goals		Clean sheets	
	League	Cups	League	Cups	League	Cups
1994/5	39	7	1	0	10	5
1993/4	12	4	1	0		

Playing strength
Strong, tough, uncompromising
A calming influence

Pen picture
Alan is a Northern Ireland international who plays a very hard game. He shook off the injury problems of last year to play a captain's part in leading the team into a very respectable 8th place. He must be happy with the 61 goals scored, but not so keen on the 59 conceded. He commands a regular place in the QPR defence, but you would not want him in your fantasy team.

Danny Maddix Centre back

Club QUEEN'S PARK RANGERS

Date of birth 11.10.67

Alternative Position Full back

	Appearances (as substitute)		Goals		Clean sheets	
	League	Cups	League	Cups	League	Cups
1994/5	21(6)	4	1	1	6	3
1993/4	0	0	0	0		

Playing strength
Skilful
Enjoys attacking

Pen picture
After missing the whole of the 1993/4 season through injury, Danny has returned to play an important part in defence. He has formed an impressive-looking partnership with McDonald which will probably start the new season. As with other QPR defenders, you should not select him.

Karl Ready Centre back

Club QUEEN'S PARK RANGERS

Date of birth 14.8.72

Alternative Position Right full back

	Appearances (as substitute)		Goals		Clean sheets	
	League	Cups	League	Cups	League	Cups
1994/5	11(2)	0(1)	1	0	4	0
1993/4	19(3)	0	1	0		

Playing strength
Steady
Young and energetic
Versatile

Pen picture
Karl is a Welsh Under-21 international who has made a number of appearances standing in for injured players in various defensive positions. It is unlikely that he will start the season as a regular, although he has impressed and certainly has potential. In any case, it is not wise to consider QPR defenders for your team.

Steve Yates Centre back

Club QUEEN'S PARK RANGERS

Date of birth 29.1.70

Alternative Position Full back

	Appearances (as substitute)		Goals		Clean sheets	
	League	Cups	League	Cups	League	Cups
1994/5	22(1)	4	1	0	2	3
1993/4	27(2)	1	0	0		

Playing strength
Determined, positive attitude

Pen picture
Steve began the season as the first choice Centre back to partner Alan McDonald, but lost his place in early December. Since then, he has stood in for a few game when other players were not available, but has been unable to win back his place. He is unlikely to start the season as first choice and you must ignore him.

Andy Pearce Centre back ◉

RECOMMENDED

Club SHEFFIELD WEDNESDAY

Date of birth 20.4.66

Alternative Position

	Appearances (as substitute)		Goals		Clean sheets	
	League	Cups	League	Cups	League	Cups
1994/5	34	7	0	0	13	2
1993/4	29(3)	9(2)	3	1		

Playing strength
Very strong tackler
Good man-to-man marker
Excellent header of the ball

Pen picture
Like Peter Atherton, Andy is a former Coventry defender. He is a solid defender who has made the perfect partner for Des Walker and has played a very significant part in developing the sound Wednesday defence. He goes forward for corners and in the 1993/4 season scored three league goals. With such superb heading ability it is almost unthinkable that he will not score a few again in the coming season. You may just find that his price is significantly reduced too. We recommend that you give him very careful consideration.

Des Walker Centre back

Club SHEFFIELD WEDNESDAY

Date of birth 26.11.65

	Appearances (as substitute)		Goals		Clean sheets	
	League	Cups	League	Cups	League	Cups
1994/5	38	5	0	0	13	2
1993/4	42	12	0	0		

Playing strength
Very fast
Superb positional sense

Pen picture
We are assured by Wednesday fans that Des is back to his wonderful best. He is lightning fast, has a great positional sense which enables him to cover the Full backs and he is a superb tackler. He is a top-class defender whose only short-coming is his weak distribution. We cannot recommend him for your fantasy selections because he very rarely scores a goal and so you might get better points elsewhere.

Richard Hall Centre back

Club SOUTHAMPTON

Date of birth 14.3.72

	Appearances (as substitute)		Goals		Clean sheets	
	League	Cups	League	Cups	League	Cups
1994/5	36(1)	6	4	0	7	3
1993/4	4	0	0	0		

Playing strength

Tremendous all-round ability

Pen picture

This remarkable talented young man was badly missed when an injury ruled him out for almost all of the previous season. He is a former England U-21 player and fans believe that he will play for the full England team. He is strong, brave, a good tackler and very powerful in the air. He also scores goals regularly. When he moves to a good defensive club he will be well worth including in your team, but not with Southampton!

Ken Monkou Centre back

Club SOUTHAMPTON

Date of birth 29.11.64

	Appearances (as substitute)		Goals		Clean sheets	
	League	Cups	League	Cups	League	Cups
1994/5	31	6	0	1	6	3
1993/4	35	2	4	0		

Playing strength

Strong character

Solid centre half

Scores a few vital goals

Pen picture

Two years ago Ken was an outstanding player who could be relied upon to turn in regular and reliable games every week. There are now more defensive errors creeping in and passes going astray. Maybe that is why Alan Ball has signed Neilsen from Newcastle. However, he is still a threat to the opposition at set-pieces.

Alan Neilson Centre back

Club SOUTHAMPTON

Date of birth 26.9.72

Alternative Position Full back

	Appearances (as substitute)		Goals		Clean sheets	
	League	Cups	League	Cups	League	Cups
1994/5 (for Newcastle)	5(1)	1	0	0	2	1
1993/4 (for Newcastle)	10(4)	0	0	0		

Playing strength

Solid defender either at centre back or right back

Good in the air

Pacey

Gives 100%

Pen picture

Alan is a Welsh international, who was born in Cyprus. He was signed from Newcastle for £550,000 at the beginning of June. He can play either Right back or Centre back, so Alan Ball has some flexibility. Presumably he is intended to replace Jeff Kenna. At Newcastle he might have been a good buy, but not at Southampton.

Colin Calderwood Centre back

Club TOTTENHAM HOTSPUR

Date of birth 20.1.65

	Appearances (as substitute)		Goals		Clean sheets	
	League	Cups	League	Cups	League	Cups
1994/5	35(1)	7	2	0	10	1
1993/4	26	8	0	0		

Playing strength

A good defender when confident

A tough tackler

Pen picture

Since Colin was introduced in mid-November, he missed only one game and the defensive record improved dramatically (they had not kept a clean sheet up to that point). He is a solid, reliable defender whose performance seems to depend very much upon his level of confidence. After such a goos season, it should be high going into 1995/6. Even so, do not include Spurs defenders in your fantasy team.

Jason Cundy Centre back

Club TOTTENHAM HOTSPUR

Date of birth 12.11.69

	Appearances (as substitute)		Goals		Clean sheets	
	League	Cups	League	Cups	League	Cups
1994/5	0	0	0	0	0	0
1993/4	0	0	0	0		

Playing strength

A solid, reliable defender

Pen picture

Jason has played regularly in the reserves, but has not been called upon for the first team. There are a number of other defenders in front of him and he may decide that a move elsewhere is his best option.

Gary Mabbutt Central defence

Club TOTTENHAM HOTSPUR

Date of birth 23.8.61

	Appearances (as substitute)		Goals		Clean sheets	
	League	Cups	League	Cups	League	Cups
1994/5	33(3)	8	0	0	11	1
1993/4	29	3	0	0		

Playing strength
Reliable defender
Good motivator

Pen picture
Gary was left out of the team at the beginning of the season and the dismal start was experienced. When he returned in early October, the team put together a run of matches in which the defensive performance improved dramatically. Even though he has lost a little pace, his experience and knowhow have helped to hold the team together during the crisis.

Stuart Nethercott Centre back

Club TOTTENHAM HOTSPUR

Date of birth 21.3.73

	Appearances (as substitute)		Goals		Clean sheets	
	League	Cups	League	Cups	League	Cups
1994/5	8(9)	2(2)	0	1	1	0
1993/4	9(1)	1	0	0		

Playing strength
A commanding, cool defender for his age

Pen picture
Stuart, having won his place at the end of the previous season, was in the team for the disastrous start to 1994/5. He played for the first six games before the defence was reshuffled, and he was one of the casualties. He has played only two games since. No doubt he will survive this setback and fulfil the expectations which were being forecast twelve months ago, but it may take a little while to recover and you certainly should not sign him on.

Gica Popescu Centre back

Club TOTTENHAM HOTSPUR

Date of birth 9.10.67

	Appearances (as substitute)		Goals		Clean sheets	
	League	Cups	League	Cups	League	Cups
1994/5	23	5	3	0	7	0
1993/4						

Playing strength
Skilful defender

Pen picture
Gica is a classy, talented footballer who has not come to terms with the physical side of the English game. Despite the fact that he scores a few goals, there is no

way that you can afford to have him in your team for two good reasons; i) his place in the Tottenham team is uncertain and ii) you should not select any Tottenham defenders.

Kevin Scott Centre back

Club TOTTENHAM HOTSPUR

Date of birth 17.12.66

	Appearances (as substitute)		Goals		Clean sheets	
	League	Cups	League	Cups	League	Cups
1994/5	4	0	0	0	0	0
1993/4	12	0	1	0		
1993/4 (for Newcastle United)	18	3	0	0		

Playing strength
Good all-round defender

Pen picture
Kevin joined Spurs in February 1994, having played more than 220 games for Newcastle United. He is a classy defender who has never really fitted in at White Hart Lane. His positional play is good and he reads the game well, but he needs to be more aggressive. His is almost totally a defensive role, although he does go forward for corners.

Alvis Martin Centre back

Club WEST HAM UNITED

Date of birth 29.7.58

	Appearances (as substitute)		Goals		Clean sheets	
	League	Cups	League	Cups	League	Cups
1994/5	24	4	0	0	7	2
1993/4	6(1)	3	2	0		

Playing strength
Vast experience
Good in the air
Joins attacks for corners

Pen picture
Alvin has suffered a succession of injuries over the past two seasons and he may now have to give way to Rieper in the Centre back position. He will find that hard after more than 20 years at the club, the vast majority of which have been right at the very top. Hopefully this incredible example of loyalty will be around for some time to come, offering cover.

Steve Potts Centre back

Club WEST HAM UNITED

Date of birth 7.5.67

	Appearances (as substitute)		Goals		Clean sheets	
	League	Cups	League	Cups	League	Cups
1994/5	42	6	0	0	13	3
1993/4	41	8	0	0		

Playing strength
An inspirational captain
Solid defender

Pen picture
Steve is another loyal, long-serving club player. He signed for West Ham in 1983 and has played over 275 games for them. He is totally reliable captain and back four defender who has missed only one game in two years. However, his record of one goal in ten years discourages us from selecting him for our fantasy team.

Marc Rieper Centre back

Club WEST HAM UNITED

Date of birth 5.6.68

	Appearances (as substitute)		Goals		Clean sheets	
	League	Cups	League	Cups	League	Cups
1994/5	17(4)	0	1	0	6	0

Playing strength
Stylish defender
Dangerous at set-pieces

Pen picture
The Danish international, signed from Brondby on loan until the end of the season, has settled remarkably well into English football. Arrangements are under way for him to sign on permanently and so we are assuming that this is what will happen. He has taken over from Alvin Martin and has impressed everyone with his stylish defending and the danger he generates at set-pieces. You could do much worse than buy him.

Simon Webster Centre back

Club WEST HAM UNITED

Date of birth 20.1.64

	Appearances (as substitute)		Goals		Clean sheets	
	League	Cups	League	Cups	League	Cups
1994/5	0(5)	0	0	0	0	0

Playing strength
Solid and reliable defender

Pen picture
Simon has only just returned from a broken leg and other injuries and is trying to force his way into the first team. It is far too early for you to consider him for your team.

Dean Blackwell Centre back

Club WIMBLEDON

Date of birth 5.12.69

Alternative Position Full back

	Appearances (as substitute)		Goals		Clean sheets	
	League	Cups	League	Cups	League	Cups
1994/5	2	0	0	0	2	0
1993/4	16(2)	1(1)	0	0		

Playing strength
A very capable all-round defender
Versatile

Pen picture
Dean has found the competion too strong and played only two games, at the tail-end of the season, standing in for Andy Thorn. He played his part well and in both games Wimbledon kept clean sheets. With his place in the team so uncertain, you certainly should not select him.

Chris Perry Centre back

Club WIMBLEDON

Date of birth 26.4.73

	Appearances (as substitute)		Goals		Clean sheets	
	League	Cups	League	Cups	League	Cups
1994/5	17(5)	5	0	0	6	2

Playing strength
Hard-working
Committed youngster with good potential

Pen picture
Chris has won the club award as the Most Improved Player of the season for Wimbledon. He has also been selected by Joe Kinnear as the Clubman of the Year because of his hard work. Furthermore, he is always first to arrive and last to leave the training ground. Having come through the Wimbledon production line, he could be another who will develop to fetch a large fee to help keep the club afloat.

Andy Thorn Centre back

Club WIMBLEDON

Date of birth 12.11.66

	Appearances (as substitute)		Goals		Clean sheets	
	League	Cups	League	Cups	League	Cups
1994/5	22(1)	4	1	0	6	2
1993/4 (for Crystal Palace)	10	2	0	1		

Playing strength
Strong, reliable, secure

Pen picture
Andy is back for his second spell at Wimbledon, having been to Newcastle and Crystal Palace. He missed most of last season at Palace through injury and rejoined the Dons during the early weeks of the season. He is now a regular and scores the occasional goal, but any member if the Wimbledon defence is not recommended for your team.

MIDFIELDERS

Jimmy Carter Right Midfield

Club ARSENAL

Date of birth 9.11.65

	Appearances (as substitute)		Goals	
	League	Cups	League	Cups
1994/5	2(1)	0	0	0
1993/4	0	0	0	0

Playing strength
Speedy, tricky winger

Pen picture
Jimmy was at Millwall with George Graham and was brought to Arsenal from Liverpool. He played only two games last season and is not popular with the fans. He will find it hard to regain a first team place and may well move on.

Paul Davis Centre Midfield

Club ARSENAL

Date of birth 9.12.61

	Appearances (as substitute)		Goals	
	League	Cups	League	Cups
1994/5	3(1)	2	1	1
1993/4	21(1)	10(2)	0	0

Playing strength
Creative midfielder
Excellent first touch

Pen picture
Although he no longer plays much of a part in the first team, Paul Davis is still revered by the fans. Now an elder statesman at Highbury, Gunners fans still remember the great skill and passing ability he had, and still has (though not the legs). By all means dream about the past, but he is not for your future fantasy teams.

Mark Flatts Left Midfield

Club ARSENAL

Date of birth 14.10.72

	Appearances (as substitute)		Goals	
	League	Cups	League	Cups
1994/5	1(2)	(1)	0	0
1993/4	2(1)	0	0	0

Playing strength
Fast winger who likes to run at defenders

Pen picture
For the second year he has spent a lot of time out on loan. He is unlikely to figure in future plans at Highbury and it is likely that he will move elsewhere.

Glenn Helder Left Midfield

Club ARSENAL

Date of birth   28.10.68

Alternative Position Right Midfield

	Appearances (as substitute)		Goals	
	League	Cups	League	Cups
1994/5	12(1)	0	0	0

Playing strength
Fast skilful winger
Good crosser of the ball

Pen picture
Glenn is a Dutch international who arrived in February having been signed from Vitesse for £2 million. His great skill is appreciated by the Highbury crowd who expect even better things of him next year. However, he is not one for your fantasy team as he is not a great goalscorer. Having said that, he did score 9 goals in 98 appearances for Sparta Rotterdam before joining Vitesse.

David Hillier Centre Midfield

Club ARSENAL

Date of birth 18.12.69

	Appearances (as substitute)		Goals	
	League	Cups	League	Cups
1994/5	5(4)	6(2)	0	0
1993/4	11(4)	5(1)	0	0

Playing strength
Good vision and accurate passer

Pen picture
David has been in and out of the team (and more out than in) during 1994/5. His passing abilities are excellent, but other areas of his game are weaker and it is unlikely that he will figure much in the first team in the coming year.

Stephen Hughes Centre Midfield

Club ARSENAL

Date of birth 18.9.76

	Appearances (as substitute)		Goals	
	League	Cups	League	Cups
1994/5	1	0	0	0

Playing strength
Young and skilful

Pen picture
Stephen is a young man who made his Premiership debut against Aston Villa at Christmas, but has to wait for another opportunity. His time will come, but it is far too early for you to consider him for your team.

John Jensen Centre Midfield

Club ARSENAL

Date of birth 3.5.65

	Appearances (as substitute)		Goals	
	League	Cups	League	Cups
1994/5	24	9(1)	1	0
1993/4	27	13(1)	0	0

Playing strength
Experienced
Tough tackling

Pen picture
1994/5 will be remembered at Highbury as the year that John Jensen scored for the Arsenal. Despite his poor record in that area, this Danish international who joined Arsenal at the start of the 1992/3 season is very highly thought of. In fact his shooting is very good, hard and usually not very far off target. However he does not get forward very often and he is certainly not one for your fantasy team.

Eddie McGoldrick Left Midfield

Club ARSENAL

Date of birth 30.4.65

Alternative Position Full back

	Appearances (as substitute)		Goals	
	League	Cups	League	Cups
1994/5	9(2)	4(3)	0	0
1993/4	23(3)	8(3)	0	1

Playing strength
A skilful, wide midfield player

Pen picture
Eddie is not a regular member of the first team and although he has undoubted ability, he has not made his mark at Highbury. He is not very popular with some sections of the crowd and, unless Bruce Rioch is able to get something extra out of him, he may well move elsewhere. Not one for your team.

Paul Merson Midfield ⊙

RECOMMENDED

Club ARSENAL

Date of birth 20.3.68

	Appearances (as substitute)		Goals	
	League	Cups	League	Cups
1994/5	24	10(1)	4	3
1993/4	24(9)	14(1)	7	5

Playing strength
Skilful

Scores and makes goals

Takes good corners and attacking free kicks

Pen picture
Arsenal's most attacking midfielder, playing on the left wing, Paul scores some classic goals and bends in centres with his right foot. After his much-publicised problems, he has struggled to regain his best form, but even so, has scored 4 goals in the 16 games since his return. He makes, as well as scores, goals and is worth your consideration.

Steve Morrow Midfield

Club ARSENAL

Date of birth 2.7.70

Alternative Position Left Full back

	Appearances (as substitute)		Goals	
	League	Cups	League	Cups
1994/5	11(4)	2(4)	1	1
1993/4	7(4)	2	0	0

Playing strengths
Dependable and versatile

Good man-marker

Tenacious tackler

Pen picture
Steve is a Northern Ireland international who plays either in central or left midfield, or at left back. He is never afraid of a 50-50 challenge and always does a reasonable job when he is brought in. However he is not a regular first team player, nor is he a goal scorer, and he should not figure in your team.

Ray Parlour Right Midfield

Club ARSENAL

Date of birth 7.3.73

	Appearances (as substitute)		Goals	
	League	Cups	League	Cups
1994/5	22(8)	13(2)	0	0
1993/4	24(3)	5	2	0

Playing strength
Young

Fast

Pen picture
Ray plays on the wide right hand side of midfield and shines with his fast bursts into the opposition half/penalty area. He creates chances for his forwards, but his shooting could be better, as is indicated by his lack of goals. This will cause him to be excluded from fantasy teams.

Stefan Schwarz Centre Midfield

Club ARSENAL

Date of birth 13.4.69

	Appearances (as substitute)		Goals	
	League	Cups	League	Cups
1994/5	34	15	2	2

Playing strength
Hard running, creative midfield general
Powerful shot
Strong in the tackle
Creative

Pen picture
Stefan is a 25-year-old Swedishn international who joined Arsenal at the end of the *1993/4* season for £1.75m from Benfica. He plays on the left hand side of midfield and has a dynamic left foot shot which is used regularly at free-kicks. There has been much speculation that he might be going abroad, but if Bruce Rioch persuades him to stay, he will be a great asset to the Arsenal. The fans love him and it is surprising that he has not scored more goals. He is probably not quite right for your team.

Ian Selley Midfield

Club ARSENAL

Date of birth 14.6.74

	Appearances (as substitute)		Goals	
	League	Cups	League	Cups
1994/5	10(3)	6	1	0
1993/4	16(2)	6(3)	0	1

Playing strength
Hard tackler
Young and energetic
Good man-marker

Pen picture
Ian is another hard-tackling midfielder who has been unable to win a regular place in the Arsenal midfield. He was unfortunate to break a leg last season just as it seemed he might get games more often and now he is back to join the fight for a place. In any case, he is a ball-winner rather than a goal scorer, and he should not figure in your plans.

Franz Carr Right Midfield

Club ASTON VILLA

Date of birth 24.9.66

	Appearances (as substitute)		Goals	
	League	Cups	League	Cups
1994/5	0(2)	0	0	0

Playing strength
Has pace
Can be a match-winner when on song

Pen picture
It is something of a mystery to fans why Brian Little brought Franz to Villa Park from Leicester, having taken him there from Sheffield United a few months earlier. He has come on as substitute twice, but has not made much impact, nor has he in the reserves. Maybe the manager knows something that we do not. In any case, avoid him in your fantasy team.

Dave Farrell Left Midfield

Club ASTON VILLA

Date of birth 11.11.71

Alternative Position Striker

	Appearances (as substitute)		Goals	
	League	Cups	League	Cups
1994/5	0	2	0	0
1993/4	4	0	0	0

Playing strength
Speedy winger
Has a good left foot

Pen picture
As we suggested last year, Dave has not made it in the first team. With Staunton moving forward to the left hand side of midfield, the prospects for the future for him at Villa Park look more bleak than ever. It would not be surprising if he were to move on.

Ian Taylor Centre Midfield ⊙

RECOMMENDED

Club ASTON VILLA

Date of birth   4.6.68

	Appearances (as substitute)		Goals	
	League	Cups	League	Cups
1994/5	21	2	1	0
1994/5 (for Sheffield Wednesday)	9(5)	2(2)	1	1

Playing strength
Goalscoring midfielder
Good in the air
Never stops running

Pen picture
Ian is a 26-year-old midfielder who has signed for Villa from Sheffield Wednesday for £1 million and fans are agreed that he is Brian Little's best signing to date. He is a box-to-box player who has a big engine and who seems to have the knack of being in the right place at the right time to score goals. He had an excellent goalscoring record when he was at Port Vale and Villa fans are expecting him to score a lot more for them. He could score them for you too, so check him out.

Andy Townsend Left or Centre Midfield

Club ASTON VILLA

Date of birth 23.7.63

	Appearances (as substitute)		Goals	
	League	Cups	League	Cups
1994/5	32	8	1	1
1993/4	32	15	3	1

Playing strength
Tough in the tackle
Industrious worker
Good tactician

Pen picture
Andy usually plays on the left hand side of midfield, but since the arrival of Taylor, he tends to play more of a defensive role. He is the midfield anchor man and scores a few goals regularly each season, but not enough for you to select him.

Dwight Yorke Midfield ⊙⊙⊙
RECOMMENDED

Club ASTON VILLA

Date of birth 3.11.71

Alternative Position Striker

	Appearances (as substitute)		Goals	
	League	Cups	League	Cups
1994/5	33(4)	6	6	2
1993/4	2(10)	0(2)	2	1

Playing strength
Great skill
Scores goals from nothing

Pen picture
Dwight was born in Tobago and signed for Aston Villa at the age of 18. He has the great combination of being competitive for every ball and having wonderful skill. This is one place where you really could pick up a bargain. Some of the fantasy games classify Yorke as a midfield player, which he sometimes is. However, he often plays as a striker and at the end of last season he had a run in that position and was a revelation. If he is still classified as such, and he starts the season "up front", you simply must have him in your team!

Mark Atkins Centre Midfield

Club BLACKBURN ROVERS

Date of birth 14.8.68

	Appearances (as substitute)		Goals	
	League	Cups	League	Cups
1994/5	30(4)	7(1)	6	0
1993/4	7(7)	1(3)	1	0

Playing strength
Good, dependable squad player
Strong in the tackle

Pen picture
Mark is one of the few players remaining from before the Dalglish era, much to the surprise of many fans. He surprised many in the footballing world, including Blackburn fans, by not only winning his place in the team for nearly the whole of the season, but also by scoring six very valuable goals. Without doubt his price will rise in 1995/6 and he may get fewer games when all of the squad are fit. So we do not recommend him, but have a sneaking feeling that he may just prove us wrong.

David Batty Centre Midfield

Club BLACKBURN ROVERS

Date of birth 2.12.68

	Appearances (as substitute)		Goals	
	League	Cups	League	Cups
1994/5	4(1)	0	0	0
1993/4	26	6	0	0

Playing strength
Midfield dynamo
Hard tackling

Pen picture
David missed most of last season due to an ankle injury, but returned for the last four matches looking as good as ever. He is the ideal player for winning the ball in midfield, he has good timing, he tackles well and his passing is reliable. He is ideal for the Premiership and vital to Blackburn Rovers, but shooting is not his strong point and he rarely scores. Therefore he is not at all suitable for fantasy football teams.

Lee Makel Centre Midfield

Club BLACKBURN ROVERS

Date of birth 11.1.73

	Appearances (as substitute)		Goals	
	League	Cups	League	Cups
1994/5	0	0(1)	0	0
1993/4	(2)	0(1)	0	0

Playing strength
Excellent midfield potential

Pen picture
Lee is an England Youth international, who has had very occasional outings in the first team. If he gets the opportunity, expect him to do well, but Blackburn have not given him much of a chance since they signed him from Newcastle in 1991. He should not figure in your considerations.

Stuart Ripley Right Midfield

Club BLACKBURN ROVERS

Date of birth 20.11.67

	Appearances (as substitute)		Goals	
	League	Cups	League	Cups
1994/5	36(1)	8	0	0
1993/4	39	9	4	0

Playing strength

Experienced winger

Good crosser

Pen picture

Stuart is an old-style winger who can operate on either flank, but usually plays on the right. He provides the ammunition from the right for the SAS, but did not score himself last season. Surely that will not happen again this season, but even so he will not find the net often enough to be worthy of consideration in your fantasy teams.

Tim Sherwood Centre or Right Midfield

Club BLACKBURN ROVERS

Date of birth 6.2.69

	Appearances (as substitute)		Goals	
	League	Cups	League	Cups
1994/5	38	7	6	0
1993/4	37	8	2	1

Playing strength

Good vision and control

Very creative

Strong tackler

Pen picture

Tim is a cultured, creative midfield player who has excellent distribution. He is the Blackburn playmaker and has had an excellent season. This season he also added a new facet to his game; he scored a few more goals. If he can continue to do this in the season ahead, he will add a new dimension to the Blackburn attacking force and will improve his own chances of improving on his England career which began this year. He might even force you into considering him for your fantasy team.

Robbie Slater Right Midfield

Club BLACKBURN ROVERS

Date of birth 23.11.64

Alternative Position Utility player

	Appearances (as substitute)		Goals	
	League	Cups	League	Cups
1994/5	12(6)	4	0	0

Playing strength

Versatile squad member

Hard-working

Pen picture

Robbie has not been a regular member of the Blackburn first team, but has made a valuable contribution whenever he has been called upon. He usually plays on the right hand side of midfield where he has deputised for Stuart Ripley, but he has also played in central midfield. His work-rate cannot be faulted as he covers the whole pitch in his efforts to retrieve the ball or set up an attack. He has not yet scored and should not be considered seriously for your fantasy team.

Paul Warhurst Centre Midfield

Club BLACKBURN ROVERS

Date of birth 26.9.69

Alternative Position Central Defence

	Appearances (as substitute)		Goals	
	League	Cups	League	Cups
1994/5	20(7)	6(1)	2	0
1993/4	4(5)	1	1	0

Playing strength

Versatile

Powerful

Pen picture

Paul has had a succession of injuries over the past two or three years. This may account for the fact that he has been unable to hold down a first team place with Blackburn. He has played in a variety of positions and has shown great pace, but, he has not been able to reproduce the goalscoring achievements that he accomplished at Sheffield Wednesday. Do not consider him for your team.

Jason Wilcox Left Midfield ⊙⊙
RECOMMEMNDED

Club BLACKBURN ROVERS

Date of birth 15.7.71

	Appearances (as substitute)		Goals	
	League	Cups	League	Cups
1994/5	27	9	5	1
1993/4	30(2)	6	6	1

Playing strength

Creative, goalscoring winger

Very speedy

An excellent crosser of the ball

Pen picture

During the early part of the season Jason was in tremendous form. He worked his way into the England squad and made a huge impact, both in creating and scoring goals. He is an ideal fantasy team member, if he is not too expensive. Unfortunately his season was ruined by cruciate ligament problems and he did not play again after early March. His contribution was badly missed in the crucial run-in. Check out his injury position and his fantasy price at the start of the season and if both are OK, buy him and start collecting points.

Neil Fisher Right Midfield

Club BOLTON WANDERERS

Date of birth 7.11.70

Alternative Position Left Midfield

	Appearances (as substitute)		Goals	
	League	Cups	League	Cups
1994/5	0	0	0	0

Playing strength
Skilful

Pen picture
Neil has not been terribly consistent and it is likely that he will be moving on. He has not appeared in the first team this year and would be unlikely to do so next season.

David Lee Right Midfield

Club BOLTON WANDERERS

Date of birth 5.11.67

	Appearances (as substitute)		Goals	
	League	Cups	League	Cups
1994/5	35(4)	8(1)	0	0

Playing strength
Very good pace
Can take on defenders
Good at crossing the ball

Pen picture
David has a lot going for him with his speed and dribbling ability, but he is too inconsistent to be able to command a regular first team place. In fact, the fans think that he will get very few games.

Jason McAteer Centre Midfield

Club BOLTON WANDERERS

Date of birth 18.6.71

	Appearances (as substitute)		Goals	
	League	Cups	League	Cups
1994/5	41(2)	8	5	3

Playing strength
The complete midfielder
(Powerful engine, good vision, speedy and accurate, fast shot with either foot)

Pen picture
Jason is an Ireland international who loves to run at defenders. He is an all-round player who scores goals and is the envy of many bigger Premiership clubs. Whether he will remain at Burnden Park remains to be seen. You may be surprised to find that we are not recommending him. He will certainly be the most expensive of the Bolton midfielders and we believe that there are others who are more suited to the fantasy games. Read on!

Neil McDonald Right Midfield

Club BOLTON WANDERERS

Date of birth 2.11.65

Alternative Position Right Full back

	Appearances (as substitute)		Goals	
	League	Cups	League	Cups
1994/5	4	0	0	0

Playing strength
Good positional sense

Pen picture
Neil was signed from Oldham at the start of the season and broke his leg in the first match. He looks to have lost his confidence (eg in the Play-Off Final at Wembley), particularly when tackling, and fans feel that he will not be in the first team.

Andy McKay Midfield

Club BOLTON WANDERERS

Date of birth 16.1.75

	Appearances (as substitute)		Goals	
	League	Cups	League	Cups
1994/5	0	0	0	0

Playing strength
Defends well
Has a good shot

Pen picture
Andy is a 20-year-old reserve who has good potential for the future, but will not figure during the coming season.

Mark Patterson Left Midfield

Club BOLTON WANDERERS

Date of birth 24.5.65

	Appearances (as substitute)		Goals	
	League	Cups	League	Cups
1994/5	23(3)	3(2)	2	0

Playing strength
Utility
"Bulldog" tackler
Has a good shot

Pen picture
Mark likes to stay in the centre of midfield, where he can be involved and go in hard looking for the ball. He is more likely to be a replacement player rather than a regular first team selection.

Richard Sneekes Central Midfield ⊙⊙⊙
RECOMMENDED

Club BOLTON WANDERERS

Date of birth 30.10.68

	Appearances (as substitute)		Goals	
	League	Cups	League	Cups
1994/5	37(1)	8(1)	6	2

Playing strength
Great shooting ability
Excellent distribution
Goalscorer

Pen picture
Richard is a Dutch star who was signed from Fortuna Sittard where he was coached by Johann Cruyff. He has been described by fans as "A revelation" and "The Glenn Hoddle of Bolton". His scoring record is impressive and he may not cost as much as the better-known McAteer. We suspect that Sneekes will score more goals.

Alan Thompson Left Midfield ⊙⊙⊙
RECOMMENDED

Club BOLTON WANDERERS

Date of birth 22.12.73

	Appearances (as substitute)		Goals	
	League	Cups	League	Cups
1994/5	34(3)	8(1)	7	2

Playing strength
Very speedy
Great shot
Always looking to score goals

Pen picture
Alan Thompson was the Bolton Wanderers Player of the Year and he was called up for the England U-21 squad. He has great potential and is certain to be in the Bolton first team. He plays on the left wing and loves to take people on and then either shoot or put in a telling cross. He is very talented and his skills are exactly those which are required in fantasy football games. We recommend him highly.

Stuart Whittaker Left Midfield

Club BOLTON WANDERERS

Date of birth 2.1.75

Alternative Position Right Midfield

	Appearances (as substitute)		Goals	
	League	Cups	League	Cups
1994/5	(1)	0	0	0

Playing strength
Remarkably quick
Takes on and beats defenders

Pen picture
He is described by one fan as "reminiscent of Ryan Giggs". He has great potential and all fans asked said that they would be disappointed if he did not get a chance in the Premiership.

Craig Burley Right Midfield

Club CHELSEA

Date of birth 24.9.71

	Appearances (as substitute)		Goals	
	League	Cups	League	Cups
1994/5	16(9)	2(1)	2	0
1993/4	20(3)	8	3	3

Playing strength
An attacking midfielder who scores spectacular long-range goals
Takes shots at goal from free kicks
Stylish, fine passer of the ball

Pen picture
It seemed that Craig had really made the breakthrough in the 1993/4 season, but he picked up an injury in the Cup Final and did not play his first Premiership match in 1994/5 until the end of November. For the remainder of the season his form has been in and out, but he has lots of class plus a fine, hard shot and there are many fans who think that he should be in the team if he is fit. He has a reasonable goalscoring record and he might just be worth consideration if his price is very low.

David Hopkin Midfield

Club CHELSEA

Date of birth 21.8.70

Alternative Position Striker

	Appearances (as substitute)		Goals	
	League	Cups	League	Cups
1994/5	7(8)	0(1)	1	0
1993/4	12(9)	3(2)	0	0

Playing strength
Hard runner, full of energy
Long throw specialist
Good distribution

Pen picture
David had just a few Premiership games last season, most of them in April and May. It is unlikely that he will play a major role this year and we could not recommend that you consider him.

Mustafa Izzet Midfield

Club CHELSEA

Date of birth 31.10.74

	Appearances (as substitute)		Goals	
	League	Cups	League	Cups
1994/5	0	0	0	0

Playing strength
Great movement
Good ball control

Pen picture
Although Mustafa has not played for the Premiership team, he has played regularly in the reserves and has impressed with his control, ability and general vision. He has also scored six goals. He must be due for a first team opportunity soon and he may just grasp it. Even so, it is too early for you to consider him.

Eddie Newton Central Midfield

Club CHELSEA

Date of birth 13.12.71

	Appearances (as substitute)		Goals	
	League	Cups	League	Cups
1994/5	22(8)	7(3)	1	0
1993/4	33(3)	10	0	0

Playing strength
Strong tackler
Very consistent

Pen picture
Eddie is mainly a defensive midfielder, quick to recover and a strong tackler. He distributes the ball well and scores the odd goal, but not enough for you to consider him.

Gavin Peacock Central Midfield ◉◉
RECOMMENDED

Club CHELSEA

Date of birth 18.11.67

	Appearances (as substitute)		Goals	
	League	Cups	League	Cups
1994/5	38	13	4	2
1993/4	37	11	8	6

Playing strength
A quality finisher who scores at vital times
Constructive attacking midfielder
Good distribution

Pen picture
Gavin had what for him was a rather anonymous season. From having scored 12 goals for Newcastle in 1992/3, his tally has reduced each year. His price in fantasy games may do the same. His strength has always been the way in which he makes runs through the middle, leading to laying on or scoring a goal. He may find that this returns with some prompting from Ruud Gullit. You may pick up a bargain.

David Rocastle Right Midfield

Club CHELSEA

Date of birth 2.5.67

	Appearances (as substitute)		Goals	
	League	Cups	League	Cups
1994/5	26(2)	10(1)	0	2
1993/4	21	2	2	0
(for Manchester City)				

Playing strength
Vast experience
Good dribbler
Great ball skills

Pen picture
David has moved around the top English clubs and his expertise on the field is noticeable. His skill is undoubted, although his form last season was in and out. He seems to have been around for years, yet he is still only 28. He battles with Burley for the right midfield slot and he may lose out to the younger man next season. Do not select him.

Nigel Spackman Defensive Midfield
Club CHELSEA
Date of birth 2.12.60

	Appearances (as substitute)		Goals	
	League	Cups	League	Cups
1994/5	36	12	0	0
1993/4	5(4)	3	0	0

Playing strength
Good tackler
Excellent distribution
Great deal of experience

Pen picture
Having had a lot of time out through injury during the previous season, Nigel returned to surprise a lot of people by winning back his place in the first team. He has provided the solid base at the back of the midfield, allowing others like Wise and Peacock to spend more time forward. He does a valuable job for Chelsea (even at 34) but not for a fantasy team.

Dennis Wise Midfield   ⊙
RECOMMENDED
Club CHELSEA
Date of birth 16.12.66

	Appearances (as substitute)		Goals	
	League	Cups	League	Cups
1994/5	18(1)	10	6	1
1993/4	35	7	4	2

Playing strength
Play-maker, with good vision and precision passing
Gives 100%
A motivating captain
Takes corners, free-kicks and penalties

Pen picture
The Chelsea fans love Dennis (although the same cannot be said for taxi drivers). His vision and distribution are brilliant and his set-pieces are superb. There are those who say that his set pieces are why Terry Venables had him in the England team. He is Chelsea's best player, according to the fans, but his influence extends to being a motivating captain as well as a great player. He always scores well in fantasy football games and you should consider him.

Willie Boland Left Midfield
Club COVENTRY CITY
Date of birth 6.8.75
Alternative position Right Midfield

	Appearances (as substitute)		Goals	
	League	Cups	League	Cups
1994/5	9(3)	1	0	0
1993/4	21(3)	3	0	0

Playing strength
Good awareness
Boundless energy

Pen picture
Still only 20, Willie seems to have been around for years, but last season his career took a step backwards. He did not develop as had been anticipated and he was selected for far fewer games. He still has time to learn, he also has time to score his first goal for the club.

Paul Cook Left Midfield
Club COVENTRY CITY
Date of birth 22.2.67

	Appearances (as substitute)		Goals	
	League	Cups	League	Cups
1994/5	33(1)	6	3	0

Playing strength
Great left foot
Takes free-kicks

Pen picture
Paul has had a disappointing season, according to the fans. His distribution has been poor and he has shown a lack of pace. Even his free-kicks have usually failed to hit the target and force a save out of the opposition goalkeeper. The suggestion is that he will find it hard to get into the team next year, in which case, do not sign him up for your team.

Julian Darby Midfield
Club COVENTRY CITY
Date of birth 3.10.67
Alternative Position Full back

	Appearances (as substitute)		Goals	
	League	Cups	League	Cups
1994/5	27(2)	4(2)	1	0
1993/4	25	1	5	0

Playing strength
An attacking midfield player who has a record of scoring goals

Pen picture
Julian who was virtually an ever present under Phil Neale has had just two games under Ron Atkinson (the last two games of the season). It would seem that Ron agrees with some of the fans who do not rate Julian, and his future could be in jeopardy. He must have some talent, he scored 36 goals in 265 games. You cannot risk him at Highfield Road, but watch out in case he goes goalscoring somewhere else.

Sean Flynn Midfield
Club COVENTRY CITY
Date of birth 13.3.68
Alternative Position Striker

	Appearances (as substitute)		Goals	
	League	Cups	League	Cups
1994/5	32	5	4	1
1993/4	30(3)	3	3	0

Playing strength
100% performer
Good in the air

Pen picture
Sean has not had the greatest of seasons, but then, neither have Coventry. At least he can be relied upon to give his all, even if things are not going his way. If he could improve his goalscoring just a little bit more, he might be worth considering.

Lee Hurst Left Midfield
Club COVENTRY CITY
Date of birth 21.9.70

	Appearances (as substitute)		Goals	
	League	Cups	League	Cups
1994/5	0	0	0	0
1993/4	0	0	0	0

Playing strength
Good but unfulfilled potential

Pen picture
It now rather looks as though the injuries following on from Lee's broken leg will end his career. It is always sad when a young player with unfulfilled potential has his career prematurely foreshortened. Now we will probably never know just how good he might have been.

Leigh Jenkinson Left Midfield
Club COVENTRY CITY
Date of birth 9.7.69

	Appearances (as substitute)		Goals	
	League	Cups	League	Cups
1994/5	10(1)	3	1	0
1993/4	10(6)	0(1)	0	0

Playing strength
Great ability

Pen picture
Leigh plays on the left wing and shows great skill, but he often wastes the chances he has created. It is this inconsistency which causes them to believe that he will not figure in Big Ron's plans.

Mike Marsh Midfield
Club COVENTRY CITY
Date of birth 21.7.69
Alternative Position Striker

	Appearances (as substitute)		Goals	
	League	Cups	League	Cups
1994/5	15	4	2	0
1993/4	33	8	1	1

Playing strength
Great skill
Reads the game well

Pen picture
Mike is a talented player with lots of skill and a footballing brain. He is a utility player whose brains and abilities enable him to adapt to other positions easily. In Ron Atkinson's first match at Highfield Road, against West Ham, in the absence of Cobi Jones, Mike was pushed into attack and responded by scoring one goal and creating the other. He will not let his manager down, whether he be real or fantasy.

David Rennie Midfield
Club COVENTRY CITY
Date of birth 29.8.64
Alternative Position Centre back

	Appearances (as substitute)		Goals	
	League	Cups	League	Cups
1994/5	28	5	0	0
1993/4	34	3(1)	1	0

Playing strength
Reads the game well and always wants to be involved

Pen picture
David has won the crowd onto his side again with some splendid performances since Ron Atkinson's arrival. These have been at Centre back, but we have listed him in midfield since some of the games put him there in their listings. Under those circumstances you should NEVER select him, but you probably would not anyway since he very rarely scores.

Kevin Richardson Midfield

Club COVENTRY CITY

Date of birth 4.12.62

| | Appearances (as substitute) | | Goals | |
	League	Cups	League	Cups
1994/5	14	0	0	0
1994/5 (for Aston Villa)	18(1)	4	0	0
1993/4 (for Aston Villa)	40	15	5	2

Playing strength
A committed 90 minute player
Likes to get forward

Pen picture
Kevin is a wholehearted competitor who likes to get forward, but who, surprisingly, has not scored this year either with Coventry or Aston Villa. He is a battler of the type of whom Ron Atkinson approves and he will doubtless bolster the Coventry defence/midfield. He will also score the odd goal or two, but not enough to cause you to show interest in him.

Sandy Robertson Midfield

Club COVENTRY CITY

Date of birth 26.4.71

| | Appearances (as substitute) | | Goals | |
	League	Cups	League	Cups
1994/5	0(1)	0	0	0

Playing strength
Hardworking and energetic

Pen picture
Sandy puts a great deal of effort into his game, but fans are concerned about his stamina. He seems to run out of steam 20 minutes from time. The jury is still out on him, but at least Ron has given him his first taste of Premiership football, even if it was as a substitute.

John Williams Midfield

Club COVENTRY CITY

Date of birth 11.5.68

Alternative Position Striker

| | Appearances (as substitute) | | Goals | |
	League	Cups	League	Cups
1994/5	3(6)	0	0	0
1993/4	27(5)	3(0)	3	0

Playing strength
Excellent pace

Pen picture
John plays as either a striker or as a winger. He hardly figured in the first team at all last season even though he has much ability and loves to score goals. Unfortunately, for a striker, he does not score often enough, whereupon he sometimes loses confidence. He should not figure in your fantasies.

John Ebbrell Midfield

Club EVERTON

Date of birth 1.10.69

| | Appearances (as substitute) | | Goals | |
	League	Cups	League	Cups
1994/5	25	3	0	0
1993/4	39	6	4	0

Playing strength
Strong in the tackle

Pen picture
John is not a favourite of Everton supporters nor, it would seem, of referees; he was booked nine times last season! Fans' comments range from "Should be sold" to "John 'I don't know how to go forward' Ebbrell has had a poor season". Nevertheless, he has played most games and obviously is well thought of by Joe Royle. Sometimes the ball-winning workers in midfield are not appreciated by the crowd. In any case, his lack of scoring precludes him from being in your fantasy team.

Tony Grant Midfield ⊙⊙⊙

RECOMMENDED

Club EVERTON

Date of birth 14.11.74

| | Appearances (as substitute) | | Goals | |
	League	Cups	League	Cups
1994/5	1(4)	0	0	0
1993/4	0	0	0	0

Playing strength
A playmaker
Strong in the tackle

Pen picture
Fans are saying that here is one to watch!! They have begun to rave about this 20-year-old playmaker who has scored 5 goals in 21 appearances for the reserves and made his Premiership debut against QPR. Since then he has been on the subs' bench regularly and he could be the find of the season for you in your fantasy

team. He could start the season in Everton's midfield and if he takes his chance, who knows? Take a long look at Everton at the outset of the season and be ready to snap up this cheap young midfielder.

Barry Horne Centre Midfield

Club EVERTON

Date of birth 18.5.62

| | Appearances (as substitute) | | Goals | |
	League	Cups	League	Cups
1994/5	30	5	0	0
1993/4	28(4)	7	1	0

Playing strength
Tigerish tackler
Defends well

Pen picture
Barry plays in central midfield and is something of a terrier, tackling hard and getting the team moving forward. He is a hard working ball-winner, underrated by some of the fans, yet loved by many others. He is essential in the middle of the park, allowing others to get forward into the opposition penalty area. He gets into good positions himself but does not shoot often enough. Some fans do not seem to mind his lack of goals, in view of the other excellent services he provides. As for my fantasy team, that is not good enough, I will not select him.

Anders Limpar Right Midfield

Club EVERTON

Date of birth 24.8.65

| | Appearances (as substitute) | | Goals | |
	League	Cups	League	Cups
1994/5	18(8)	5	2	0
1993/4	9	0	0	0
1993/4 (for Arsenal)	9(1)	2	0	0

Playing strength
Very quick
Direct
Skilful

Pen picture
On his day, Anders is a match-winner with his speed, skill and flair. Unfortunately, on other days he is terribly frustrating, drifting out of a game and sometimes failing to tackle back and defend. Due to his inconsistency he is not certain to keep his place in the team and in any case, his lack of goalscoring threat means that he should not be considered for your fantasy team.

Joe Parkinson Centre Midfield

Club EVERTON

Date of birth 11.6.71

| | Appearances (as substitute) | | Goals | |
	League	Cups	League	Cups
1994/5	32(2)	8	0	1
1993/4	0	0	0	0

Playing strength
Hard-tackling ball-winner
Skilful

Pen picture
Described by one fan as "the find of the season", Joe has slotted in alongside Barry Horne in the centre of midfield to provide a very solid hub of the Everton team. He does not always get the credit for his skill, being mainly recognised as a hard tackler. His goals tally is not adequate to justify his selection for your team.

Vinny Samways Centre Midfield

Club EVERTON

Date of birth 27.10.68

| | Appearances (as substitute) | | Goals | |
	League	Cups	League	Cups
1994/5	13(3)	2	2	0
1993/4 (for Tottenham)	39	8	3	0

Playing strength
Outstanding passing ability
Constructive attacker

Pen picture
Vinny has been in and out of the team all season and it would appear that he does not figure in Joe Royle's plans. It seems that he is likely to move, but a number of fans hope that that will not be the case as he has skill which could be well used in the Everton midfield. Although he is a creative player, he does not score enough goals to be good value in the fantasy league and you should not consider him for your team.

Graham Stuart Midfield

Club EVERTON

Date of birth 24.10.70

Alternative Position   Striker

| | Appearances (as substitute) | | Goals | |
	League	Cups	League	Cups
1994/5	20(8)	4(2)	3	3
1993/4	26(4)	3(1)	3	0

Playing strength
Hard tackler
Creative

Pen picture

Graham is appreciated by the fans at Goodison Park, who prefer to see him playing in midfield going forward, rather than in attack. Any chances he gets are likely to be in that area. He is popular at Everton, but will not be among fantasy managers.

Mark Ford Right Midfield

Club LEEDS UNITED

Date of birth 10.10.75

	Appearances (as substitute)		Goals	
	League	Cups	League	Cups
1994/5	0	0	0	0
1993/4	0(1)	0	0	0

Playing strength
Strong in the tackle
Prepared to shoot

Pen picture
Mark was captain of United's 1993 Youth Cup-winning team but he has not yet had a chance to prove himself in the first team. This cannot be far away and at only 19, time is on his side. He is one to watch for the future, but not yet ready for consideration for your team.

Gary McAllister Central Midfield

Club LEEDS UNITED

Date of birth 25.12.64

	Appearances (as substitute)		Goals	
	League	Cups	League	Cups
1994/5	41	6	6	0
1993/4	42	5	8	0

Playing strength
A constructive attacking midfield player with excellent vision.
Excellent positional sense
Inspirational captain

Pen picture
Gary is a midfield supremo, he seems to have everything. He has excellent distribution and superb vision and he can change the pace and direction of the game with one sweet pass. He is not afraid to shoot on sight and he takes very good set-pieces. He always does reasonably well in the various fantasy games, but is not outstanding and is usually quite highly priced. You may do better elsewhere.

Carlton Palmer Right Midfield

Club LEEDS UNITED

Date of birth 5.12.65

Alternative Position Centre back

	Appearances (as substitute)		Goals	
	League	Cups	League	Cups
1994/5	39	5	3	1
1993/4	37	12	5	2

Playing strength
Hard tackler
Runs well with the ball
Boundless energy

Pen picture
Carlton is one of the game's personalities and is very popular with the Elland Road fans. He joined Leeds from Sheffield Wednesday for £2.6 million a year ago and began the season at Centre back. By the end of the season he had reverted to his best position, in midfield, and his performances improved considerably. Although his strengths, as stated above, are his energy, enthusiasm and tackling, he scores a few goals too. He scored three last season and might be expected to produce a few more in a full season in midfield; not enough, however, for you to consider him.

Matthew Smithard Midfield

Club LEEDS UNITED

Date of birth 13.6.76

Alternative Position Striker

	Appearances (as substitute)		Goals	
	League	Cups	League	Cups
1994/5	0	0	0	0
1993/4	0	0	0	0

Playing strength
Good runs up the right wing, also scores goals.

Pen picture
At 19, Matthew has still to make his first team debut. He is an old-fashioned winger, who makes good runs up the wing and can deliver a good cross or shoot well. It is too early for you to select him this year, but watch out for him in the future.

Gary Speed Left Midfield

Club LEEDS UNITED

Date of birth 8.9.69

	Appearances (as substitute)		Goals	
	League	Cups	League	Cups
1994/5	39	6	3	0
1993/4	35(1)	4	10	2

Playing strength
He finds good goalscoring positions and creates chances for others.

Pen picture
A talented left-sided midfield player, who is very highly rated by Howard Wilkinson. Not all of the Leeds fans agree with him, criticising his work-rate.

He is very attack minded and is at his best when he is able to play wide on the left. His goal tally last season was disappointing. Surely he will score more next year, so look out for his price, it may be reduced to make him good value for money.

Mark Tinkler Right Midfield

Club LEEDS UNITED

Date of birth 24.10.74

	Appearances (as substitute)		Goals	
	League	Cups	League	Cups
1994/5	3	0	0	0
1993/4	0(3)	0	0	0

Playing strength
A strong tackler
Good positional strength

Pen picture
Mark is a ball-winning, defensive midfielder and as such is not appropriate to fantasy football games. He has recovered from a broken leg which threatened his career, just as he was breaking through into the first team. He had only three games this year, but may have more opportunities in 1995/6.

David White Right Midfield

Club LEEDS UNITED

Date of birth 30.10.67

Alternative Position Striker

	Appearances (as substitute)		Goals	
	League	Cups	League	Cups
1994/5	18(5)	3	3	1
1993/4	9(6)	3	5	1

Playing strength
An attacking right-sided midfielder
Creative player who can also score goals

Pen picture
David ended the previous season on a high note, with a flurry of goals, thus raising great hopes for 1994/5. Unfortunately his season was devastated by injuries and, in view of the wealth of midfield talent and potential at Elland Road, it is possible that he may move on. Maybe a change of club would refresh his proven goalscoring ability.

John Barnes Midfield

Club LIVERPOOL

Date of birth 7.11.63

Alternative Position   Striker

	Appearances (as substitute)		Goals	
	League	Cups	League	Cups
1994/5	38	12	7	2
1993/4	24(2)	4	3	0

Playing strength
Good passer
Versatile
A footballing brain

Pen picture
A few years ago John would have been an ideal choice for your fantasy team, a midfield player who guaranteed goals. Nowadays he still scores a reasonable number each season, but his main task is to play a holding role in the centre of midfield. He plays a mixture of simple short passes and occasionally a devastating long through ball, splitting the defence. His talent still shines through, but you will do better to look elsewhere.

Phil Charnock Left Midfield

Club LIVERPOOL

Date of birth 14.2.75

	Appearances (as substitute)		Goals	
	League	Cups	League	Cups
1994/5	1	0	0	0

Playing strength
Skilful and a good passer

Pen picture
Phil came into the side for the penultimate game of the season against West Ham. He showed promise, but a 3-0 defeat was hardly what he would have wished. Look at him again in a year or two.

Nigel Clough Midfield

Club LIVERPOOL

Date of birth 19.3.66

Alternative Position Striker

	Appearances (as substitute)		Goals	
	League	Cups	League	Cups
1994/5	3(7)	1	0	1
1993/4	25(2)	4	7	1

Playing strength
Excellent vision
Great passer
Cool finisher

Pen picture
There were times when it seemed that Nigel would be an England star. Liverpool fans say that he does a good job although he can drift out of a game. Some feel that he has not been given a fair crack of the whip. It seems that if he stays at Anfield, he is destined to be a perpetual deputy. If he was playing regularly, as a midfielder he would have some attraction in fantasy teams.

Mark Kennedy Left Midfield ⊙⊙

RECOMMENDED

Club LIVERPOOL

Date of birth 15.5.76

	Appearances (as substitute)		Goals	
	League	Cups	League	Cups
1994/5	4(2)	0	0	0

Playing strength
Powerful runner
Strong left foot
Accurate crosser

Pen picture
The fans are agreed. Mark looks to be an exciting prospect and Jack Charlton has already called him into the Ireland squad. He is a very direct player with a powerful shot which he does not hesitate to use. Assuming that he will be classified as a midfield player, here is a real possibility to pick up fantasy points. He should not be too expensive and he is likely to score goals. He scored five league and three cup goals for Millwall last season. Check him out!

Steve McManaman Midfield ⊙⊙

RECOMMENDED

Club LIVERPOOL

Date of birth 11.2.72

	Appearances (as substitute)		Goals	
	League	Cups	League	Cups
1994/5	40	15	7	2
1993/4	29(1)	3(1)	2	0

Playing strength
Great skill
Good pace
All-round ability

Pen picture
Since being given a free role in midfield, Steve has been a revelation. He is speedy, tricky and very difficult to stop when he goes on one of his powerful runs. His confidence in his own ability has grown, particularly in front of goal, and the future looks remarkably bright for Steve and for Liverpool. It could also look bright for you, but at quite a cost.

Jan Molby Centre Midfield

Club LIVERPOOL

Date of birth 4.7.63

Alternative Position Centre back

	Appearances (as substitute)		Goals	
	League	Cups	League	Cups
1994/5	12(2)	2	2	0
1993/4	11	2	2	1

Playing strength
Great skill
Excellent vision
Good passer
Expert with penalties and free-kicks

Pen picture
Once again the fans agree that Jan is the best passer (both long and short) at the club. With his great vision, he can break down defences with one superlative pass. No wonder one of our contributors says, with typical Scouse humour "When he's fit, he's worth his weight in gold; and that's a lot of gold!". Unfortunately he will not be of that value to you in a fantasy team.

Jamie Redknapp Centre Midfield ⊙⊙

RECOMMENDED

Club LIVERPOOL

Date of birth 25.6.73

	Appearances (as substitute)		Goals	
	League	Cups	League	Cups
1994/5	36(4)	14	3	2
1993/4	29(6)	6	4	0

Playing strength
Great vision
Very mobile
Powerful right-foot shot

Pen picture
Jamie made real progress last season, breaking into the England squad and showing excellent form for Liverpool throughout the season. He is going to get better and better, so expect more goals next year. Well worth checking out.

Paul Stewart Centre Midfield

Club LIVERPOOL

Date of birth 7.10.64

Alternative Position Striker

	Appearances (as substitute)		Goals	
	League	Cups	League	Cups
1994/5	0	0	0	0
1993/4	7(1)	3	0	0

Playing strength
Powerful ball winner

Pen picture
Paul did not figure in the Liverpool team last season and it is most unlikely that he will do so with the midfield talent available at Anfield. He could be moving on, and you should move on to the next contender.

Michael Thomas Centre Midfield

Club LIVERPOOL

Date of birth 24.8.67

Alternative Position Right Full back

	Appearances (as substitute)		Goals	
	League	Cups	League	Cups
1994/5	15(5)	3(2)	0	0
1993/4	1(6)	0	0	0

Playing strength
Times his runs from midfield very well
Energetic all-action performer

Pen picture
Michael plays in midfield and is a hard worker who can make penetrating runs into the penalty area. He makes more goals than he scores these days. Certainly not one for you to spend much time on.

Francis Tierney Midfield

Club LIVERPOOL

Date of birth

Pen picture
As we go to print we hear that Francis, a teenage midfield player from Crewe has signed for Liverpool for £700,000, another footballing talent from the Crewe production line. We know little about him except that he scored four goals last season. This is just the type of player to check out. If he does get into the team and score a few goals, he will certainly have been a cheap buy.

Mark Walters Left Midfield

Club LIVERPOOL

Date of birth 2.6.64

	Appearances (as substitute)		Goals	
	League	Cups	League	Cups
1994/5	7(14)	3(1)	0	0
1993/4	7(10)	1(2)	0	0

Playing strength
Pace and skill
Has a good shot

Pen picture
Fans feel that he has speed and a good shot, but not the consistency or commitment to warrant a regular first team place. He should not be considered for your team

Peter Beagrie Left Midfield

Club MANCHESTER CITY

Date of birth 29.11.65

	Appearances (as substitute)		Goals	
	League	Cups	League	Cups
1994/5	33(4)	10(2)	2	2
1993/4	9	0	1	0
1993/4	295 (for Everton)		4	1

Playing strength
Runs at defenders and takes them on
Always willing to shoot

Pen picture
Playing on the left side of midfield, Peter made a significant contribution to City's cause. He is always likely to bring a good number of assists and a few goals. Last season's scoring was lower than expected, but maybe he has something of an excuse since he played for about a third of the season with a broken foot! You could certainly do worse than have him in your team, but you could probably do better.

Garry Flitcroft Centre Midfield ◉◉

RECOMMENDED

Club MANCHESTER CITY

Date of birth 6.12.72

	Appearances (as substitute)		Goals	
	League	Cups	League	Cups
1994/5	37	9	5	0
1993/4	19(2)	5	3	0

Playing strength
Good with both feet
Competitive

Pen picture

Still only 22 years old, Garry is the ideal type of player for your fantasy team. He scores goals regularly and will not be expensive. Last season, four of his five goals came during the early part of the season when he and Steve Lomas were in tandem, winning the ball and moving forward with the attack. Lomas was injured early in the New Year and Garry was forced to play more of a holding role, thus preventing him from getting forward anywhere near as much. If Steve Lomas is back for the 1995/6 season, expect more goals from Garry and cash in on them.

Maurizio Gaudino Midfield

Club MANCHESTER CITY

Date of birth 12.12.66

	Appearances (as substitute)		Goals	
	League	Cups	League	Cups
1994/5	17(3)	4(1)	3	1

Playing strength
A classy player

Pen picture

Since he joined City just before Christmas, fans have come to appreciate the skills of this talented midfielder. Unfortunately he struggled because the team generally were struggling. If the team plays well, his class will bring many goals, otherwise he may become an expensive luxury. Watch how City start before you decide about Maurizio. His strike rate last season of three in 17 games was pretty good. If City get off to a good start, he might be worth quite a fantasy fee. Check the price and see the early season form.

David Kerr Midfield

Club MANCHESTER CITY

Date of birth 6.9.74

Alternative Position Right Full back

	Appearances (as substitute)		Goals	
	League	Cups	League	Cups
1994/5	2	0	0	0
1993/4	2	0	0	0
1992/3	8	0	0	0

Playing strength
Young and versatile

Pen picture

David plays on the right side of midfield or at right back. Last season, his two appearances were in the troublesome Right back position. He will probably get only the occasional game and therefore you should avoid him.

Paul Lake Midfield ◉◉

RECOMMENDED

Club MANCHESTER CITY

Date of birth 2.10.68

	Appearances (as substitute)		Goals	
	League	Cups	League	Cups
1994/5	0	0	0	0
1993/4	0	0	0	0

Playing strength
Versatile
Very highly-rated all-round player

Pen picture

Last year we told you that this is the player that the Maine Road fans rave about. In his 106 league games (mainly in midfield) he has scored 27 goals. Unfortunately, he has been in and out of action for four years through severe ligament damage. He had to abandon plans to return at the end of the 1993/4 season, but we understand that he is ready to return and he expects to be available for August, so watch out for an explosive start at Maine Road. If you are prepared to take a risk with his fitness you may get a real bargain and lots of goals.

Steve Lomas Midfield

Club MANCHESTER CITY

Date of birth 18.1.74

	Appearances (as substitute)		Goals	
	League	Cups	League	Cups
1994/5	18(2)	7	2	1
1993/4	17(6)	5(1)	0	1

Playing strength
Midfield ball-winner
Energetic dynamo

Pen picture

1994/5 was quite a season for Steve. On the positive side, he established himself in midfield, in tandem with Garry Flitcroft, as the driving force within the City engine room, each of them getting forward and creating or scoring goals, while the other stayed back to mop up potential problems. They looked a most impressive duo and City started with a flourish. In January, just before his 21st birthday, Steve was knocked unconscious in the Quarter-Final of the Coca Cola Cup at Crystal Palace and needed the kiss of life (after swallowing his tongue) and broke his fibia. He then had contract squabbles and a further small operation to remove a nerve problem in his toe. Not bad for one season, eh? Now he is raring to get back and help City back on their way to winning ways. He is certainly worth considering.

Fitzroy Simpson Left Midfield

Club MANCHESTER CITY

Date of birth 26.2.70

	Appearances (as substitute)		Goals	
	League	Cups	League	Cups
1994/5	10(6)	0(1)	2	0
1993/4	12(3)	2(1)	0	0

Playing strength
A busy player - all action

Pen picture
According to fans, it seems unlikely that Fitzroy will win a regular place because of his inconsistency. When he is on song, he looks very good, but often he seems to be very busy without achieving a great deal. When there is a full squad (no injuries) the competition for midfield places will be too strong for him.

Nicky Summerbee Midfield

Club MANCHESTER CITY

Date of birth 26.8.71

Alternative Position Right Full back

	Appearances (as substitute)		Goals	
	League	Cups	League	Cups
1994/5	39(2)	10	1	2
1993/4	36(2)		3	

Playing strength
Creative wing play
Very good crosser of the ball

Pen picture
Nicky has kept his place in the team throughout the season but some of the fans are far from happy with his contribution. He is good on the ball, particularly when crossing or shooting, but very often he tends to drift out of the game, without seeming to make the effort to get involved. If they are right, it will be up to the new manager to get the best out of him. He does not score often enough for you to consider him seriously.

Scott Thomas Right Midfield

Club MANCHESTER CITY

Date of birth 30.10.74

Alternative Position Right Full back

	Appearances (as substitute)		Goals	
	League	Cups	League	Cups
1994/5	0(1)	0	0	0
1993/4	0	0	0	0

Playing strength
Skilful winger
Hard shot
Tackles back

Pen picture
Last season Scott won the Young Player of the Year award and could well break into the first team this season. In the final few games of the season he was played at Left back in the reserves and there was speculation that Brian Horton might use him in that troublesome spot. Now that Brian has gone, we must just wait and see. Keep a look-out for this promising youngster.

David Beckham Midfield

Club MANCHESTER UNITED

Date of birth 2.5.75

	Appearances (as substitute)		Goals	
	League	Cups	League	Cups
1994/5	2(2)	5(1)	0	1
1993/4	0	0	0	0

Playing strength
Highly talented
Confident on the ball

Pen picture
David has not made promotion to the first team quite as quickly as Nicky Butt, the other young midfielder. His time will come. In the few games which he has played, he has shown a level of maturity which belies his years and this will stand him in good stead for the future. You should not buy him this year, but keep an eye on him for the future.

Nicky Butt Midfield ◉

RECOMMENDED

Club MANCHESTER UNITED

Date of birth 21.1.75

	Appearances (as substitute)		Goals	
	League	Cups	League	Cups
1994/5	11(11)	10(2)	1	0
1993/4	0(1)	0(1)	0	0

Playing strength
Tigerish tackler
Good footballing brain
Gets involved

Pen picture
Nicky has made dramatic progress this year, having been involved in all five European Cup matches. Not bad for a 20-year-old? His commitment and ball-winning may be the reason why (at the time of writing) it seems that Alex Ferguson is prepared to let Paul Ince go. He is the ready replacement. It is likely that he will have a place for much of the season ahead, and so, if his price is right, it may be worth an investment.

Simon Davies Midfield

Club MANCHESTER UNITED

Date of birth 23.4.74

	Appearances (as substitute)		Goals	
	League	Cups	League	Cups
1994/5	3(2)	5	0	1

Playing strength
Good control on the ball
Good passing skills

Pen picture
One of our contributors says that he does not lack confidence and that he "looks a lot like Giggs when on the ball". Simon likes to attack and here is another skilful young midfielder of whom we are going to hear a great deal in the future. However, as with the others (apart from Butt), this year is too early for your fantasy team.

Craig Dean Midfield

Club MANCHESTER UNITED

Date of birth 1.7.75

	Appearances (as substitute)		Goals	
	League	Cups	League	Cups
1994/5	0	0	0	0
1993/4	0	0	0	0

Playing strength
Highly skilful

Pen picture
Although Craig has not yet appeared for United, he is another young midfielder to watch. He is described by one of our Old Trafford contacts as 'the new Glenn Hoddle' but he has been unlucky with injuries and has therefore missed out.

Ryan Giggs Midfield

Club MANCHESTER UNITED

Date of birth 29.11.73

	Appearances (as substitute)		Goals	
	League	Cups	League	Cups
1994/5	29	9	1	3
1993/4	32(6)	17(2)	13	4

Playing strength
He has everything, skill, speed and a great left foot

Pen picture
For the incredible young Welshman last season became something of a frustration. He was plagued by injury and loss of form, the former undoubtedly affecting he latter. The great skill, speed, balance and ball control are all still there, but somehow the cutting edge seemed to have disappeared. The one area of his play which needs to be improved is his crossing of the ball. To often this was inaccurate. We hope that the coming season shows a return to the level of brilliance of which we all know this young man to be capable. This downturn in his form may even bring him into the price range which you can afford.

Paul Ince Central Midfield

Club MANCHESTER UNITED

Date of birth 21.10 67

	Appearances (as substitute)		Goals	
	League	Cups	League	Cups
1994/5	36	10	5	0
1993/4	39	16	8	2

Playing strength
Midfield dynamo
Highly competitive

Pen picture
Throughout the summer the question of whether Paul Ince will be staying at Old Trafford lingered on. At the time of going to print he was lined up for Inter Milan, if only his wife could find a house that she liked! On the reputed millions of pounds that he will be earning, we cannot see how that could be a problem. The author heard a fan on Radio 5 Live deploring Paul's move on the basis that he was irreplaceable. (Cantona could possibly have been replaced by Le Tissier etc but there is no-one who could pick up the mantle of Paul Ince.) We think that Alex Ferguson sees it differently; that he already has his replacement on board and tested out. As we see it, Nicky Butt is the same type of player and there may well not be room for them both in the United line-up. Transferring Paul may be saving him a great deal of conflict (and bringing in £8 or £9 million).

Andrei Kanchelskis Right Midfield ◉◉
RECOMMENDED

Club MANCHESTER UNITED

Date of birth 23.1.69

	Appearances (as substitute)		Goals	
	League	Cups	League	Cups
1994/5	25(5)	7(1)	14	1
1993/4	28(3)	15	6	4

Playing strength
Electrifying pace
Great dribbling skills

Pen picture
Andrei is the enigma of the United team. He ended up as the top scorer, despite playing in only 25 league matches. This was not due to injury, but because he could not keep his place in the team. He has blistering pace, great ball control and a tremendous shot, yet frequently Alex Ferguson leaves him out. The rumours of him being unsettled and leaving Old Trafford have lingered on for months. Expect a queue of goal-hungry managers if there is a hint that United

are prepared to sell him. Be ready to buy him wherever he goes. Now that he has got the goal-bug, it will not go away.

Roy Keane Right Midfield

Club MANCHESTER UNITED

Date of birth 10.8.71

Alternative Position Right Full back

	Appearances (as substitute)		Goals	
	League	Cups	League	Cups
1994/5	22(2)	10(1)	2	1
1993/4	34(3)	15(1)	5	3

Playing strength
Strong and energetic
Very strong in the tackle
Good in the air

Pen picture
Roy never stops running, and some of his well-timed ventures into the opposition penalty box have a devastating effect. But he is not just about power and energy. He has excellent positional sense and timing and he is building up a wealth of experience at the very highest level. It is easy to forget that he is still only 23. The one area of his game which seems to have taken a step backwards is his goalscoring, which means that, as an expensive United Midfielder, he is not for your team.

Brian McClair Midfield

Club MANCHESTER UNITED

Date of birth 8.12.63

Alternative Position Striker

	Appearances (as substitute)		Goals	
	League	Cups	League	Cups
1994/5	35(5)	10(1)	4	3
1993/4	12(14)	12(4)	1	4

Playing strength
Intelligent, hard-working striker
Totally reliable

Pen picture
After a frustrating *1993/4* season, most of which was spent sitting on the substitute's bench, Brian had virtually a full season in the first team. He is a faithful servant of the club, he never stops running, never complains if he is dropped and always puts the team before his own glory. Some fans say "He would always be in my team". Others do not always appreciate his value and are less complimentary. Brian still has much to offer to Manchester United, but not to you.

Lee Sharpe Left Midfield

Club MANCHESTER UNITED

Date of birth 27.5.71

Alternative Position Left Full back

	Appearances (as substitute)		Goals	
	League	Cups	League	Cups
1994/5	26(2)	8(3)	3	3
1993/4	26(3)	12(3)	9	2

Playing strength
Penetrating wing runs
Great creativity
Very versatile
Excellent crosser of the ball

Pen picture
Lee is a multi-talented player who will turn out in whatever position he is asked. His best position is on the left wing, where he is one of the best in the country, on his day. This season he has suffered from injuries which have affected his pace. Expect to see him back to his glorious best when he is fully fit. He is probably not for your team.

Ben Thornley Left Midfield

Club MANCHESTER UNITED

Date of birth 21.4.75

Alternative Position Striker

	Appearances (as substitute)		Goals	
	League	Cups	League	Cups
1994/5	0	0	0	0
1993/4	0(1)	0	0	0

Playing strength
Great speed and skill
A great goalscorer

Pen picture
Ben is potentially another great left wing talent, but last season had to be virtually written off because of horrific cruciate ligament injuries. He was showing excellent promise and if he can overcome these difficulties, he may be a real star for the future. You cannot afford to risk him this season.

Clayton Blackmore Midfield

Club MIDDLESBROUGH

Date of birth 23.9.64

	Appearances (as substitute)		Goals	
	League	Cups	League	Cups
1994/5	30	2	2	0

Playing strength
Versatile
Good awareness

Pen picture

Clayton was brought to Middlesbrough by his old Manchester United team-mate, Bryan Robson. His vast experience gives him an awareness of attacking opportunities, enabling him to set up a good number of goals. His powerful shot is useful at set-pieces and he links up well with the manager when he plays. He will not be a feature in your team.

Craig Hignett Midfield ◉◉

RECOMMENDED

Club MIDDLESBROUGH

Date of birth 12.1.70

Alternative position Striker

	Appearances (as substitute)		Goals	
	League	Cups	League	Cups
1994/5	26	6	8	1

Playing strength

Brilliant dead-ball specialist (penalties and free-kicks)

Very skilful

Pen picture

Craig is an ideal fantasy football player apart from one thing; he is not guaranteed a game. His record of eight league goals from 26 games is fantastic for a midfielder. He is not just a dead-ball specialist. On his day he can tear defences apart with his skilful play and he puts chances away, almost at will. Unfortunately he is inconsistent and on a bad day, he drifts out of the game and makes little or no contribution. Have a word with Robbo and tell him to pick Craig because you want him in your fantasy team. I certainly want him in mine.

Graham Kavanagh Midfield

Club MIDDLESBROUGH

Date of birth 2.12.73

Alternative Position Striker

	Appearances (as substitute)		Goals	
	League	Cups	League	Cups
1994/5	7	3	0	0

Playing strength

Strong tackler

Scores spectacular goals

Pen picture

Graham normally plays in midfield and only on very rare occasions in attack. He is a strong young man, who tackles well but sometimes lacks awareness of the positions of other players. He has scored some cracking goals. He is not a regular enough player for you to consider him.

Craig Liddle Midfield

Club MIDDLESBROUGH

Date of birth 21.10.71

	Appearances (as substitute)		Goals	
	League	Cups	League	Cups
1994/5	1	2	0	0

Playing strength

Strong tackler

Pen picture

He has made the transition from non-league football successfully and came into the first team at the close of last season. He battles for the ball and he also scores the occasional goal. It is a little too early for you to select him.

Alan Moore Midfield ◉◉

RECOMMENDED

Club MIDDLESBROUGH

Date of birth 25.11.74

Alternative Position Striker

	Appearances (as substitute)		Goals	
	League	Cups	League	Cups
1994/5	37	4	4	2

Playing strength

Takes on the whole defence

Blasts in wonderful goals

Pen picture

One of our contacts describes Alan as "Boro's answer to Ryan Giggs". Still only 20, he has two seasons behind him in which he has scored 15 league goals in 78 games. When he is on form, he can dance past an entire back four and bang in goals. If he is described as a midfielder, buy him quickly.

Robbie Mustoe Midfield

Club MIDDLESBROUGH

Date of birth 28.8.68

	Appearances (as substitute)		Goals	
	League	Cups	League	Cups
1994/5	27	6	3	1

Playing strength

Powerful engine

Fearless tackler

Distributes with accuracy

Pen picture

Cast in the Bryan Robson mould, he is a good player to have in the team when the Boss is out. He never stops running and one minute he is tackling back preventing a goal, then the next, he is in the opponent's penalty area setting up a chance for the strikers. He is a great asset to have in the team.

Jamie Pollock Midfield

◉◉

Club MIDDLESBROUGH

Date of birth 16.2.74

	Appearances (as substitute)		Goals	
	League	*Cups*	*League*	*Cups*
1994/5	41	6	5	1

Playing strength
Ferocious tackler
Energetic worker
Goalscorer

Pen picture
Jamie is a Boro boy through and through. He regards pulling on their jersey as an honour, and he plays like it! Sometimes his combative tackling takes it a bit too far, but he never stops grafting, and he scores a few goals. He is as solid as a rock and Robbo must have reserved a place on the teamsheet for him. I might well do the same.

Bryan Robson Midfield

Club MIDDLESBROUGH

Date of birth 11.1.57

	Appearances (as substitute)		Goals	
	League	*Cups*	*League*	*Cups*
1994/5	22	0	1	0

Playing strength
He has everything

Pen picture
This young lad definitely looks as though he has potential. If he is properly looked after, he could go far in the game. He has a thunderous shot, seems to read the game as if he had an old head on those young shoulders and manages to tell everyone what to do as well as to play his own game extremely well. Now all that he needs to do is to build up some experience. When he has done so, you can think about signing him up. The only problem with him is that he keeps on getting injured.

Philip Stamp Midfield

Club MIDDLESBROUGH

Date of birth 12.12.75

	Appearances (as substitute)		Goals	
	League	*Cups*	*League*	*Cups*
1994/5	3	4	0	0

Playing strength
Very competitive
Creative

Pen picture
Philip is a local lad who has made his way to the fringe of the first team squad. He is not a regular, yet.

However he is a committed, all-action midfield dynamo who will be challenging for a regular place.

Richard Appleby Left Midfield

Club NEWCASTLE UNITED

Date of birth 18.9.75

Alternative Position Left Full back

	Appearances (as substitute)		Goals	
	League	*Cups*	*League*	*Cups*
1994/5	0	0	0	0

Playing strength
Very good pace

Pen picture
Richard does not appear to have maintained his original progress, which was considerable. His passing is below standard and it now seems likely that he will not make an immediate impact on the first team. You should rule him out of your considerations.

Lee Clark Midfield

Club NEWCASTLE UNITED

Date of birth 27.10.72

	Appearances (as substitute)		Goals	
	League	*Cups*	*League*	*Cups*
1994/5	8(9)	6(2)	1	1
1993/4	29	5	2	0

Playing strength
Constructive midfield player
Good blindside runs
Creative passing ability

Pen picture
Lee is not certain to stay at St James' Park as he wants first team football and that cannot be guaranteed in the competitive environment at Newcastle. Some fans feel that he should be played more often since he is a 'busy' player who creates lots of chances. One reason why he is missing out may be that his finishing is not all that it might be, nevertheless at another Premiership club, he could well be playing much more often.

James Crawford Midfield

Club NEWCASTLE

Date of birth 1.5.73

	Appearances (as substitute)		Goals	
	League	*Cups*	*League*	*Cups*
1994/5	0	0	0	0

Playing strength
Constructive midfielder

Pen picture
James was bought by Kevin Keegan as one of his "Swingers" (could go either way). The general opinion of the fans is that he is rather slow and they cannot see him making it. Nevertheless, fans do get it wrong, so see what happens.

Ruel Fox Right/Left Midfield ◉◉
RECOMMENDED

Club NEWCASTLE UNITED

Date of birth 14.1.68

Alternative Position Striker

	Appearances (as substitute)		Goals	
	League	Cups	League	Cups
1994/5	40	11	10	2
1993/4	14	0	2	0
1993/4 (for Norwich)	25	12	7	2

Playing strength
Very fast
Skilful
Excellent crosser
Scores goals

Pen picture
Ruel usually plays on the right wing/midfield and has made a big impression, since he arrived at Newcastle in February, as a fast tricky winger, who knows how to cross a ball and how to find the net. He creates chances both in open play and from set-pieces, in which he is frequently involved. He has also played as a striker. It is difficult to imagine what the format will be in midfield and in attack with all of the new personnel at Newcastle, but one thing is for sure, there will be a place for Ruel, and just watch him go, with all of the extra support. Expect more than last year's ten goals, and try to afford him.

Keith Gillespie Right Midfield

Club NEWCASTLE UNITED

Date of birth 18.2.75

Alternative Position Striker

	Appearances (as substitute)		Goals	
	League	Cups	League	Cups
1994/5	15(2)	2	2	2
1994/5 (for Manchester United)	3(6)	3	1	0

Playing strength
Speedy
Good shot
Plenty of confidence to take on a man

Pen picture
According to Geordie fans, Andy Cole was the makeweight in the deal to bring Keith Gillespie to St James' Park! His speed, ability to beat a man and good shot with either foot cause Newcastle fans to believe that he will provide plenty of points from goals and assists. It is by no means certain that he will be in the starting line-up when the season begins and we suggest that you wait and see how he develops. You can always transfer him in later on.

Chris Holland Right Midfield

Club NEWCASTLE UNITED

Date of birth 11.9.75

	Appearances (as substitute)		Goals	
	League	Cups	League	Cups
1994/5	0	0	0	0
1993/4	2(1)	0	0	0

Playing strength
Good constructive right winger

Pen picture
In 1993/4 he deputised for Ruel Fox on two occasions, and on his debut laid on two goals. He has not had another chance and is unlikely to again in the foreseeable future. With Fox, Gillespie and possibly Hottiger and Watson all competing for the position on the right of midfield, Chris has very little room for optimism. If he does get in, he has a powerful motor and crosses the ball well, but rarely gets into goalscoring positions. You have to ignore him.

Mike Jeffrey Midfield

Club NEWCASTLE UNITED

Date of birth 11.8.71

Alternative Position Striker

	Appearances (as substitute)		Goals	
	League	Cups	League	Cups
1994/5	0	1(2)	0	1
1993/4	2	0	0	0

Playing strength
Good in the air
Creates chances
Can play wide

Pen picture
Some fans feel that Mike would have done well if he had been given the chance, maybe when Sellars was injured. He is somewhat of a utility player, playing in central midfield or on the left or alternatively, up front. He takes players on and has a tremendous shot and has had many outstanding games for the reserves, but last season's squad number of 31 probably says it all, and new faces have joined. Not one for your team.

Robert Lee Midfield

●●
RECOMMENDED

Club NEWCASTLE UNITED

Date of birth 1.2.66

Alternative Position Striker

	Appearances (as substitute)		Goals	
	League	Cups	League	Cups
1994/5	34	9	9	5
1993/4	41	6	7	1

Playing strength
Scores plenty of goals from midfield

Pen picture
Another player whom we suggested for an England cap last season, and then it happened. (We did not know that Terry had bought the book.) Robert's season started with a bang. He scored eleven goals in the first eleven games and then it all seemed to fall apart after he was injured while playing for England. He is a real powerhouse when he is on song and with the remarkable line-up of talent which will be on display at Newcastle this season, he could score a huge number of goals. He is well worth having in any fantasy team.

Scott Sellars Left Midfield

Club NEWCASTLE UNITED

Date of birth 27.11.65

	Appearances (as substitute)		Goals	
	League	Cups	League	Cups
1994/5	12	7	0	1
1993/4	29(1)	4(1)	3	1

Playing strength
Outstanding crosser of the ball
Takes corners
Shoots from free-kicks

Pen picture
People outside Newcastle probably do not realise just how important Scott is to them. All of our contacts agree that the injury to him at the beginning of November was the biggest factor in the team's decline. Certainly, at the end of November, with Sellars in the team, they were top of the league and after that they slipped right away. Apparently, at the time of his injury he was playing the best football of his career. He will get you plenty of assists with his sweet left foot and his superb vision, but he rarely scores goals.

Barry Venison Centre Midfield

Club NEWCASTLE UNITED

Date of birth 16.6.64

Alternative Position Centre back

	Appearances (as substitute)		Goals	
	League	Cups	League	Cups
1994/5	28	8	1	0
1993/4	36(1)	5	0	0

Playing strength
Highly experienced
Creative utility player (three different positions in three seasons; Full back, Centre back and Midfield)

Pen picture
Barry is always prepared to play where he is needed by the club. He is a brilliant example to younger players (also with his hair style and fashion sense!). Last season he took up a holding position in midfield just in front of the back four and took to it as though he had played there all his life. Venables liked what he saw and picked him for England. We understand that Pavel is worried in case he decides to take up goalkeeping! However, he is not a great fantasy points scorer.

Steve Watson Midfield

Club NEWCASTLE UNITED

Date of birth 1.4.74

Alternative Position Full back

	Appearances (as substitute)		Goals	
	League	Cups	League	Cups
1994/5	21(5)	4(4)	4	1
1993/4	29(3)	5(1)	2	0

Playing strength
Very strong utility player who enjoys attacking
Joins the attack for corners

Pen picture
Watch out for his categorisation in the various fantasy football games. In some games he was called a Full back, which was where he had played the previous season, whereas, last year he played in midfield. If he can get into the first team (which seems to be getting more and more difficult) and if he is classified as a full back, he is well worth buying. Five goals from his 25 starts last season is a very good strike rate. As a midfielder, he is less attractive.

Kingsley Black Left Midfield

Club NOTTINGHAM FOREST

Date of birth 22.6.68

Alternative Position Right Midfield

	Appearances (as substitute)		Goals	
	League	Cups	League	Cups
1994/5	5(5)	2	2	0
1993/4	30(7)	6(2)	3	2
(Endsleigh League Div 1)				

Playing strength
Industrious
Can beat a man

Pen picture
Kingsley usually plays on the right hand side of midfield, although he can play on the left. He came to Forest as an expensive, high-profile player and has not really fulfilled the expectation of the fans. He is out of favour and is unlikely to figure in future plans; indeed, if a suitable offer comes in, Kingsley could be on his way.

Lars Bohinen Centre Midfield ⊙

RECOMMENDED

Club NOTTINGHAM FOREST

Date of birth 8.9.66

	Appearances (as substitute)		Goals	
	League	Cups	League	Cups
1994/5	30(4)	5	6	1
1993/4	22(1)	3(1)	1	0

(Endsleigh League Div 1)

Playing strength
Classy midfield playmaker
Excellent ball-control and distribution

Pen picture
Lars plays in the centre of midfield and is a skilful passer of the ball who weighs in with a few goals which are usually spectacular ones such as an impertinent chip or lob. Last season he scored twice direct from corners! It seems that he has now won the battle with Gemmill for the central midfield spot and his price may rise in some of the fantasy games. Nevertheless, with his newly-found goalscoring touch, he has to warrant your consideration.

Scot Gemmill Centre Midfield

Club NOTTINGHAM FOREST

Date of birth 2.1.71

	Appearances (as substitute)		Goals	
	League	Cups	League	Cups
1994/5	19	3	1	1
1993/4	30(1)	8	8	2

(Endsleigh League Div 1)

Playing strength
Good distribution
A goalscoring midfielder
Good vision

Pen picture
Scot failed to hold down a regular place last season because of his inconsistency, yet he was recalled to the Scotland team. He has flair and ability and is an intelligent passer of the ball who likes to get forward. Unfortunately he sometimes lacks the bite and determination to make the most of his undoubted talent. I f he does get back into the side you might pick up an inexpensive goalscoring midfielder.

Paul McGregor Right Midfield

Club NOTTINGHAM FOREST

Date of birth 17.12.74

Alternative Position Left Midfield or Striker

	Appearances (as substitute)		Goals	
	League	Cups	League	Cups
1994/5	(10)	0	1	0

Playing strength
Has an eye for goal
A good crosser of the ball
Not afraid to take on a Full back

Pen picture
Paul is a 20-year-old, who plays as a winger, or alternatively as a striker. In 1992/3 he scored a remarkable 45 goals in the Youth team, but had a quieter year in the reserves the following season. Last season he came on as substitute in ten games and scored his first goal. He also scored six goals in sixteen appearances for the reserves. He may not start too many matches, but look out for his name. Anyone who scores the number of times that he has already done is worth watching.

David Phillips Centre Midfield

Club NOTTINGHAM FOREST

Date of birth 29.7.63

Alternative Position Full back or Centre back

	Appearances (as substitute)		Goals	
	League	Cups	League	Cups
1994/5	38	6	1	0
1993/4	40(3)	10	4	0

(Endsleigh League Div 1)

Playing strength
Totally dependable
Versatile

Pen picture
David is a solid, reliable utility midfielder who usually plays just in front of the back four where his ability to read the game can be exploited to the full. He has also played in both full back positions and at centre back. In view of this and the fact that he rarely scores, you should not consider him for your fantasy team, although he is extremely valuable to Frank Clark.

Bryan Roy Midfield ⊙⊙

RECOMMENDED

Club NOTTINGHAM FOREST

Date of birth 12.2.70

Alternative Position Striker

	Appearances (as substitute)		Goals	
	League	Cups	League	Cups
1994/5	37	6	13	1

Playing strength
Very fast
Goalscorer
Exciting dribbler
Unselfish passer

Pen picture
Bryan enjoyed a hugely successful first season in English football. He is a flair player, with great speed, a wonderful first touch and a willingness to work hard. Also, he is unselfish, providing penetrating passes which frequently split opposition defences. His pairing with Collymore became one of the, if not the, most exciting in the FA Carling Premiership and it will be interesting to see how he teams up with a new partner. Last year, in some fantasy games, he was generously described as a midfielder; they may not be so generous this season! If they are, you are almost obliged to have him, if you can afford him.

Steve Stone Right Midfield ⊙

RECOMMENDED

Club NOTTINGHAM FOREST

Date of birth 20.8.71

Alternative Position Centre Midfield

	Appearances (as substitute)		Goals	
	League	Cups	League	Cups
1994/5	41	6	5	0
1993/4	45	9	5	0
(Endsleigh League Div 1)				

Playing strength
Tough tackling
Always gives 100% effort
Hardest worker and fittest member of the team

Pen picture
Steve operates on the right hand side of midfield and is renowned for his phenomenal work-rate. This highly popular player was voted Player of the Season by the supporters. He is a good crosser of the ball and provides many assists. His five goals last season was the same as in *1993/4*, and should have been much higher if his composure in front of goal had been what it should. You certainly have to consider him for your team.

Neil Webb Centre Midfield

Club NOTTINGHAM FOREST

Date of birth 30.7.63

	Appearances (as substitute)		Goals	
	League	Cups	League	Cups
1994/5	0	(1)	0	0
1993/4	17(4)	5(3)	3	1
(Endsleigh League Div 1)				

Playing strength
Very experienced
Great vision

Pen picture
Once a great player and exquisite passer, Neil is not likely to figure in Frank Clark's plans for the coming season. We understand from fans that he has been told that he can leave if the offer is right. The message is that Neil is far from fit (they use the word "overweight") and is unlikely even to get on the bench.

Ian Woan Left Midfield ⊙

RECOMMENDED

Club NOTTINGHAM FOREST

Date of birth 14.12.67

	Appearances (as substitute)		Goals	
	League	Cups	League	Cups
1994/5	35(2)	3(1)	5	0
1993/4	23(1)	7	5	0
(Endsleigh League Div 1)				

Playing strength
Can be brilliant
Great left foot, particularly for crosses

Pen picture
Playing on the left hand side of midfield, Ian has tremendous ability and scores a few goals, but his inconsistency is frustrating for the fans. His passing can be brilliant, switching the direction of the attack with effortless ease. However he lacks the consistency, and sometimes it seems, the desire, to fulfil the great potential of his ability.

Simon Barker Centre Midfield

Club QUEEN'S PARK RANGERS

Date of birth 4.11.64

	Appearances (as substitute)		Goals	
	League	Cups	League	Cups
1994/5	37	7	4	0
1993/4	35(2)	5	5	3

Playing strength
A goalscoring midfielder
Very skilful

Pen picture

Simon is a skilful midfielder who has always scored a few goals. Over his long career, he has averaged just over five per season, which is not quite enough to make him of interest to you. However, he will probably be quite cheap and he certainly is consistent in his goal supply. You never know, he may find a few more. The risk is yours to take.

Steve Hodge   Right Midfield

Club QUEEN'S PARK RANGERS

Date of birth 25.10.62

Alternative Position Centre Midfield

| | Appearances (as substitute) | | Goals | |
	League	Cups	League	Cups
1994/5	15	1	0	0
1993/4	7(1)	2(1)	1	0

Playing strength
A creative ball-player.

Pen picture
Steve has always been a skilful player who is not totally appreciated by the supporters. He sometimes appears to be giving less than 100%. Maybe that is just the way he plays. He won a place in the first team at the end of October, but Holloway took over again at the end of January, since when his central midfield pairing with Barker has stood firm. It is most unlikely that that situation will change for the start of the new season. You should avoid him.

Ian Holloway   Right Midfield

Club QUEEN'S PARK RANGERS

Date of birth 12.3.63

| | Appearances (as substitute) | | Goals | |
	League	Cups	League	Cups
1994/5	28(3)	6(1)	1	0
1993/4	19(6)	0(1)	0	0

Playing strength
Aggressive tackler
Wholehearted player
Good distribution

Pen picture
Ian's main role is that of ball-winner, but he also distributes the ball well for strikers running through. He has now made one of the midfield places his own and if his determination on the ball is anything to go by, he will not be ousted easily. However, he rarely scores and will not be of interest to fantasy managers.

Andy Impey   Right Midfield

Club QUEEN'S PARK RANGERS

Date of birth 13.9.71

| | Appearances (as substitute) | | Goals | |
	League	Cups	League	Cups
1994/5	40	6	3	1
1993/4	31(3)	4	3	1

Playing strength
Very fast
Skilful

Pen picture
Andy is QPR's Most Improved Player of the Year. Particularly towards the end of the season, his confidence had grown so that he would regularly take on his Full back and deliver an accurate cross. He does not score many goals and so you should not select him, but keep an eye on him; at only 23, there is plenty of time for him to develop that side of his game, as his confidence continues to improve. If he does that, do not hesitate to transfer him in.

Michael Meaker   Left Midfield   ⊙

RECOMMENDED

Club QUEEN'S PARK RANGERS

Date of birth 18.8.71

| | Appearances (as substitute) | | Goals | |
	League	Cups	League	Cups
1994/5	7(1)	3	0	1
1993/4	11(3)	2	1	0

Playing strength
Very determined
Good skills

Pen picture
Michael is one of those players who has great ability, yet frequently frustrates the fans. When he has a good day he is outstanding, running at defenders, tackling back, shooting powerfully. Yet on other days he seems to drift out of the game. It would be a pity if his great potential remains unfulfilled. You may be prepared to take a risk on him. If he gets in the team, and if he has a number of good days, the small outlay that you have made would have been well rewarded. Listen out for reports at the start of the season and possibly take a gamble.

Trevor Sinclair   Left Midfield

Club QUEEN'S PARK RANGERS

Date of birth 2.3.73

Alternative Position Striker

| | Appearances (as substitute) | | Goals | |
	League	Cups	League	Cups
1994/5	32(1)	4	4	1
1993/4	30(2)	4	4	1

Playing strength

Makes good forward runs

Scores goals

Pen picture

Trevor is a big favourite at Loftus Road. He helped England win the Toulon U-21 Tournament in 1994 and his career has gone on from there. He has great skill and flair and scores a few goals. He is considered by some fantasy games to be a striker, in which case you must ignore him, but as a midfielder he will give you good returns at a reasonable rate. However, from a fantasy point of view, he is not a high-flyer and we think that you could do better elsewhere.

Chris Bart-Williams Right Midfield ◉◉
RECOMMENDED

Club SHEFFIELD WEDNESDAY

Date of birth 16.6.74

Alternative Position Striker

	Appearances (as substitute)		Goals	
	League	Cups	League	Cups
1994/5	32(6)	7	2	2
1993/4	30(7)	7(2)	8	2

Playing strength

Excellent ball skills, good dribbler

Instinctive goal scorer

Pen picture

Chris is only just 21 and yet has a tremendous amount of experience. He has exceptional skill with the ability to take on a man, provide a telling pass or shoot at goal. During the two previous seasons he had scored 14 goals from 51 appearances and yet he only scored twice last season. Perhaps this was because he was kept out on the right wing rather than being able to break forward from central midfield, which is his preferred position. Even so, he scored very well in most fantasy games because of the large number of assists which he provided. If David Pleat can get the best out of this man, he could be one of the really greats.

Lee Briscoe Left Midfield

Club SHEFFIELD WEDNESDAY

Date of birth 30.9.75

	Appearances (as substitute)		Goals	
	League	Cups	League	Cups
1994/5	6	0	0	0
1993/4	0(1)	0	0	0

Playing strength

Very quick

A good crosser of the ball

Pen picture

Lee broke into the team towards the end of the season, but had a poor game against Ipswich. His speed helps him to get back well to cover. With excellent crossing ability and great speed, he has a bright future.

Graham Hyde Centre Midfield

Club SHEFFIELD WEDNESDAY

Date of birth 10.11.70

	Appearances (as substitute)		Goals	
	League	Cups	League	Cups
1994/5	33(2)	7	5	1
1993/4	27(9)	11(1)	1	2

Playing strength

Hard tackler

Always gives 100%

Big engine

Pen picture

Graham is a very competitive, local player who is popular with the fans. He has always been a solid tackler, an energetic midfield dynamo and one who loved to go forward. This year there has been an extra bonus as he has started to score goals for the first time. His place in the team is now assured (unless his face does not fit with the new manager) and you can expect more of the same next year. Unfortunately it is not quite enough for us to recommend that you buy him.

Klas Ingesson Centre Midfield ◉◉
RECOMMENDED

Club SHEFFIELD WEDNESDAY

Date of birth 20.8.68

	Appearances (as substitute)		Goals	
	League	Cups	League	Cups
1994/5	9(4)	2	2	0

Playing strength

Very fast

A thunderous shot

Pen picture

Klas has played only a handful of games since joining Wednesday from PSV Eindhoven, because of injury. He is a Swedish international whose craft and guile have served his clubs and country well over the years. He is very quick and powerful and breaks forward with a will to score, frequently with his own thunderous shot. He has a good goalscoring record for clubs and country. If he has overcome his injury problems, you may have a high points scorer here.

Ryan Jones Centre Midfield

Club SHEFFIELD WEDNESDAY

Date of birth 23.7.73

Alternative Position Right Midfield

	Appearances (as substitute)		Goals	
	League	Cups	League	Cups
1994/5	3(2)	0(1)	0	0
1993/4	24(3)	7	6	1

Playing strength
Brave and energetic
Hard-tackling

Pen picture
Ryan, a Welsh international, has played only a few games this season due to injury. He is a brave young player who is prepared to throw himself around in the box. With a good record of goalscoring from midfield, he is ideal for fantasy football games, but you need to be sure that his injuries are behind him.

Adam Poric Right Midfield

Club SHEFFIELD WEDNESDAY

Date of birth 22.4.73

	Appearances (as substitute)		Goals	
	League	Cups	League	Cups
1994/5	1(3)	0	0	0
1993/4	2(4)	0(2)	0	0

Playing strength
Skilful player
Breaks forward well

Pen picture
Adam is a young Australian midfielder who has been a member of the first team squad for three years, but has been unable to establish himself in it. He is unfortunate to find such a wealth of midfield talent at Hillsborough which means that he gets relatively few first team games. He breaks from midfield well, but has a weakness in his tackling. You should not consider him.

John Sheridan Centre Midfield

Club SHEFFIELD WEDNESDAY

Date of birth 1.10.64

	Appearances (as substitute)		Goals	
	League	Cups	League	Cups
1994/5	34(2)	6(1)	1	0
1993/4	19(1)	2	3	0

Playing strength
Great vision
Excellent distribution
Deadly free-kick specialist

Pen picture
John is a Republic of Ireland international with much experience. He rarely gives the ball away and his vision and passing are superb. He spots gaps in the defence and threads the ball accurately through. He never breaks through himself and very rarely shoots at goal. Not at all ideal for the fantasy game.

Andy Sinton Left Midfield

Club SHEFFIELD WEDNESDAY

Date of birth 19.3.66

	Appearances (as substitute)		Goals	
	League	Cups	League	Cups
1994/5	22(3)	4	0	0
1993/4	25	10	3	0

Playing strength
Very good pace
Crosses the ball well

Pen picture
Andy, an England international, has suffered badly with injuries last season, which must have been as big a disappointment to him as it was to the fans. His great speed and excellent crosses cause any defence trouble, but he falls over a lot (according to fans) and is easily moved off the ball. For £2.75m the fans would have expected more.

Chris Waddle Right Midfield

Club SHEFFIELD WEDNESDAY

Date of birth 14.12.60

	Appearances (as substitute)		Goals	
	League	Cups	League	Cups
1994/5	20(5)	3	4	1
1993/4	19	6(1)	3	0

Playing strength
Great pace
Excellent vision

Pen picture
The fans continue to rave about Chris. Whether it is his vision, crossing ability, passing ability, taking of free-kicks, corners etc, whatever the area, they reckon that he is second to none. They really do go on! There is no doubt whom they think is their top man. They are prepared to overlook his heading inability and the fact that he is not quite as fast as he used to be. They still want him in any team that is chosen. So steer clear of Wednesday fans or else they will try to persuade you to have him in your team and in my opinion, that would be a mistake.

Michael Williams Centre Midfield

Club SHEFFIELD WEDNESDAY

Date of birth 21.11.69

Alternative Position Right Midfield

	Appearances (as substitute)		Goals	
	League	Cups	League	Cups
1994/5	8(2)	0	1	0
1993/4	4	1(1)	0	0

Playing strength
Great pace

Pen picture
After a number of years at the club, Michael broke through into the first team at the end of the season; then the manager is fired and he has to start all over again. His speed helps him to get into some good goalscoring positions and he scored his first goal for the club in the last match of the season against Ipswich. He is not one for your team.

Neil Heaney Midfield

Club SOUTHAMPTON

Date of birth 3.11.71

Alternative Position Striker

	Appearances (as substitute)		Goals	
	League	Cups	League	Cups
1994/5	21(13)	7(1)	2	
1993/4	2	0	0	0

Playing strength
Promising young player
Great pace

Pen picture
It is difficult to know how Neil will be classified. Southampton call him a striker, but he is more of a winger and may be put in midfield by the newspaper games. He was signed from Arsenal for £300,000 in March 1994, just before the transfer deadline. He is a favourite with the fans at the Dell because of his skill and great pace. If he scored a few more goals, he could be of interest to you.

David Hughes Midfield

Club SOUTHAMPTON

Date of birth 30.12.72

	Appearances (as substitute)		Goals	
	League	Cups	League	Cups
1994/5	2(10)	0(4)	2	1
1993/4	0(2)	0	0	0

Playing strength
Good constructive player
Scores some remarkable goals

Pen picture
David signed from non-league Weymouth in the summer of 1991, but his progress was interrupted by twice breaking an ankle. He spent the summer of 1993 on loan to a Swedish club and made his debut in February 1994, soon after playing his first match for the Welsh Under-21 team. He spent most of last season sitting on the bench, but found the net three times. He needs a run in the first team to establish his career.

Matt Le Tissier Midfield ◉◉◉

RECOMMENDED

Club SOUTHAMPTON

Date of birth 14.10.68

Alternative Position Striker

	Appearances (as substitute)		Goals	
	League	Cups	League	Cups
1994/5	41	8	20	10
1993/4	38	2	25	0

Playing strength
Outstanding skill
He scores more goals from midfield than any other player in the country
The quality of his goals is amazing

Pen picture
What else is there to be said about this incredible talent? Suffice it to say that if he is classified in midfield and you do not select him, do not blame me if you fail to win your fantasy. This incredible talent has everything, except a regular place in the England team. Maybe Tel is living in Fantasyland. Or maybe he could not see him playing alongside David Platt, David Batty and Paul Gascoigne in midfield. How could he possibly cope with a midfield of Matty,

Batty, Platty and Fatty? If you want a top striker's goal tally, added to points for numerous assists, plus vision, skill, creativity, etc, etc, etc sign up Le Matt.

Paul McDonald Midfielder ◉◉
RECOMMENDED

Club SOUTHAMPTON

Date of birth 20.4.68

	Appearances (as substitute)		Goals	
	League	Cups	League	Cups
1994/5	0(2)	0	0	0

Playing strength
Goalscorer
Skill
Pace

Pen picture
Paul plays on the left wing and may be classified as either a Striker or a Midfielder. He has scored 15 goals in 33 games in the reserves and if he gets into the first team and is classified in midfield, you should certainly buy him.

Neil Maddison Midfield ◉
RECOMMENDED

Club SOUTHAMPTON

Date of birth 2.10.69

	Appearances (as substitute)		Goals	
	League	Cups	League	Cups
1994/5	35	6	3	0
1993/4	41	4	7	0

Playing strength
Hard-working
Consistent and reliable
Midfield playmaker

Pen picture
Neil is yet another home-grown player. He is a positive individual who has overcome serious knee injury problems to gain a regular place in the first team. If he can keep clear of any further trouble, he has a very bright future. Not only does he battle for everything in midfield, he can be relied upon to score a few goals each season. He is worth your consideration.

Jim Magilton Centre Midfield ◉
RECOMMENDED

Club SOUTHAMPTON

Date of birth 6.5.69

	Appearances (as substitute)		Goals	
	League	Cups	League	Cups
1994/5	42	8	6	1
1993/4	15	0	0	0

Playing strength
Gifted ball-player
Excellent distribution
Good finisher

Pen picture
Jim was signed from Oxford in February 1994 for a fee of £600,000 as Alan Ball's first signing. The verdict from the fans is a very positive one. He is seen as the midfield playmaker, who does not shoot as often as he might. Yet in his career he has scored 34 goals in 165 games. It could be that this will be the season when he really makes his mark in the Premiership, and maybe in your fantasy team. Potentially a cheap goalscoring midfield player.

Paul Tisdale Midfield

Club SOUTHAMPTON

Date of birth 14.1.73

	Appearances (as substitute)		Goals	
	League	Cups	League	Cups
1994/5	0(7)	0(2)	0	0

Playing strength
Great skill
Wonderful vision

Pen picture
This young man is a very exciting midfielder. He has come through the Youth team and the reserves and last season spent quite a lot of time on the bench. Will he make the breakthrough in the coming season? He may well do so, but if so, do not be tempted to select him for your fantasy team, as he is not much of a goalscorer.

Tommy Widdrington Midfield

Club SOUTHAMPTON

Date of birth 1.10.71

Alternative Position Centre back

	Appearances (as substitute)		Goals	
	League	Cups	League	Cups
1994/5	23(5)	6	0	0
1993/4	11	2	1	0

Playing strength
Strong in the tackle
A young battler

Pen picture
Tommy is the supporters' sponsored player and very popular. His never-say-die spirit and his determined approach have won the fans over. He plays either in the centre of the back four, or in midfield. He is a young battler for the future, but not for your fantasy team, as he does not score enough goals.

Darren Anderton Right Midfield

Club TOTTENHAM HOTSPUR

Date of birth 3.3.72

Alternative Position Striker

	Appearances (as substitute)		Goals	
	League	Cups	League	Cups
1994/5	37	8	5	2
1993/4	35(2)	8	6	0

Playing strength
Excellent creator of opportunities
Very good at set-pieces (he takes both free-kicks and corners)

Pen picture
The 1994/5 season was very eventful for Darren as he established his name as a fixture (for the time being, at least) in the England team. He must also have found it interesting and a fantastic experience playing alongside Jurgen Klinsmann. His performances improved, although his goalscoring stayed at the same level as in the two preceding years. He is on the way to becoming a legend at Spurs, but we think that he will be too expensive for you to include in your fantasy team.

Darren Caskey Midfield ◉

RECOMMENDED

Club TOTTENHAM HOTSPUR

Date of birth 21.8.74

	Appearances (as substitute)		Goals	
	League	Cups	League	Cups
1994/5	1(3)	0(1)	0	0
1993/4	17(8)	5(1)	4	1

Playing strength
An attacking midfielder

Pen picture
It must have been a disappointment to Darren that, after breaking into the first team in the *1993/4* season, he failed to capitalise on it and he has spent a year in the reserves. Fortunately time is on his side, but it would be a great pity if his undoubted talent does not find a suitable stage on which to display it. His skills are as an attacking Midfielder, and as such he might be of interest to managers of fantasy teams if he held a regular place in the first team.

Jason Dozzell Midfield ◉◉

RECOMMENDED

Club TOTTENHAM HOTSPUR

Date of birth 9.12.67

Alternative Position Striker

	Appearances (as substitute)		Goals	
	League	Cups	League	Cups
1994/5	6(1)	2	0	0
1993/4	28(4)	6	8	1

Playing strength
An adaptable player, midfield or striker
A constructive player who also scores goals
Takes attacking free-kicks

Pen picture
When Jason joined Spurs from Ipswich in the 1993 close season for £1.75 million, great things were expected of him. At Ipswich he had a superb goalscoring record for a midfield man and he kept that up at Spurs in his first season. Even during 1994/5 he scored 10 goals in 15 games in the reserves. Some fans criticise his attitude and so he may not regain his place. If he does get a chance in the first team as a result of the departure of Klinsmann, he will be very cheap and just the type of player who is suited to fantasy football games. Under those circumstances, snap him up quickly. As long as he is in the team, you are guaranteed cheap goals.

Ilie Dumitrescu Midfield

Club TOTTENHAM HOTSPUR

Date of birth 6.1.69

Alternative Position Striker

	Appearances (as substitute)		Goals	
	League	Cups	League	Cups
1994/5	11(2)	2	4	1

Playing strength
A goalscoring midfielder
Great skill
Good pace

Pen picture
Ilie joined Spurs during the 1994 close season and made an impact with four goals in eleven games. After Gerry Francis took over and he lost his place in the team, he was allowed to go on loan to Seville. It is most likely that he will move out permanently but, at the time of going to print, this has not been finalised and Ilie is such an ideal fantasy player that he must be included, just in case he stays. He scores lots of goals from midfield and therefore is worth his weight in gold. If he is around and likely to play, you MUST include him.

Danny Hill Midfield

Club TOTTENHAM HOTSPUR

Date of birth 1.10.74

	Appearances (as substitute)		Goals	
	League	Cups	League	Cups
1994/5	1(2)	0(2)	0	0
1993/4	1(2)	0	0	0

Playing strength
Hard working
Highly skilful
Tremendous potential

Another of a string of highly-talented young players trying to break through into the first team ranks. He has been on the fringe of the first team for three seasons and this really does need to be his year. He was on the fringe of the England U-21 team in June 95. Even so, buying him for your team has to be something of a gamble. Maybe you should wait and transfer him in later if he makes it.

David Howells Defensive Midfield

Club TOTTENHAM HOTSPUR

Date of birth 15.12.67

	Appearances (as substitute)		Goals	
	League	Cups	League	Cups
1994/5	26	7	1	0
1993/4	15(3)	1(1)	1	1

Playing strength
Hard-working
Skilful

Pen picture
It was David's introduction into midfield in November that made the biggest difference to the change in the club's fortunes. He bolstered up the defensive capabilities by slotting in, just in front of the back four, to provide a ball-winner in midfield, rather than all creative players. The difference was instantaneous and dramatic, the season was transformed. However, having sung his praises, I must now warn you not to pick him. That defensive midfield role is simply not the type that you would want your fantasy footballers to have to play.

Andy Turner Left Midfield

Club TOTTENHAM HOTSPUR

Date of birth 23.3.75

Alternative Position Striker

	Appearances (as substitute)		Goals	
	League	Cups	League	Cups
1994/5	1	0	0	0
1993/4	0(1)	0	0	0

Playing strength
Speedy
Versatile

Pen picture
Andy is a classy young left winger (he can play as a striker) who is highly thought of by many fans. Two years ago he had a run in the first team, but then suffered a loss of form which affected his confidence. He was brought in for the last match of last season and may have more opportunities in 1995/6. However, it would be too much of a gamble to include him in your team.

Martin Allen Midfield

Club WEST HAM UNITED

Date of birth 14.8.65

	Appearances (as substitute)		Goals	
	League	Cups	League	Cups
1994/5	26(3)	4	2	0
1993/4	20(6)	6(2)	5	2

Playing strength
Boundless energy
Tremendous strength of shot
Scores goals

Pen picture
The effervescent Martin Allen loves football. He wants to be involved, wherever the ball is, but particularly if it is near the opposition goal. He has a very hard shot and loves to use it. He gets a number of goals and if he could hold a regular place in the first team, he would be the type of player that you would want in your fantasy team. Unfortunately he is too inconsistent and attracts too many Yellow Cards.

Ian Bishop Midfield

Club WEST HAM UNITED

Date of birth 29.5.65

	Appearances (as substitute)		Goals	
	League	Cups	League	Cups
1994/5	31	5	1	0
1993/4	36	8	1	0

Playing strength
Great distribution
Very influential player

Pen picture
Ian has played many good games for West Ham, but our contributor reports that the final ten games of last season were the best that he had ever played. It seems that this excellent passer of the ball loves to play against the better club. Unfortunately, unless it is the final one before a goal, good passing does not win you any points in fantasy football games. He does not score enough goals to be worth buying.

Dale Gordon Right Midfield

Club WEST HAM UNITED

Date of birth 9.1.67

	Appearances (as substitute)		Goals	
	League	Cups	League	Cups
1994/5	0	0	0	0
1993/4	8	1	1	0

Playing strength
An attacking right winger

Pen picture

Dale remains something of a mystery to most Hammers fans as he has played only a handful of games in two years, due to injury. You certainly should not show interest in him.

Matt Holmes Left Midfield

Club WEST HAM UNITED

Date of birth 1.8.69

| | Appearances (as substitute) | | Goals | |
	League	Cups	League	Cups
1994/5	24	2	1	0
1993/4	33(1)	7	3	0

Playing strength

Hard worker

Likes to attack

Pen picture

Big-hearted Matt is an unassuming, hard-working midfielder who loves to go forward. He usually plays wide on the left and he creates many chances for the strikers. Unfortunately, he does not take many himself. Not one for the fantasy games, I am afraid.

Michael Hughes Midfield

Club WEST HAM UNITED

Date of birth 2.8.71

Alternative position Striker

| | Appearances (as substitute) | | Goals | |
	League	Cups	League	Cups
1994/5	15(2)	2	2	0

Playing strength

Tremendous pace

Skill on the ball

A rocket shot

Pen picture

It seems almost certain that Michael will be returning to Strasbourg, which will disappoint Hammers fans who have really taken to heart this influential Irishman. He was one of the sensations of the 1991/2 season when he was playing for Manchester City. He moved to Strasbourg on loan when he failed to re-negotiate a contract at Maine Road. Here is a talent that it would be good to get back into the English game. Let us hope he stays.

Don Hutchison Midfield ⊙⊙⊙
RECOMMENDED

Club WEST HAM UNITED

Date of birth 9.5.71

Alternative Position Striker

| | Appearances (as substitute) | | Goals | |
	League	Cups	League	Cups
1994/5	22(1)	3(1)	9	2
1993/4	6(5)	2(2)	0	0

Playing strength

Competitive player

Good runs from midfield

Has lots of skill

Pen picture

Last year we recommended that, if Don was given the right blend of midfield and attacking work, he could be a very valuable asset for you. Did you sign him up? We did! This year you may get another bargain with him. He has made a success of playing as a striker, and if the newspaper games fail to pick up on that, you could get a lot of valuable points for a very reasonable outlay. We suggest that you check him out and probably buy him.

John Moncur Centre Midfield ⊙
RECOMMENDED

Club WEST HAM UNITED

Date of birth 22.9.66

| | Appearances (as substitute) | | Goals | |
	League	Cups	League	Cups
1994/5	30	5	2	1
1993/4	(for Swindon)		4	0

Playing strength

An excellent passer

Intelligent reader of the game

Pen picture

John is immensely talented and the Hammers fans believe that he could break into the England squad this season. He needs to score more goals before he breaks into my squad. He is certainly worth checking out, but he is recommended as a borderline case only.

Matthew Rush Right Midfield

Club WEST HAM UNITED

Date of birth 6.8.71

| | Appearances (as substitute) | | Goals | |
	League	Cups	League	Cups
1994/5	15(8)	3	2	0
1993/4	9(1)	0	1	0

Playing strength

Good strength and pace

Pen picture

Matthew plays on the right wing and has played a few games, usually standing in when someone is injured. He is very fast, very clever and has a good shot in either foot, so why is he not a regular in the team? Some fans question his attitude and if there is a problem there, it is a pity if it is preventing a talent from fulfilling its potential. In any case, you should pass him by.

Danny Williamson Midfield

Club WEST HAM UNITED

Date of birth 5.12.73

	Appearances (as substitute)		Goals	
	League	Cups	League	Cups
1994/5	4	0	0	0
1993/4	0	0	0	0

Playing strength
Skill and enthusiasm

Pen picture
Danny is a young prospect with a great deal of potential who seems unable to get a run in the first team. He is a great tackler and shows a great deal of skill, yet he rarely gets an opportunity. You cannot afford to risk buying him.

Neil Ardley Left Midfield

Club WIMBLEDON

Date of birth 1.9.72

	Appearances (as substitute)		Goals	
	League	Cups	League	Cups
1994/5	9(5)	4(1)	1	0
1993/4	14(2)	6(1)	1	1

Playing strength
A classic young winger who can cross the ball with either foot

Pen picture
Neil is a former England Under-21 international who 'ardley played at all last season (sorry!). He operates on the left wing and is a creator rather than a scorer of goals. He will not figure in your fantasy team.

Stewart Castledine Midfield

Club WIMBLEDON

Date of birth 22.1.73

	Appearances (as substitute)		Goals	
	League	Cups	League	Cups
1994/5	5(1)	0	1	0
1993/4	3	0	1	0

Playing strength
A highly promising youngster

Pen picture
22-year-old Stewart made a few more appearances last season, but his progress from the previous season seems to have slowed down. He is young and so there is still time, but he needs to establish himself in the first team this season.

Gerald Dobbs Midfield

Club WIMBLEDON

Date of birth 24.1.71

Alternative Position Striker

	Appearances (as substitute)		Goals	
	League	Cups	League	Cups
1994/5	0	0	0	0
1993/4	3(7)	0	0	0

Playing strength
Hard worker
Has pace

Pen picture
Gerald has somewhat fallen out of favour and did not appear for the first team last season. He has turned out regularly for the reserves and scored a few goals, but it looks as though his future at Wimbledon is uncertain. You must not select him.

Robbie Earle Midfield ⊛⊛⊛
RECOMMENDED

Club WIMBLEDON

Date of birth 27.1.65

	Appearances (as substitute)		Goals	
	League	Cups	League	Cups
1994/5	9	4	0	1
1993/4	41	9	9	3

Playing strength
A powerful, goalscoring midfield player

Pen picture
Robbie has had a miserable season, ruined by injury. He is a vital cog in the Wimbledon machinery and

always scores lots of goals from midfield. He averaged over ten per season for the previous twelve years. If he is fit, he is an ideal fantasy footballer and after this season, he is likely to be much less expensive. He must be a prime contender for a place in your team.

Peter Fear Right Midfield

Club WIMBLEDON

Date of birth 10.9.73

	Appearances (as substitute)		Goals	
	League	Cups	League	Cups
1994/5	8(6)	2(2)	1	0
1993/4	23	3	1	0

Playing strength
Promising young right winger

Pen picture
Quite surprisingly, Peter has been in and out of the Wimbledon team this year. During the *1993/4* season, he had won his place in the team, played an important part in their successful end of season run in and played a part in winning the Toulon Under 21 Tournament with the successful England team. This season was quite an anti-climax for him. He has potential, but he is of no use to your fantasy team if he is in the reserves.

Marcus Gayle Midfield ◉

RECOMMENDED

Club WIMBLEDON

Date of birth 27.9.70

Alternative Position Striker

	Appearances (as substitute)		Goals	
	League	Cups	League	Cups
1994/5	22(1)	2	2	1
1993/4	10	0	0	0

Playing strength
Tall, powerfully-built

Pen picture
His first full season with Wimbledon must have been something of a disappointment for Marcus, as it would have been for Joe Kinnear and the managers who selected him as a cheap fantasy midfielder. Described, at the start of the 1994/5 season, by manager Joe Kinnear as 'a future Fash, once we've worked with him', and a former striker-turned-midfielder, many were expecting to pick up a number of goals from this big 6'2", physical forward. In fact, he scored only twice in 22 games and missed out on the middle part of the season. Maybe he will do better next year. He is a borderline recommendation.

Vinnie Jones Midfield

Club WIMBLEDON

Date of birth 5.1.65

	Appearances (as substitute)		Goals	
	League	Cups	League	Cups
1994/5	33	4	3	0
1993/4	32	8	2	1

Playing strength
Aggressive midfield ball-winner
Excellent passer of the ball
Good motivator

Pen picture
Much has been said and written about Vinnie Jones which emphasises his tough approach to the game. Not so much is said about the skill and midfield talent of this dedicated worker. Last season he won his first cap - for Wales! Whatever your views about his approach to the game, we can ease your conscience about whether or not to buy him by confirming that he does not score many goals and should be ignored when selecting your team.

Oyvind Leonhardsen Midfield ◉◉

RECOMMENDED

Club WIMBLEDON

Date of birth 17.8.70

	Appearances (as substitute)		Goals	
	League	Cups	League	Cups
1994/5	18(2)	3	4	1

Playing strength
Goalscoring midfielder

Pen picture
Oyvind joined Wimbledon on loan from Rosenborg, Norway in October, having been an ever-present member of the Norway team at the 1994 World Cup. The intention is to make the loan into a permanent transfer for £400,000. He made a big impact in the team and scored four goals in 17 games. He is certainly one to consider for your team.

STRIKERS

Dennis Bergkamp Striker ⊙⊙⊙
RECOMMENDED

Club ARSENAL

Date of birth 10.5.60

Playing strength
Remarkable strike-rate
Great skill on the ball

Pen picture
Dennis is a truly world-class striker and has won most of the top honours in the game. During his stay at Ajax from 1981–1993, he helped them to win the European Cup-Winners' Cup (1987), Dutch League Championship (1990), UEFA Cup (1992) and Dutch Cup (1993). Since moving to Inter Milan in 1993, he has had less success but still played in the UEFA Cup-winning team in 1994. His goalscoring feats in Holland were amazing – 103 in 185 league matches and 23 in 39 internationals for Holland. However, since moving to Italy, he has managed only 11 goals in 52 Serie A games. Arsenal believe that his game is much more suitable to the English game than that of Italy and that Dennis will resume his prolific goalscoring feats alongside Ian Wright. We agree and recommend him very strongly.

Kevin Campbell Striker
Club ARSENAL

Date of birth   4.2.70

| | Appearances (as substitute) | | Goals | |
	League	Cups	League	Cups
1994/5	19(4)	9(2)	4	1
1993/4	29(9)	11(4)	14	5

Playing strength
Strong and steady
A good foil for Ian Wright

Pen picture
1994/5 was a very bad year for Kevin. He began the season as the first choice striker, but lost his form and his confidence. Now that Hartson and Kiwomya have arrived to join Ian Wright and with other young strikers waiting in the wings, it is probably time for him to move on. He is not one to think about for long.

Paul Dickov Striker
Club ARSENAL

Date of birth 1.11.72

| | Appearances (as substitute) | | Goals | |
	League	Cups	League	Cups
1994/5	4(5)	2(2)	0	3
1993/4	0	1	0	0

Playing strength
Scores goals
Brave and tenacious

Pen picture
A promising young striker who scored 16 goals in 18 reserve team games in *1993/4* and has 13 from 19 starts in *1994/5*. He has not had a long run in the first team, but has certainly been on the fringe. With a great deal of competition for places as a striker at Highbury, Paul may get only few opportunities. This is a pity since he has the potential to score goals at the highest level. Unfortunately we cannot recommend that you select him, but watch out in case he manages to force his way in, he may be worth transferring in as a cheap striker if he does.

John Hartson Striker ⊙
RECOMMENDED

Club ARSENAL

Date of birth 5.4.75

| | Appearances (as substitute) | | Goals | |
	League	Cups	League	Cups
1994/5	14(1)	5(1)	7	0

Playing strength
Very good in the air
Excellent first touch
Natural goal scorer

Pen picture
Gunners fans quote the signing of John Hartson as a reminder of what a good manager George Graham was. Many doubted the wisdom of paying £2.5 million for a 19 year old, but Hartson has already started to repay that fee. His heading ability is the thing that fans highlight first in comments about him, but also that he is strong on the ground, being very difficult to knock off the ball. A decent strike rate in his first few games, he will surely get better in 1995/6. You ought to consider him as a possible cheap striker.

Chris Kiwomya Striker
Club ARSENAL

Date of birth 2.12.69

| | Appearances (as substitute) | | Goals | |
	League	Cups	League	Cups
1994/5	5(9)	1(2)	3	0
1993/4 (for Ipswich)	34(3)	3	5	1

Playing strength
Tremendous pace over the first 10 yards

Pen picture
It is difficult to see why Chris came to Highbury. From the start it has seemed unlikely that he would win a regular first team place, With Hartson and Wright apparently settled as the first choice pair of strikers, and with Dickov waiting in the wings (not to

mention Read) opportunities for him will be scarce. This is unfortunate because fans love his speed and his touch. He is a good asset for Arsenal to have on the bench, but not for you to have in your squad.

Paul Read Striker

Club ARSENAL

Date of birth 25.9.73

	Appearances (as substitute)		Goals	
	League	Cups	League	Cups
1994/5	0	0	0	0

Playing strength
Scores lots of goals
Lots of pace

Pen picture
Now here is a real fantasy prospect! Although he has not yet made it into the first team, this 21-year-old is a prolific goalscorer. He has managed to score 23 goals in 25 games for the reserves and combines good skill and pace. Maybe Bruce Rioch will be more likely to give him a chance than George Graham would have been. He has the problem of a string of good strikers ahead of him in the queue, but just watch out if he gets a chance! Unfortunately the strength of the opposition prevents us from suggesting that you select him.

Alan Smith Striker

Club ARSENAL

Date of birth 21.11.62

	Appearances (as substitute)		Goals	
	League	Cups	League	Cups
1994/5	17(2)	8		2 2
1993/4	20(4)	12(4)		3 4

Playing strength
Good in the air
Holds up the ball well

Pen picture
Alan is an experienced striker who has scored almost 200 league goals in his long career, but whose strength now lies in creating opportunities for others. He is a loyal club servant who is thought very highly of at Highbury, but he has not played since the New Year and it would seem that his playing career at Arsenal is probably over.

Ian Wright Striker   ◉◉

RECOMMENDED

Club ARSENAL

Date of birth 3.11.63

	Appearances (as substitute)		Goals	
	League	Cups	League	Cups
1994/5	20(1)	8	18	12
1993/4	39	13	23	11

Playing strength
Skilful at high speed
An instinctive and deadly striker
A great enthusiast

Pen picture
Ian scores spectacular goals, often when they are least expected. He is a prolific goal scorer, particularly in cups where his amazing total of 38 in the past three seasons must be some sort of record. He always gives100% and he is almost guaranteed to score 20+ goals in the season ahead. You must consider selecting him very seriously.

Dalian Atkinson Striker

Club ASTON VILLA

Date of birth 21.3.68

	Appearances (as substitute)		Goals	
	League	Cups	League	Cups
1994/5	11(5)	5	3	4
1993/429	15		8	7

Playing strength
He has everything, pace, skill, goalscoring ability

Pen picture
Dalian is fast, powerful, has a great shot, in fact, he really does have everything. Yet many of the fans are fed up with him and have nicknamed him "Sicknote" on the basis of their claim that he regularly fails to turn up. Despite his skill, you, like Villa, cannot afford to include him.

John Fashanu Striker

Club ASTON VILLA

Date of birth 18.9.62

	Appearances (as substitute)		Goals	
	League	Cups	League	Cups
1994/511(2)	3		3	0
1993/4	36(1)	9	11	1
(for Wimbledon)				

Playing strength
Strong and physical
Fast

Pen picture
'Fash' is probably the striker whom most Premiership central defenders least like to face. His physical presence and speed and strength make him a real handful. Since joining Villa at the start of the season, he has played only a handful of games and now has a career-threatening injury. You should certainly not consider him for your team.

Graham Fenton Striker

Club ASTON VILLA
Date of birth 22.5.74
Alternative Position Midfield

	Appearances (as substitute)		Goals	
	League	Cups	League	Cups1
1994/5	7(10)	1(2)	2	0
1993/4	9(3)	1(1)	1	0

Playing strength
Aggressive
Energetic

Pen picture
Graham plays just off the front line, but will probably be categorised as a striker in most fantasy games. He is raw, aggressive and at 21 he has time on his side. By the end of the season he had just about won his place in the team and if he is classified as a midfield player he might be worth considering. As a striker, steer clear of him.

Nil Lamptey Striker

Club ASTON VILLA
Date of birth 10.12.74

	Appearances (as substitute)		Goals	
	League	Cups	League	Cups
1994/5	1(5)	2(1)	0	3

Playing strength
Exciting tricky player

Pen picture
Nil, a Ghanaian, was signed from PSV Eindhoven during the summer of 1994. His exciting skills have dazzled the fans at times, but he has not been given enough opportunities and it is likely that his work permit will not be renewed.

Tommy Johnson Striker

Club ASTON VILLA
Date of birth 15.1.71

	Appearances (as substitute)		Goals	
	League	Cups	League	Cups
1994/5	11(3)	0(1)	4	0

Playing strength
Hard worker
Very mobile

Pen picture
Tommy was Brian Little's most expensive signing, (for £2 million, from Derby) but he has struggled to adapt to the Premiership. He is an unorthodox striker, often trying to do something different, but he frequently seems to drift out of the game and subsequently he has not claimed a regular place. You should not give him one in your team either.

Dean Saunders Position Striker

Club ASTON VILLA
Date of birth 21.6.64

	Appearances (as substitute)		Goals	
	League	Cups	League	Cups
1994/5	39	9	15	2
1993/4	37(1)	14	10	6

Playing strength
Energetic
Committed runner

Pen picture
Dean is a very unselfish striker who does a lot of running for others. He is a workaholic, with an incredible work rate. He is not a prolific scorer and is not the type to include in a fantasy team.

Kevin Gallacher Striker

Club BLACKBURN ROVERS
Date of birth 23.11.66
Alternative Position Midfield (either wing)

	Appearances (as substitute)		Goals	
	League	Cups	League	Cups
1994/5	1	0	1	0
1993/4	27(3)	8	7	1

Playing strength
Quick-thinking striker
Versatile
Pacey

Pen picture
Kevin missed most of the season through a broken leg. He made his comeback against Crystal Palace in April, scored a goal and then suffered another broken leg. No matter how skilful a player might be and Gallacher is certainly that, you do not want anyone that unlucky in your team!

Mike Newell Striker

Club BLACKBURN ROVERS
Date of birth 27.1.65

	Appearances (as substitute)		Goals	
	League	Cups	League	Cups
1994/5	2(10)	0(3)	0	0
1993/4	27(1)	4	6	2

Playing strength
Tremendous commitment
Hard worker
Holds the ball up well

Pen picture
Destined to be a squad player once the SAS was formed, Mike has had very few opportunities in 1994/5. The situation is likely to remain the same for

the season ahead unless one of the two first choices is injured.

Alan Shearer Striker ⊙⊙⊙
RECOMMENDED

Club BLACKBURN ROVERS

Date of birth 13.8.70

	Appearances (as substitute)		Goals	
	League	*Cups*	*League*	*Cups*
1994/5	42	7	34	3
1993/4	33(6)	8	31	3

Playing strength
Brilliant striker
Scores goals from anywhere

Pen picture
What more can be said about Alan Shearer? Undoubtedly the best striker in England, the coming season and the European Champions Cup will answer the question as to whether he is the best in Europe. Certainly most fantasy managers want him in their team, the only problem being that he will undoubtedly be the most expensive player in every game. Only if he is handicapped sufficiently by a very high price can you risk leaving him out.

Chris Sutton Striker ⊙⊙
RECOMMENDED

Club BLACKBURN ROVERS

Date of birth 10.3.71

	Appearances (as substitute)		Goals	
	League	*Cups*	*League*	*Cups*
1994/5	40	8	15	6
1993/4	41	11(1)	25	3
(for Norwich City)				

Playing strength
Strong
Good pace
Excellent work rate

Pen picture
After his move from Norwich in the close season, football fans throughout England (and probably much further afield) wondered how successful the Sutton/Shearer partnership would prove to be. The first few matches told them, 20 goals in the opening fourteen league and cup games, and the rate never let up. Over the season they scored 49 league and 9 cup goals between them. The only difference being that after scoring 12 of those first 20, Chris turned provider and scored only a further 9 while Shearer was scoring 29. His heading ability, which had been so praised at Norwich, is being questioned at Ewood Park. Nevertheless, the overwhelming success of the partnership has been dramatically proven. He may be cheaper next year and just possibly a better buy for your fantasy team.

Owen Coyle Striker

Club BOLTON WANDERERS

Date of birth 14.7.66

	Appearances (as substitute)		Goals	
	League	*Cups*	*League*	*Cups*
1994/5	8(11)	3(1)	5	1

Playing strength
Good running off the ball
Skilful

Pen picture
Owen is likely to be used as cover rather than as an automatic member of the first team. He has been unable to command a regular place in the senior side, but has never let them down when called upon. He has had a very good season in the reserves. The main problem is that he is slightly-built and easily knocked off the ball. You should not consider him for your team.

Fabian De Freitas Striker

Club BOLTON WANDERERS

Date of birth 28.7.72

	Appearances (as substitute)		Goals	
	League	*Cups*	*League*	*Cups*
1994/5	7(6)	3	2	2

Playing strength
Very fast
Great skills
Good with head and feet

Pen picture
Fabian was signed from Holland for £350,000 and has shown great pace and skill. The Play-Off Final at Wembley was a case in point. Bolton looked a totally different team when he came on at half time. Fans believe that he has high potential for next year and that the manager must find room for him in the team.

Gary Martindale Striker

Club BOLTON WANDERERS

Date of birth 24.6.71

Alternative Position Midfield

	Appearances (as substitute)		Goals	
	League	*Cups*	*League*	*Cups*
1994/5	0	0	0	0

Playing strength
Has a good shot
A fine header of the ball

Pen picture
Although he has a good goalscoring record in the reserves, he has never made it into the first team. The fans who know him would like him to have an

opportunity to play a few games. He is certainly one for the future.

John McGinlay Striker ⊙
RECOMMENDED

Club BOLTON WANDERERS

Date of birth 8.4.64

	Appearances (as substitute)		Goals	
	League	Cups	League	Cups
1994/5	34(3)	8(1)	16	6

Playing strength
Regular goalscorer
Creative
A thinker
Good with head and feet

Pen picture
John is a Scotland international and a regular goalscorer at all levels. He was with Bruce Rioch at Millwall and followed him to Bolton. The fans claim that John is good at every aspect of the job of Striker. You could certainly do worse than to buy him, but we suspect that you could probably do a lot better.

Mixu Paatelainen Striker

Club BOLTON WANDERERS

Date of birth 3.2.67

	Appearances (as substitute)		Goals	
	League	Cups	League	Cups
1994/5	43(1)	8(1)	13	3

Playing strength
Holds the ball up well
Spreads the play well

Pen picture
The fans are really divided over Mixu. Some give very positive comments and others do not want to know him. Some say that he is good in the air whilst others say he rarely wins anything in the air. Some criticise his strike rate, yet he scored only three less than John McGinlay, (admittedly from more games) about whom they rave. And so it goes on. The author is confused! One thing is certain, Bruce Rioch thought highly of him, his place was virtually guaranteed. Furthermore, he has scored goals at all levels; he got four for Finland in an international match against San Marino last December. Whatever the outcome, Mixu is not for you. There are more suitable strikers elsewhere.

Robert Fleck Striker

Club CHELSEA

Date of birth 11.8.65

	Appearances (as substitute)		Goals	
	League	Cups	League	Cups
1994/5	0	0	0	0
1993/4	7(2)	1	1	0

Playing strength
Hard worker
Creative talent

Pen picture
Robert has been out on loan to Bristol City and it seems most unlikely that he will be in the mind of Glenn Hoddle for the coming season.

Paul Furlong Striker

Club CHELSEA

Date of birth 1.10.68

	Appearances (as substitute)		Goals	
	League	Cups	League	Cups
1994/5	30(6)	10(1)	10	3

Playing strength
A forceful, goalscoring centre forward.
Good control in the air

Pen picture
Paul has had a reasonable first season in the Premiership. He is the target man, laying the ball off to either Stein or Spencer. The battle for the second striker's place will be between them. It seems that Paul, a much taller man, is assured of his. However his strike rate is not good enough to make him attractive to you.

John Spencer Striker

Club CHELSEA

Date of birth 11.9.70

Alternative Position Midfield

	Appearances (as substitute)		Goals	
	League	Cups	League	Cups
1994/5	26(3)	8(1)	11	2
1993/4	13(6)	6(5)	5	2

Playing strength
Excellent control
Quick feet
A goal maker

Pen picture
John is a cultured striker who has an impressive strike rate and who causes opposition defences a lot of trouble. He teams up well with Furlong.
Alternatively, if Stein partners Furlong and Spencer reverts to midfield, he is a busy ball winner who tackles hard and distributes the ball well. The fans prefer him up front, but with the issue in doubt, he is certainly not for you.

Mark Stein Striker

Club CHELSEA

Date of birth 28.1.66

	Appearances (as substitute)		Goals	
	League	Cups	League	Cups
1994/5	21(3)	5(1)	8	3
1993/4	18	7	13	1

Playing strength
Natural instinctive goal scorer
Very quick on the turn and off the mark

Pen picture
Mark's season was plagued by injuries and he did not start a game until after Christmas. His strike rate was not as good as last year and fans complain that he sometimes shoots without due thought to the placement of the shot. He played his part in a reasonable run-in and will almost certainly keep his place in the team. However, his decreased strike-rate should not persuade you to buy him.

Iyseden Christie Striker

Club COVENTRY CITY

Date of birth 14.11.76

	Appearances (as substitute)		Goals	
	League	Cups	League	Cups
1994/5	0	0	0	0
1993/4	0	0	0	0

Playing strength
Strong runner with pace and skill

Pen picture
Not yet 19, there is no doubt in the mind of our contact at Highfield Road that this young man will make the grade. He looks to be the complete striker. Unfortunately Big Ron is not renowned for giving youth a chance and so Iyseden may have a while to wait. The thought of Dublin and Christie up front with Ndlovu slotting in behind sounds pretty exciting to me. But there again, Ron isn't one for excitement.

Dion Dublin Striker

Club COVENTRY CITY

Date of birth 22.4.69

	Appearances (as substitute)		Goals	
	League	Cups	League	Cups
1994/5	31	7	13	3
1993/4	1(	1(3)	1	1
(for Manchester United)				

Playing strength
Good in the air
Good strike rate

Pen picture
Do you remember our recommendation last year? Did you buy him? Surely he was the best value-for-money striker in any of the fantasy lists. Unfortunately, we expect his price to rocket and we cannot recommend him again this year. That does not mean that he will not do a good job for Coventry; we are sure that he will. But rate per £, he is unlikely to be anywhere near as profitable as last season.

Peter Ndlovu Striker

Club COVENTRY CITY

Date of birth 25.2 73

	Appearances (as substitute)		Goals	
	League	Cups	League	Cups
1994/5	28(2)	4	11	2
1993/4	40	3	11	0

Playing strength
Highly skilful and forceful striker who runs at players
Lethal striker of the ball

Pen picture
People in the Premiership are now well aware of this amazing talent. How long Coventry will be able to hang onto him we do not know, but Dublin and Ndlovu together is a dynamic partnership. In the 25 games where they were attacking partners, they scored 21 goals between them. That is not bad for a new partnership. Expect the ratio of goals per game to increase in the coming season. It is just possible that Ndlovu's price will stay within range, in which case, make up your own mind.

Roy Wegerle Striker

Club COVENTRY CITY

Date of birth 19.3.64

	Appearances (as substitute)		Goals	
	League	Cups	League	Cups
1994/5	21(5)	4(2)	3	2
1993/4	20(1)	4	6	0

Playing strength
Great skill on the ball

Pen picture
Roy is a classy player, but he has struggled with injuries over the last season or two. You cannot consider him for your team because not only does he miss a lot of games, he rarely scores, for a striker.

Daniel Amokachi Striker

Club EVERTON

Date of birth 30.12.72

Alternative Position Midfield

	Appearances (as substitute)		Goals	
	League	Cups	League	Cups
1994/5	16(1)	2(1)	4	2

Playing strength

Running with the ball

Pen picture

Daniel is a twenty-two-year-old Nigerian who is a great favourite with the crowd. Many feel that "Amo's" best position is in a free role just behind the two strikers. Joe may not be able to afford such an attacking luxury, although it would certainly lead to exciting football. He is almost certain to be classified as a striker and as such, he may not be a regular in the team. You cannot justify selecting him for your team.

Stuart Barlow Striker

Club EVERTON

Date of birth 16.7.68

	Appearances (as substitute)		Goals	
	League	Cups	League	Cups
1994/5	7(3)	2(1)	2	0
1993/4	6(16)	2(3)	3	2

Playing strength

Lightning fast

Good first touch

Pen picture

Stuart has had plenty of chances but fans are not happy with his contribution. It is unlikely that he will be in the team very often next year and he should certainly not be in your fantasy team.

Duncan Ferguson Striker ⊙⊙
RECOMMENDED

Club EVERTON

Date of birth 27.12.71

	Appearances (as substitute)		Goals	
	League	Cups	League	Cups
1994/5	22(1)	4	7	1

Playing strength

Great in the air

Holds the ball up well

Excellent on the ground

Pen picture

The Everton fans are expecting great things from Duncan Ferguson; already they are talking of him as being as great as Dixie Dean. According to them, he will score 25+ goals next season and is the complete centre forward, excellent in the air and great on the ground. He both scores and sets up chances for others. Let us hope that their optimism is well-founded and that he produces the goods and controls his behaviour. If he does all that Everton supporters are claiming, you should have him in your team.

Paul Rideout Striker

Club EVERTON

Date of birth 14.8.64

	Appearances (as substitute)		Goals	
	League	Cups	League	Cups
1994/5	24(4)	5(1)	13	1
1993/4	21(3)	4	6	5

Playing strength

Strong in the air

Makes good forward runs

Pen picture

Paul is a tall, strong, physical player who is good running at defences, or when challenging in the air. Opinions about him are mixed. For some he is the perfect partner for Ferguson, strong runs off the ball, finding space, while others do not rate him. No-one can argue with the facts that he was the club's leading scorer last season, his best for many years. Even so, we cannot recommend him for your fantasy team.

Brian Deane Striker

Club LEEDS UNITED

Date of birth 7.2.68

	Appearances (as substitute)		Goals	
	League	Cups	League	Cups
1994/5	33(2)	4(1)	8	1
1993/4	41	5	11	1

Playing strength

Excellent control

Good pace

Pen picture

Brian was voted the Supporters' Club Player of the Year, even though he has not hit the prolific goalscoring form which he exhibited at Sheffield United. He showed a tremendous improvement after the arrival of Tony Yeboah, as he was able to become the provider, rather than the target man. His confidence regained, he seems to be assured his place in the Leeds front line, but not in yours!

Jamie Forrester Striker

Club LEEDS UNITED

Date of birth 1.11.74

	Appearances (as substitute)		Goals	
	League	Cups	League	Cups
1994/5	0	0	0	0
1993/4	2(1)	1(1)	0	2

Playing strength

An out-and-out goal scorer.

Pen picture

Jamie is an aggressive player who has been a prolific goalscorer at junior and reserve level, but has not yet shown the same ability in his few first team games.

Phil Masinga Striker

Club LEEDS UNITED

Date of birth 28.6.69

	Appearances (as substitute)		Goals	
	League	Cups	League	Cups
1994/5	15(7)	3(2)	5	4

Playing strength
Good positional sense
Accurate shot

Pen picture
Phil has had few opportunities since signing for Leeds last summer and with the arrival of Tony Yeboah, his future must be in doubt. He endeared himself to Elland Road fans with a sensational extra time hat trick against Walsall in the F A Cup and they would be disappointed if he were to move on. You cannot afford to risk buying him.

Rod Wallace Striker

Club LEEDS UNITED

Date of birth 2.10.69

Alternative Position Midfield

	Appearances (as substitute)		Goals	
	League	Cups	League	Cups
1994/5	30(2)	4(1)	4	0
1993/4	34(3)	2	17	0

Playing strength
Great pace
Aggressive striker

Pen picture
After scoring 17 goals the previous season, this year's total was very disappointing. His strength is his pace and being able to run past defenders. This year his finishing has let him down and frustrated the fans and his main contribution has been in creating chances for others. In many fantasy games he is classified as a striker and as such you cannot consider him.

Noel Whelan Striker

RECOMMENDED

Club LEEDS UNITED

Date of birth 30.12.74

	Appearances (as substitute)		Goals	
	League	Cups	League	Cups
1994/5	18(4)	4	4	0
1993/4	7(9)	1	0	1

Playing strength
A goal scorer
Good pace

Pen picture
Still only 20, Noel has great potential. He has an excellent goalscoring record at lower levels but has not yet made a big impact in the big time. Given the right opportunity (such as playing alongside Tony Yebooah) he might do so this year, and he will be inexpensive in fantasy games. Check out whether he will be playing at the start of the season and, if so, be prepared to try him out in your team.

Tony Yeboah Striker

RECOMMENDED

Club LEEDS UNITED

Date of birth 6.6.66

	Appearances (as substitute)		Goals	
	League	Cups	League	Cups
1994/5	16(2)	0(2)	12	1

Playing strength
Scoring goals!

Also creates opportunities for others

Pen picture
Tony Yeboah is the great hope for Leeds United, he could prove to be an inspirational signing by Howard Wilkinson. After being the leading scorer in the Bundesliga with 20 goals for Eintracht Frankfurt, he moved to Elland Road for a reported £3.4 million, an incredible bargain at today's inflated prices. His impact has been little short of phenomenal, scoring 13 goals from 16 starts. Although he will be expensive in fantasy games, he should not cost as much as Shearer, Cole etc and his points return may well match theirs. You almost certainly have to have him.

Stan Collymore Striker ◉◉
RECOMMENDED

Club LIVERPOOL

Date of birth 22.1.71

	Appearances (as substitute)		Goals	
	League	Cups	League	Cups
1994/5	37	6	22	3
1993/4	27(1)	7	19	6

Playing strength
Electrifying speed
Great skill running with the ball
Great shot with either foot

Pen picture
After a summer of, not so much "Will he, won't he?", but more "Where and when?", Stan the Man has finally made his choice; well, we believe that he has. At the time of going to print, he has not actually signed for Liverpool, but apparently, Everton have now given up and Stan will sign within a week. Therefore, we are making assumptions and with Stan Collymore that is dangerous; on or off the pitch, he is totally unpredictable! He is one of that breed of footballers who is either a genius or is on the fringe of being completely out of line. Amongst our glowing tributes last year we said, "His suspect temperament may be a problem, ...". We were proved right again. As a star striker, Liverpool could not have done much better. The mouth waters at the thought of a front line of Collymore and Fowler. They could get 50+ goals between them. Which of them will benefit most by the partnership, or will it be one of the midfielders? Take your own pick, but do not leave Stan out of your considerations.

Robbie Fowler Striker ◉◉
RECOMMENDED

Club LIVERPOOL

Date of birth 9.4.75

	Appearances (as substitute)		Goals	
	League	Cups	League	Cups
1994/5	42	15	25	6
1993/4	27(1)	6	12	6

Playing strength
Lethal striker, good with either foot

Pen picture
Robbie Fowler is still only 20 and has already climbed to the top of the tree as far as strikers are concerned. Only Alan Shearer beat him last season and he will have to watch out this time. He scores goals from all angles and distances, his potential is breathtaking. We hold our breath to see the results of the Collymore/Fowler partnership. What will it do for Robbie? At his age, he can only get better, so buy him if you can afford him, unless you can get better value for money.

Lee Jones Striker

Club LIVERPOOL

Date of birth 29.5.73

	Appearances (as substitute)		Goals	
	League	Cups	League	Cups
1994/5	0(1)	0(1)	0	0
1993/4	0	0	0	0

Playing strength
Good pace
Has an eye for goal
Great first touch

Pen picture
Lee was most unfortunate to break a leg just as he was about to get into the first team. He has lots of ability, but of course, at 22 he is rather "past it" compared with Robbie Fowler. He might find it a struggle to get a regular game!

Ian Rush Striker

Club LIVERPOOL
Date of birth 20.10.61

| | Appearances (as substitute) | | Goals | |
	League	Cups	League	Cups
1994/5	38	14	12	7
1993/4	41(1)	7	13	5

Playing strength
Committed captain who gives his all

Pen picture
"Tosh", as he is known by the fans, works exceptionally hard and still gets a reasonable number of goals, but he has lost the sharpness which made him great. Some fans are saying that he should stop now, but what a marvellous substitute to have sitting on the bench waiting to come on for Fowler or Collymore. However, whatever he does, he is not for your team.

Carl Griffiths Striker

Club MANCHESTER CITY
Date of birth 24.11.69

| | Appearances (as substitute) | | Goals | |
	League	Cups	League	Cups
1994/5	0(2)	0(1)	0	0
1993/4	11(5)	2	4	0

Playing strength
Good positional sense
Effective goalscorer

Pen picture
Carl Griffiths has not really made the most of his first team opportunities, according to fans at Maine Road. They feel that his strike rate from reasonable chances is not high enough for a Premiership striker and they feel that he may well move on. He will certainly not get enough chances for you to consider him for your fantasy team.

Adie Mike Striker

Club MANCHESTER CITY
Date of birth 16.11.73

| | Appearances (as substitute) | | Goals | |
	League	Cups	League	Cups
1994/5	1(1)	(1)	0	0
1993/4	1(8)	1(1)	1	0

Playing strength
Young, nimble striker

Pen picture
Fans believe that Adie has not made the progress that was expected of him. He cannot get many chances in the first team and the future does not look too good for him at Maine Road. Perhaps it is time for a move.

Niall Quinn Striker

Club MANCHESTER CITY
Date of birth 6.10.66

| | Appearances (as substitute) | | Goals | |
	League	Cups	League	Cups
1994/5	24(11)	5(5)	8	2
1993/4	14(1)	3	5	1

Playing strength
Excellent in the air and on the ground

Pen picture
Will he, won't he? The question of whether Niall would be going to Portugal has been around for much of the summer. It looks to have fallen through, but what the position will be at the start of the season remains unknown at the time of writing. City have an embarrassment of riches in attack and one of Brian Horton's problems was that he never found out and settled on the best way to use them. Now that he has gone, the future for Niall looks uncertain, despite his excellent contribution last year. You must not risk buying him.

Uwe Rösler Striker   ◉◉
RECOMMENDED

Club MANCHESTER CITY
Date of birth 15.11.68

| | Appearances (as substitute) | | Goals | |
	League	Cups	League	Cups
1994/5	29(2)	7(1)	15	7
1993/4	12	0	5	0

Playing strength
Strong in the air
Powerful on the ground

Pen picture
Uwe is a natural goalscorer who gives 100% and he is expected to have another fine season. When we recommended him last year, we said that the only constraint might be the price. The same question arises this season, only more so after his impressive goalscoring feats in 1994/5. Even at a high price, you have to consider him.

Paul Walsh Striker

Club MANCHESTER CITY

Date of birth 1.10.62

	Appearances (as substitute)		Goals	
	League	Cups	League	Cups
1994/5	39	9	12	3
1993/4	11	0	4	0

Playing strength

A 'busy' player

A good foil for another striker

Good opportunist

Pen picture
Many would be surprised that, of the three main strikers at Maine Road, it is Paul who played by far the most games last season. Most people would not have expected that. He is not a prolific goalscorer and many feel that they may have already seen the best of him. Nevertheless, on his day he can still turn the defence and lay on the telling pass which leads to a goal for Rösler or Quinn. Fans felt that he struggled towards the end of the season and so you should not expect too much for the season ahead.

Eric Cantona Striker

Club MANCHESTER UNITED

Date of birth 24.5.66

	Appearances (as substitute)		Goals	
	League	Cups	League	Cups
1994/5	21	3	12	1
1993/4	34	14	18	7

Playing strength

Tremendous vision

Outstanding skill

Scores great goals

Great creative talent

Pen picture
There can be no doubt about Eric's footballing genius. He is one of the finest players in the world, excellent vision and awareness, breathtaking skill on the ball and the ability to do what ordinary mortals would only dream about. Having showered him with praise, the author cannot condone his outrageous behaviour. It is ludicrous to claim that fans' provocation in any way excuses the sort of reaction which he displayed at Selhurst Park. In my opinion, that type of behaviour deserves a life ban from the game.

Andy Cole Striker ⊙⊙
RECOMMENDED

Club MANCHESTER UNITED

Date of birth 15.10.71

	Appearances (as substitute)		Goals	
	League	Cups	League	Cups
1994/5	17(1)	0	11	0
1994/5 (for Newcastle United)	18	9	9	6
1993/4 (for Newcastle United)	40	5	34	7

Playing strength

Outstanding goalscoring talent

Creates goals for others

Very quick over the first five yards

Pen picture
The footballing world was amazed when Kevin Keegan allowed the Tyneside folk-hero Andy Cole to join rivals Manchester United. Perhaps the £7 million had something to do with it. Due to being cup-tied, Andy has not played a full part in United's season, even since he joined them. Next year will tell whether Ferguson was right to spend that kind of money on him. The evidence so far is promising, but not conclusive. You may have to spend a large proportion of your budget on him if you want him in your team. With Cantona, Giggs etc laying on chances, he may break all goalscoring records this coming season. Think about him carefully.

Mark Hughes Striker

Club MANCHESTER UNITED

Date of birth 1.11.63

	Appearances (as substitute)		Goals	
	League	*Cups*	*League*	*Cups*
1994/5	33(1)	10	8	4
1993/4	36	11	12	9

Playing strength

Great ability to shield the ball and hold up play for others

Scores spectacular goals

Pen picture

Mark is a great player for United, but not in fantasy football games. He is the target man who holds up the ball magnificently for others, but will never be a prolific goalscorer. Whether or not he will get a regular place in the United line-up this year, facing competition from Cantona and Cole, remains to be seen, but we cannot recommend that you give him a place in yours.

Paul Scholes Striker ◉◉

RECOMMENDED

Club MANCHESTER UNITED

Date of birth 16.11.74

	Appearances (as substitute)		Goals	
	League	*Cups*	*League*	*Cups*
1994/5	6(11)	4(3)	5	2
1993/4	0	0	0	0

Playing strength

Outstanding goal scorer.

Takes on defenders

Aggressive tackler

Pen picture

Well, now do you believe us? Last year we said "You read it here first! This young man will be a star! United's Young Player of the Year *1993/4*, he is a good dribbler, fights for the ball and scored 25 times in 25 appearances for the 'A' team. Watch this space." Five goals from only six starts in the Premiership says it all. With a goalscoring knack such as he has, you only have to write his name on the scoresheet and you have goals. Was it really necessary to spend £7 million on Cole? The problem here is how he is going to find his way into the team. If he were to be transferred (like Dublin last season) he would be the bargain of the season. As it is, you may have to ignore him because of the competition, but do not forget him, just in case.

Jan Aage Fjortoft Striker ◉◉

RECOMMENDED

Club MIDDLESBROUGH

Date of birth 10.1.67

	Appearances (as substitute)		Goals	
	League	*Cups*	*League*	*Cups*
1994/5	8	0	3	0
1994/5	36	10	17	10
(for Swindon, Endsleigh League Div 1)				

Playing strength

Natural goalscorer

Pen picture

Jan took months before he scored his first goal in English football, and he has not stopped since. He showed at Swindon that he could even score goals for a team which was struggling against relegation. He gets many of his goals from near-impossible situations. He is also very good at holding up the ball for others; and his plane impression celebrations are second-to-none. You had better consider him carefully.

Chris Freestone Striker

Club MIDDLESBROUGH

Date of birth 4.9.71

	Appearances (as substitute)		Goals	
	League	*Cups*	*League*	*Cups*
1994/5	0	0	0	0

Playing strength

Goalscorer

Speed

Pen picture

Chris is another player who is making the transition from non-league to the top grade. He has scored dozens of goals in non-league and reserve team football and some of the fans are waiting to see him let loose on the Premiership defences. He is like lightning and he knows where to find the net. You cannot afford to risk signing him on, but he is one to watch in the future.

Uwe Fuchs Striker

Club MIDDLESBROUGH

Date of birth 23.7.66

	Appearances (as substitute)		Goals	
	League	Cups	League	Cups
1994/5	15	0	9	0

Playing strength
Goalscorer

Pen picture
It was largely due to his goals late in the season that Middlesbrough won promotion. He does not look particularly pretty, but he is strong and he scores goals. It is likely that he will be going back to Germany, but just in case he stays, we have included him. It would be an interesting battle to see which of the strikers won the day. He would probably find things hard in the Premiership and we would not recommend you buying him.

John Hendrie Striker

Club MIDDLESBROUGH

Date of birth 24.10.63

	Appearances (as substitute)		Goals	
	League	Cups	League	Cups
1994/5	39	4	15	2

Playing strength
Speed
Goalscoring ability

Pen picture
John is a striker who occasionally finds himself stuck on the wing. He can terrorise defences with his great turn of speed and he knows where to find the net. He is a threat to anyone and Boro await with interest the impact that he will have in the Premiership.

Jaime Moreno Striker

Club MIDDLESBROUGH

Date of birth 19.1.74

Alternative Position Midfield

	Appearances (as substitute)		Goals	
	League	Cups	League	Cups
1994/5	14	4	1	1

Playing strength
Very skilful

Pen picture
Jaime is a Bolivian international who is still finding his feet in English football, but shows great promise. He is extremely skilful and determined and sets up lots of chances. However, he must gain the confidence to shoot more often himself.

Paul Wilkinson Striker

Club MIDDLESBROUGH

Date of birth 30.10.64

	Appearances (as substitute)		Goals	
	League	Cups	League	Cups
1994/5	30	6	6	3

Playing strength
Target man
Aerial power

Pen picture
Paul struggled a little last season, but still managed to score a few goals. He is a target man who makes up for his lack of pace and ball control with strong physical presence and aerial power. He may find it hard to get into the first team, and even harder if he does.

Tommy Wright Striker

Club MIDDLESBROUGH

Date of birth 10.1.66

Alternative Position Midfield

	Appearances (as substitute)		Goals	
	League	Cups	League	Cups
1994/5	1	6	0	0

Playing strength
Can beat a defender
Good crosser of the ball

Pen picture
Tommy has not played regular first team football for the past two years, but is now on his way back. He is a tricky winger who takes on his man and then puts in a good cross. Sometimes he plays as a striker, but his lack of physical presence does not help him. You will not consider him for very long.

Malcolm Allen Striker

Club NEWCASTLE UNITED

Date of birth 21.3.67

	Appearances (as substitute)		Goals	
	League	Cups	League	Cups
1994/5	0(1)	0(1)	0	0
1993/4	9	3	5	2

Playing strength
Reliable goalscorer
Takes penalties (in Beardsley's absence)

Pen picture
Malcolm is the reserve striker but missed the whole of the season through injury. With the arrival of Ferdinand, plus Kitson, Beardsley and Fox ready to take over up front, he has little or no chance of playing many games.

Peter Beardsley Striker

Club NEWCASTLE UNITED

Date of birth 18.1.61

Alternative Position Midfield

	Appearances (as substitute)		Goals	
	League	*Cups*	*League*	*Cups*
1994/5	33	10	13	2
1993/4	35	6	21	3

Playing strength
Great creativity
Reliable goalscorer
Takes penalties and free-kicks

Pen picture
At age 34, Peter still runs around like someone half his age, is still inspirational (ask Kevin Keegan!) and still scores spectacular goals. He now plays a deeper game and just watch the service that Les Ferdinand will get. One thing is for certain, if Peter can walk, he will be in the team. That is one advantage of your manager being your biggest fan. He is not so appropriate to a fantasy team.

Paul Brayson Striker

Club NEWCASTLE UNITED

Date of birth 15.9.77

	Appearances (as substitute)		Goals	
	League	*Cups*	*League*	*Cups*
1994/5	0	0	0	0

Playing strength
Scores goals

Pen picture
Seventeen-year-old Paul has scored more than 50 goals for the Youth team and the Reserves (who both won their Championships). That suggests that he might soon start pushing for a place.

Les Ferdinand Striker ⊙⊙⊙
RECOMMENDED

Club NEWCASTLE UNITED

Date of birth 18.12.66

	Appearances (as substitute)		Goals	
	League	*Cups*	*League*	*Cups*
1994/5	37	5	24	2
1993/4	35(1)	4	16	2

Playing strength
Good in the air, he just hangs there
Good on the ground
Great goalscorer

Pen picture
When Andy Cole went to Manchester United, the fans were demanding a big name striker. In Les Ferdinand, they have got, not only a big name, but a big heart. With the support that he will be getting from people like Beardsley, Sellars, Fox etc, etc, expect him to break his personal goalscoring record this season; and that means a lot of goals. You have to think about buying him.

Paul Kitson Striker

Club NEWCASTLE UNITED

Date of birth 9.1.71

	Appearances (as substitute)		Goals	
	League	*Cups*	*League*	*Cups*
1994/5	24(2)	7(1)	8	4

Playing strength
Works hard
Good in the air

Pen picture
Most Newcastle fans are very sympathetic towards Paul, who was put in Andy Cole's role and although he did a good job and scored a reasonable number of goals, he was onto a loser from day one. Our contributors think that, if he is given the chance to play alongside Ferdinand, he could be lethal. He might even be worth buying as a cheap striker.

Gary Bull Striker

Club NOTTINGHAM FOREST

Date of birth 12.6.66

	Appearances (as substitute)		Goals	
	League	*Cups*	*League*	*Cups*
1994/5	1	(1)	1	0
1993/4	3(8)	2(2)	0	0
(Endsleigh League Div 1)				

Playing strength
Goal poacher

Pen picture
Gary is the cousin of Steve Bull of Wolves, and made a name for himself as a goalscorer at Barnet. He has never really shone on his few opportunities at the City Ground and rumours persist of his pending transfers (usually to Birmingham where he went on loan). If he stays at Nottingham, he is highly unlikely to figure in the first team.

Jason Lee Striker

Club NOTTINGHAM FOREST

Date of birth 9.5.71

	Appearances (as substitute)		Goals	
	League	*Cups*	*League*	*Cups*
1994/5	5(17)	0(2)	3	0
1993/4	10(3)	0	2	0
(Endsleigh League Div 1)				

Playing strength
Good header
Hard worker

Pen picture
Jason is 6'4" and is something of a cult hero at the City Ground where he is known as the Dreadlocked Destroyer, on account of his distinctive hairstyle and his ability to come off the bench and cause havoc. He is not the best of shooters and certainly not a prolific goalscorer, but he has a terrific work rate and is an excellent header of the ball. He may be a "super sub", but he is not the replacement for Stan.

Robert Rosario *Striker*
Club NOTTINGHAM FOREST
Date of birth 4.3.66

| | Appearances (as substitute) | | Goals | |
	League	Cups	League	Cups
1994/5	(1)	0	0	0
1993/4	15(1)	3	2	0
(Endsleigh League Div 1)				

Playing strength
Gives 100%
Good goalmaker

Pen picture
Robert is renowned for not scoring goals. His career is in the balance after a serious knee injury and he is highly unlikely to feature next season.

Bradley Allen *Striker*
Club QUEEN'S PARK RANGERS
Date of birth 13.9.71

| | Appearances (as substitute) | | Goals | |
	League	Cups	League	Cups
1994/5	2(3)	1(1)	2	1
1993/4	14(7)	3	7	3

Playing strength
Opportunist goalscorer
Great skill

Pen picture
Bradley Allen must wonder what he has to do to secure a regular place in the QPR first team. From the famous Allen footballing family, he has obviously inherited some of their natural talent in the form of snatching goals. From about 60 league games he has scored 25 goals, and he is still only 23. Apparently, our contributors tell us that he does not have the vision of the other strikers. It looks as though you have to forget him, but he will be cheap and if he is given a chance, you may find that you have picked up a goalscoring bargain.

Danny Dichio *Striker* ◉◉
RECOMMENDED

Club QUEEN'S PARK RANGERS
Date of birth 19.10.74

| | Appearances (as substitute) | | Goals | |
	League	Cups	League	Cups
1994/5	4(5)	2	3	0

Playing strength
Good young goalscorer

Pen picture
Danny is the lesser known partner of the former QPR Youth team strike partnership. Kevin Gallen has already made his mark in the Premiership. This season it could be Danny's turn. His strike rate may not be quite as prolific as Kevin's, but it is not far behind and two goals from his four league games so far is not a bad start. Furthermore, they have played together so often that their understanding must be great. Will Ray Wilkins risk giving youth a chance? If so you may get bargain points from one, or even both, of this young partnership.

Kevin Gallen *Striker* ◉◉◉
RECOMMENDED

Club QUEEN'S PARK RANGERS
Date of birth 21.9.75

| | Appearances (as substitute) | | Goals | |
	League	Cups	League	Cups
1994/5	31(6)	5(1)	10	2

Playing strength
Outstanding goalscorer
Creative supplier

Pen picture
Kevin has burst upon the Premiership scene during 1994/5 and forced his way into the England U-21 team. He is described by one of our contributors as "the best young hope in the country". That is some claim with all of the young footballing talent that seems to be coming through at the moment; but it may just be true. Perhaps it is the vast potential of Kevin that has persuaded Ray Wilkins to part with Ferdinand (apart from the little matter of £6 million). At this stage we do not know what price will be asked for Kevin, but we feel that 1995/6 will see him hit the big time and more than double his 1994/5 goal tally of ten. In that case, he will almost certainly give you a huge profit on your outlay. We recommend him very strongly.

Gary Penrice *Striker*
Club QUEEN'S PARK RANGERS
Date of birth 23.3.64

	Appearances (as substitute)		Goals	
	League	Cups	League	Cups
1994/5	9(10)	1(2)	3	1
1993/4	23(3)	2	8	0

Playing strength
A very 'nippy' striker

Pen picture
Only 5'8", Gary is a sharp, speedy striker who scores most of his goals from close range. In the past he has scored most of his goals from lay-offs from a big front man such as Ferdinand or Devon White. They are no longer around and so how will he combine with Gallen, or will he lose his place? We suggest that you give him a miss.

Mark Bright Striker

Club SHEFFIELD WEDNESDAY

Date of birth 6.6.62

	Appearances (as substitute)		Goals	
	League	Cups	League	Cups
1994/5	34(3)	6	11	2
1993/4	36(4)	10	19	4

Playing strength
Good in the air
Holds up the ball well under pressure

Pen picture
Mark has always been a great goalscorer, having totalled more than 150 goals in first class games, 50 of them for Wednesday. He leads the line well and his heading ability is superb. However he is now very slow and, from time to time, he misses real sitters. At 33, fans are asking whether the end of the line is near.

O'Neil Donaldson Striker

Club SHEFFIELD WEDNESDAY

Date of birth 24.11.69

	Appearances (as substitute)		Goals	
	League	Cups	League	Cups
1994/5	0(1)	0	0	0

Playing strength
Very quick
Tricky

Pen picture
Having recently signed from Doncaster Rovers, O'Neil is making quite an impact in the reserves and has been given a brief run in the first team. He is small and tricky to handle, but it is too early for you to consider him.

David Hirst Striker

Club SHEFFIELD WEDNESDAY

Date of birth 7.12.67

	Appearances (as substitute)		Goals	
	League	Cups	League	Cups
1994/5	13(2)	1(1)	3	0
1993/4	6(1)	2(1)	1	0

Playing strength
Lethal finisher
Times his runs well from deep or wide

Pen picture
David is known by some at Hillsborough as Lord Lucan; they have never seen him. He is always injured; always. When he plays, he is superb, very quick, tremendous shot, excellent dribbling and heading skills, he seems to have everything. If only he was fit! You cannot afford to have someone so injury-prone in your team.

Guy Whittingham Striker

Club SHEFFIELD WEDNESDAY

Date of birth 10.11.64

	Appearances (as substitute)		Goals	
	League	Cups	League	Cups
1994/5	16(5)	2(1)	9	0
1994/5 (for Aston Villa)	4(3)	3(2)	2	1
1993/4 (for Aston Villa)	13(5)	3	3	0

Playing strength
An out-and-out goalscorer

Pen picture
Guy is a big powerful striker who was a prolific scorer with Portsmouth, where he netted more than 100 goals in four seasons. He never settled at Villa Park and he has not established a regular first team place at Hillsborough. However, he is quick, strikes a good ball and is composed in front of goal. Although some fans say that he is not a Premiership striker, his goals did keep them up and he deserves a chance. David Pleat might just give him one. You may find that he will be inexpensive and provide you with good points.

Craig Maskell Striker

Club SOUTHAMPTON

Date of birth 10.4.68

Alternative Position Midfield

	Appearances (as substitute)		Goals	
	League	Cups	League	Cups
1994/5	2(4)	1	0	0
1993/4	6(4)	0	1	0

Playing strength
Prolific goalscorer in lower divisions

Pen picture
He rejoined Saints in February 1994, after scoring many goals in lower divisions, for Huddersfield, Reading and Swindon. He did not make a great impact, but no doubt Alan Ball will be hoping for better things. Time must be running out for Craig at this level.

Neil Shipperley Striker ◉
RECOMMENDED

Club SOUTHAMPTON
Date of birth 30.10.74

| | Appearances (as substitute) | | Goals | |
	League	Cups	League	Cups
1994/5	19	4	4	2
1994/5 (for Chelsea)	6(4)	4(1)	2	0
1993/4 (for Chelsea)	18(6)	5(1)	4	2

Playing strength
Quick and lively

Pen picture
When he was at Chelsea, our contacts described him as "the most promising younger player at the club". Fans at the Dell are equally excited about this 20-year-old. Once again, Chelsea fans reckoned that he played better off a big robust striker, who took the physical weight. It will be interesting to see how he gets on with Gordon Watson. He may be worth buying at a low price.

Gordon Watson Striker ◉
RECOMMENDED

Club SOUTHAMPTON
Date of birth 20.3.71

| | Appearances (as substitute) | | Goals | |
	League	Cups	League	Cups
1994/5	12	0	3	0
1994/5 (for Sheffield Wednesday)	5(18)	2(2)	2	0
1993/4 (for Sheffield Wednesday)	15(8)	5(3)	12	2

Playing strength

Hard worker

Great personality

Pen picture

Gordon is a strong bustling type of striker who makes life uncomfortable for defenders. He niggles and chases and generally puts them under pressure as well as going in hard for the ball. He also finds the net regularly. He and Shipperley should work well together. He might even be worth buying.

Chris Armstrong Striker
Club TOTTENHAM HOTSPUR
Date of birth 19.6.71

| | Appearances (as substitute) | | Goals | |
	League	Cups	League	Cups
1994/5 (for Crystal Palace)	40	11	8	10
1993/4 (for Crystal Palace in Endsleigh League Div 1)	43	6	23	2

Playing strength
A natural striker
Good positional play

Pen picture
Chris is good on the ground, in the air and has great pace. He was unable to reproduce his goalscoring feats of the previous season, which was a significant contribution to Palace's problems last season. Spurs fans should not put undue pressure on him by expecting him to emulate Jurgen Klinsmann, but, with the superior service which he will undoubtedly receive at White Hart Lane, he may just surprise a few doubters. We do not give him a recommendation, but will watch with interest.

Nick Barmby Striker
Club TOTTENHAM HOTSPUR
Date of birth 11.2.74

| | Appearances (as substitute) | | Goals | |
	League	Cups	League	Cups
1994/5	37(1)	8	9	2
1993/4	27	6	4	3

Playing strength
Clever, unselfish goalmaker
Goalscorer

Pen picture
Nick is unlikely to be a high-scoring striker and so should not be considered for your fantasy team. However, he has improved his strike rate this season and this will have been readily welcomed by Spurs. He has improved considerably under Gerry Francis and, no doubt, it helped having Jurgen Klinsmann around to spot his unselfish running off the ball and to occasionally slot the ball through to him.

Ronny Rosenthal Striker
Club TOTTENHAM HOTSPUR
Date of birth 11.10.63

| | Appearances (as substitute) | | Goals | |
	League	Cups	League	Cups
1994/5	14(6)	3(2)	0	4
1993/4	11(4)	0	2	0
1993/4	30 (for Liverpool)		0	0

Playing strength
Very pacey
An experienced goalscoring forward

Pen picture
There is little doubt about what was the highlight of Ronny's year. In the FA Cup 5th Round replay at The Dell, he came on as substitute and scored a hat-trick. Unfortunately in his other 17 games (plus 7 substitute appearances), he managed only one more goal. Talk about inconsistency! So far as fantasy football is concerned, you can forget about Ronny.

Teddy Sheringham Striker

Club TOTTENHAM HOTSPUR

Date of birth 2.4.66

	Appearances (as substitute)		Goals	
	League	Cups	League	Cups
1994/5	41(1)	8	17	5
1993/4	17(2)	2	13	2

Playing strength
An outstanding goalscorer

Pen picture
Teddy can usually be relied upon for 20+ goals per season, providing he escapes injury. He is one of the few genuine out-and-out goalscorers in the Premiership and his claim to be a member of your fantasy team must be taken very seriously. Do not expect him to be cheap. Of course, he will have a new partner this season and at the time of writing, it is not known who that will be. That will obviously affect his scoring potential. Look out for who it is and then decide whether or not to buy.

Jeroen Boere Striker

Club WEST HAM UNITED

Date of birth

	Appearances (as substitute)		Goals	
	League	Cups	League	Cups
1994/5	15(5)	3	6	0
1993/4	0(4)	0(1)	0	1

Playing strength
Good in the air

Pen picture
Jeroen is a big Dutch striker who reaches the ball well in the air, but often his control and direction are at fault. Fans are not convinced about his performance with his feet, but he must be doing something right, his strike rate is not that bad. Nevertheless you should avoid him.

Tony Cottee Striker

Club WEST HAM UNITED

Date of birth 11.7.65

	Appearances (as substitute)		Goals	
	League	Cups	League	Cups
1994/5	31	5	13	2
1993/4	36(3)	7	16	3

Playing strength
An instinctive goalscorer
Good close control

Pen picture
Tony has scored plenty of goals throughout his career. He is small for a target man, but he is very good at shielding the ball and holding up play. He is quick on the turn and his great first touch and excellent close control have served him well in his outstanding career. He will be a medium cost, medium point scorer in the fantasy football games.

Trevor Morley Striker

Club WEST HAM UNITED

Date of birth 20.3.61

	Appearances (as substitute)		Goals	
	League	Cups	League	Cups
1994/5	10(4)	0(2)	0	0
1993/4	39(3)	5(1)	13	3

Playing strength
Reliable
Hard-working

Pen picture
How things can change in a year. This time last year, Trevor had been declared Hammer of the Year. Now he has been given a free transfer. Obviously you will not be including him in your team, even if you can get him for nothing.

Andy Clarke Strike

Club WIMBLEDON

Date of birth 22.7.67

	Appearances (as substitute)		Goals	
	League	Cups	League	Cups
1994/5	8(17)	5(1)	1	1
1993/4	8(12)	4(3)	2	1

Playing strength
Explosive pace
Good close control

Pen picture
Andy Clarke seems to be destined to become the eternal substitute. He certainly makes his biggest contribution in that capacity, as his blistering pace towards the end of a match can tear opposition defences apart. His irregular inclusion in the first

team means that you should not include him in your team.

Efan Ekoku Striker

Club WIMBLEDON

Date of birth 7.6.67

| | Appearances (as substitute) | | Goals | |
	League	Cups	League	Cups
1994/5	24	3	9	0
1994/5 (for Norwich)	5(1)	1	0	0
1993/4 (for Norwich)	20(7)	6(1)	12	2

Playing strength
Blistering pace
A born striker

Pen picture
When he signed from Norwich, Efan Ekoku seemed to be heading for a lucrative goalscoring partnership with Dean Holdsworth. So far, this is largely unfulfilled. Efan has scored nine goals in 23 games, which is not bad, but not good enough for you to consider buying him.

Jon Goodman Striker

Club WIMBLEDON

Date of birth 2.6.71

Alternative Position Midfield

| | Appearances (as substitute) | | Goals | |
	League	Cups	League	Cups
1994/5	13(6)	0(1)	4	0

Playing strength
A regular goalscorer

Pen picture
Jon had been a regular goalscorer for Millwall since joining them from Bromley in 1992. In November 1994, when he had scored eight goals in 15 outings, he was signed by Wimbledon. The partnership in attack has continually changed, but he has made a good start and, given a run in the team, could become a regular fixture and consistent goalscorer at the top level. But we cannot recommend him as a fantasy star.

Mick Harford Striker

Club WIMBLEDON

Date of birth 12.5.59

| | Appearances (as substitute) | | Goals | |
	League	Cups	League	Cups
1994/5	17(10)	4(3)	6	2
1993/4 (for Coventry)	0(1)	0	1	0

Playing strength
Great heading ability
Has a good shot
A regular goalscorer

Pen picture
Mick has a great goalscoring record stretching back over 18 years and ten clubs. The hammering which he has taken from hard defenders over the years has begun to take its toll and he has suffered badly with injuries in recent times. He joined Wimbledon at the start of the season and made a good contribution, mainly as a substitute. With considerable competition for a place as a striker, he is unlikely to figure much in 1995/6.

Dean Holdsworth Striker

Club WIMBLEDON

Date of birth 8.11.68

| | Appearances (as substitute) | | Goals | |
	League	Cups	League	Cups
1994/5	27(1)	3(2)	7	1
1993/4	42	9	17	7

Playing strength
Hard worker
Prolific goalscorer

Pen picture
After scoring 24 goals the previous year, and almost one every two games throughout his career, Dean must have been very disappointed with last season. Maybe he was missing the service that he had received from Fash and that affected him badly. Alternatively, perhaps it was just a ruse to get his price in fantasy games reduced so that you would select him for this year. I reckon that he will be a bargain this year and with a goalscoring record like his, you have to be ready to buy him in, as a "cheapy".

WORK SHEETS

This section consists of two types of worksheets which you should use when making your fantasy league team(s) selections. There are Short-list sheets and Proposed team sheets. You may prefer to extract these from the book in order to refer more easily to the club and player details while compiling your lists.

The Short-list sheets should be used to produce an initial list from which you will ultimately make your final selection. Each of the five positions in fantasy football games, (Goalkeeper, Full back, Centre back, Midfielder and Striker,) have a separate sheet which is divided into three sections, Budget, Medium-priced and Star. You are invited to list players who are suitable for these categories, whom you would like to consider when selecting your team(s). The names of some of the likely contenders for each position/category have been given to assist you in compiling your lists. Suggested price ranges for each category have also been noted. These may be adjusted, as you think suitable.

The Proposed team sheets are to be used to list and check your selected team(s). From the Short-list sheets you should make your selections and double check the following:-

i) Cross check the value of each player selected to make sure that you have not written it down wrongly.

ii) Check the total to ensure that you have added it correctly.

iii) Check that you have not included more than two players from any one club.

iv) Check that you have the correct make-up of the team, eg:-

    1 Goalkeeper

    2 Full backs

    2 Centre backs

    4 Midfield players

    2 Strikers

Goalkeepers

Consider the following goalkeepers carefully

Budget goalkeepers
Branagan - Bolton
Miklosko - West Ham
Miller - Middlesbrough

Medium priced goalkeepers
Bosnich - Aston Villa
Lukic - Leeds
Southall - Everton
Srnicek - Newcastle

Star goalkeepers
Flowers - Blackburn
Schmeichel - Manchester United
Seaman - Arsenal

Select budget goalkeepers in the range £1.0M–£1.6M				Select medium priced goalkeepers in the range £1.7M–£2.2M				Select star goalkeepers in the range £2.3M–£3.0M			
Player	Code	Club	Price	Player	Code	Club	Price	Player	Code	Club	Price

Full backs

Consider the following full backs carefully

Budget full backs
Cox - Middlesbrough
R Elliott - Newcastle
Green - Bolton
Haaland - Nottingham Forest
Jackson - Everton
Sharp - Leeds

Medium priced full backs
Ablett - Everton
Atherton - Sheffield Wednesday
Breacker - West Ham
Dicks - West Ham
Nolan - Sheffield Wednesday
Staunton - Aston Vills

Star full backs
Dixon - Arsenal
Hinchcliffe - Everton
Irwin - Manchester United
Le Saux - Blackburn
Pearce - Nottingham Forest
Winterburn - Arsenal

Select budget full backs in the range £1M–£1.6M				Select medium priced full backs in the range £1.7M–£2.2M				Select star full backs in the range £2.3M–£3.0M			
Player	Code	Club	Price	Player	Code	Club	Price	Player	Code	Club	Price

Centre backs

Consider the following centre backs carefully

Budget centre backs
Coleman - Bolton
Pearson - Middlesbrough
Vickers - Middlesbrough

Medium priced centre backs
Ehiogu - Aston Villa
Howey - Newcastle
Pearce - Sheffield Wednesday
Stubbs - Bolton
Watson - Everton

Star centre backs
Adams - Arsenal
Albert - Newcastle
Bould - Arsenal
Gullit - Chelsea
Hendry - Blackburn
Pallister - Manchester United

Select budget centre backs in the range £1.0M–£1.6M				Select medium priced centre backs in the range £1.7M–£2.2M				Select star centre backs in the range £2.3M–£3.0M			
Player	Code	Club	Price	Player	Code	Club	Price	Player	Code	Club	Price

Midfielders

Consider the following midfielders carefully

Budget midfielders

Dozzzell - Tottenham
Flitcroft - Manchester City
Gayle - Wimbledon
Grant - Everton
Hignett - Middlesbrough
Lake - Manchester City
Leonhardsen - Wimbledon
Meaker - QPR
Moore - Middlesbrough
Pollock - Middlesbrough
Sneekes - Bolton

Thompson - Bolton

Medium priced midfielders

Bart-Williams - Sheffield Wed
Bohinen - Nottingham Forest
Butt - Manchester United
Earle - Wimbledon
Hutchison - West Ham
Ingesson - Sheffield Wednesday
Kennedy - Liverpool
Maddison - Southampton
Magilton - Southampton
Merson - Arsenal
Moncur - West Ham

Peacock - Chelsea
RedKnapp - Liverpool
Stone - Taylor - Aston Villa
Wise - Chelsea
Woan - Nottingham Forest
Yorke - Aston Villa

Star midfielders

Fox - Newcastle
Kanchelskis - Manchester United
Lee - Newcastle
Le Tissier - Southampton
McManaman - Liverpool
Roy - Nottingham Forest
Wilcox - Blackburn

Select budget midfielders in the range £1M–£1.6M				Select medium priced midfielders in the range £1.7M–£2.4M				Select star midfielders in the range £2.5M–£3.5M			
Player	Code	Club	Price	Player	Code	Club	Price	Player	Code	Club	Price

Strikers

Consider the following strikers carefully

Budget Strikers

Dichio - QPR
McGinley - Bolton
Scholes - Manchester United
Whelan - Leeds

Medium-priced Strikers

Ferguson - Everton
Fjortoft - Middlesbrough
Gallen - QPR
Hartson - Arsenal
Rösler - Manchester City
Shipperley - Southampton
Watson - Southampton

Star strikers

Bergkamp - Arsenal
Cole - Manchester United
Collymore - Liverpool
Ferdinand - Newcastle
Fowler - Liverpool
Shearer - Blackburn
Sutton - Blackburn
Wright - Arsenal
Yeboah - Leeds

Select budget strikers in the range £1.0M–£1.7M				Select medium priced strikers in the range £1.8M–£2.7M				Select star strikers in the range £2.8M–£4.0M			
Player	Code	Club	Price	Player	Code	Club	Price	Player	Code	Club	Price

INDEX OF PLAYERS